JAMES
BEARD'S
SIMPLE
FOODS

BOOKS BY JAMES BEARD

EDITED BY
HAL KENDIG

FOREWORD BY
JULIA CHILD

INTRODUCTION BY
JOHN MINAHAN

MACMILLAN PUBLISHING COMPANY
New York

Maxwell Macmillan Canada
Toronto

Maxwell Macmillan International
New York Oxford Singapore Sydney

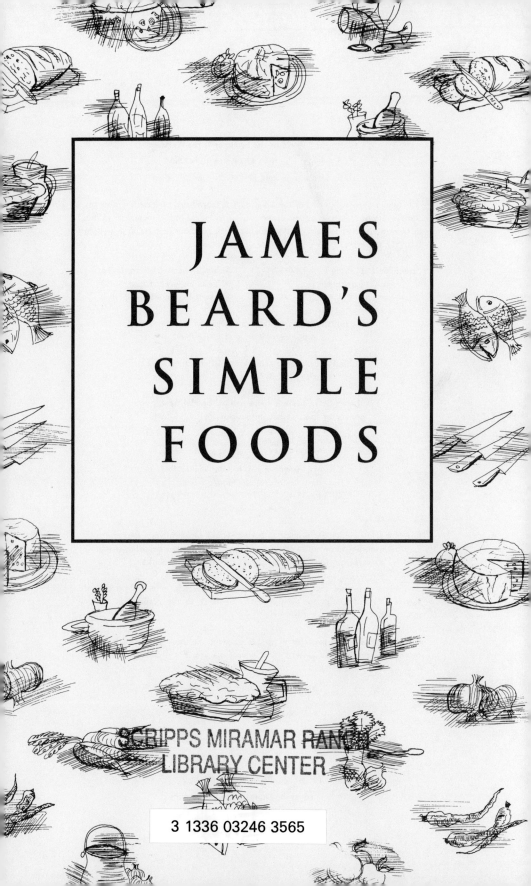

JAMES
BEARD'S
SIMPLE
FOODS

Macmillan Publishing Company
866 Third Avenue
New York, NY 10022

Maxwell Macmillan Canada, Inc.
1200 Eglinton Avenue East, Suite 200
Don Mills, Ontario M3C 3N1

Macmillan Publishing Company is part of the Maxwell Communication Group of Companies.

Library of Congress Cataloging-in-Publication Data
Beard, James, 1903–
[Simple foods]
James Beard's simple foods / edited by Hal Kendig : preface by Julia Child ; introduction by John Minahan.
p.   cm.
Includes index.
ISBN 0-02-508070-9
1. Cookery, American.   I. Kendig, Hal, 1948–   .
II. Title.   III. Title: Simple foods.
TX715.B3718   1993   92-33280
641.5—dc20

Grateful acknowledgment is made to Barbara Kafka for permission to reprint two excerpts from her foreword to *Delights and Prejudices* by James Beard, copyright © 1964 by James Beard, foreword copyright © 1990 by Barbara Kafka.

The editor expresses his gratitude to Carolyn Brownstein, John Bedrosian, and Kenneth Gale Hawkes for their valuable assistance in the preparation of the manuscript.

Book design by Anne Scatto

Illustrations by Richard Truscott

10 9 8 7 6 5 4 3 2 1

Printed in the United States of America

One of the phrases I loathe most is "gourmet cooking." What gourmet cooking is I will never know. There is fabulous cooking, good cooking, mediocre cooking, and bad cooking, and I'm convinced that some people can never rise above bad, probably because they don't really like to cook. It is the urge to get into the kitchen and the delight of making something work out ... that makes for good cooking.

James Beard

CONTENTS

FOREWORD
BY JULIA CHILD

Reading this book is like hearing James Beard talk, and I've had such a good time going over these pages since I feel I've been with him again, gossiping about food and recipes and happy reminiscences.

Although I had of course heard of him and read him during my formative years as a cook, I didn't meet him until 1961, with my colleague Simone Beck, when our first book was published. By then he was, with the exception of Craig Claiborne of *The New York Times*, the major figure on the American gastronomic scene. He was famous through his numerous books on food and cooking, his articles in the leading magazines, and his travels and cookery demonstrations throughout the country. Beard was friend and advisor to many a great hotel and restaurant, as well as companion to chefs and wine merchants. Yet, despite his renown, he was a most generous and approachable man. He loved people, loved to share his vast knowledge, and he loved to teach.

America had never quite awakened to the glories of good food until after World War II, and in the early 1950s two renowned cooking schools reigned in New York. One was that of Dione Lucas, a most talented but difficult Englishwoman, who had trained in the French cuisine. The other was The James Beard Cooking School, which Beard started with André Surmain, of Lutèce. By the way, for anyone in need of a sourcebook on the great food and wine personalities of that awakening period in American life, I recommend Evan Jones's *Epicurean Delight: The Life and Times of James Beard* (Knopf, 1990).

Jim loved teaching, took a great personal interest in his pupils, and they adored him in return. The series of chapters we have here are his teaching lessons, taken from the very popular series that appeared in the 1970s for the airline magazine *American Way*.

Although they reflect the cooking of that era, they seem just as pertinent now as they did then. Of course in those happy days one was not afraid of the good things in life—such as the free use of cream, butter, and pork fat; however, it is easy enough to adapt his informally written recipes to the spartan rules of contemporary nutritional dictums. It is his love of the good life and his lusty enthusiasm for food and drink that show infectiously through these pages.

He starts the novice cook on the basics he so strongly believed in, and the very first chapter is "Good Cooking Is in Your Hands." "Hands were the earliest of all implements for preparing food," he says, "and they are still the most versatile, efficient, and sensitive." He follows with hands-on examples, such as dipping an impeccably clean finger into the sauce to check for seasoning, for hand-mixing doughs and folding egg whites into cake batters, and concludes with how to hand-form hamburgers, a green salad, and a strawberry short-cake. The next lesson discusses the knives one needs, and each chapter includes an illustrative menu. Chapter 3 is on meat cuts, including descriptions of special cuts one might not know about, like the triangular broilable piece known as the beef tip, at the rump end of the sirloin. This chapter ends with a beautiful recipe for a simple boiled dinner—and a French version of the boiled dinner *pot-au-feu* appears in the chapter on simmering. Barbecuing was a Beard specialty, and since he published several books on the subject, "Cooking on the Outdoor Grill," Chapter 6, conveniently encapsulates his theories. How welcome to have complete directions for baking one's first loaf of bread, for roasting and stuffing one's first holiday turkey, for making ice cream.

This is a book with patient detail for the eager gastronome just starting out, and it is also a book of pleasure for cooks of any ability—you want to see how *he* did it, and what clever little tricks and esoteric bits of information he comes forth with. The mini-Reuben sandwich, for instance, is a splendid cocktail tidbit idea, and I've always lazily wondered on the significant difference between corned beef and pastrami.

Nice Beardian asides give the book a personal character: "The best pastrami I've ever eaten was one I made myself." Speaking of Thanksgiving he writes, "I like a holiday meal that is both simple and elegant . . . something very simple but very expensive first: caviar, if I can afford it. . . . He admits that it may be heresy, but he often likes chili with pasta rather than beans, at times will thicken his chili with ground nuts, and has even been known to flavor it Mexican-*mole*-style with grated bitter chocolate.

This book is James Beard as I like to remember him, Beard at his entertaining, conversational, and educational best. How lucky we are to have these articles resurrected at last, and gathered together in book form.

INTRODUCTION
BY JOHN MINAHAN

Early in 1974, when I was editor and publisher of *American Way*, the in-flight magazine of American Airlines, I asked James Beard if he would be interested in writing a monthly column in the format of "cooking lessons" that would at some time in the future be published as a hardcover book under the imprint of *American Way*. He agreed. We never signed a formal contract to this effect, but that was the long-term goal, clearly understood by our editorial staff at the time.

I left the magazine in 1976, but the core of the editorial staff remained intact until 1978, when American Airlines began the process of moving its corporate headquarters from New York to Dallas. At that time, none of the original editorial staff elected to relocate to Dallas. Consequently, the entire staff was replaced by local editors, artists, and production personnel.

Although Beard's columns continued, the original idea of the cookbook was either discarded or (more likely) never known by the new editorial staff in Dallas during the three-year period that Beard continued to write for the magazine.

In 1988, as a consultant to Management International, Inc., I suggested to the firm's president, Harold L. Kendig, that the idea of a cookbook based on the *American Way* columns was still viable and should be vigorously explored.

Subsequently, Hal Kendig invested a significant amount of time and money in researching the possibility of acquiring the reprint rights to these columns. After forming the KMB Corporation in 1988, he met with various executives at American Airlines in Dallas and was granted official reprint rights to all the columns by Lowell C. Duncan, Jr., who was American's vice president of corporate communications.

Next, Kendig discussed the project with Morris J. Galen, of the law firm of Tonkon, Toorp, Galen, Marmaduke & Booth, in Portland, the executors of the James Beard Estate, and received that firm's authority to proceed with the project. At that point, Kendig approached Peter Kump in New York, president of the James Beard Foundation, which also administers the James Beard House in Greenwich Village, and received his enthusiastic support.

Beard wrote a total of seventy monthly columns for *American Way*. Each column was approximately 2,500 words in length. Therefore, in theory, the book could have totalled about 175,000 words, or about 700 manuscript pages. However, after a careful study of the seventy columns, and keeping in mind the calorie- and cholesterol-conscious audience of today, Kendig elected to use only thirty-nine, representing the most health-oriented stories and "timeless" recipes.

Over the years, I read most of Beard's books, and I started lengthy tape-recording sessions with him that were intended to provide the basis for a proposed biography. Unfortunately, we did not complete those sessions. He died in 1985 at the age of eighty-one. However, following are some excerpts from one of the earliest tapes that give candid insights into his childhood, his parents, his adolescence, and his most formative years.

Q: You grew up in Portland, Oregon. What kind of food do you remember enjoying as a child?

A: We lived in a nice section that wasn't overbuilt. The people had very comfortable homes and there was a lot of vacant property around, so much so that our "sometime" Chinese cook would go off in the morning, in the fall, and come back with a five-gallon pail of mushrooms that we'd have for breakfast.

We had all sorts of fruit trees in the garden. We had great, enormous Bing cherries and Gravenstein apples and May Duke cherries and English walnuts, and all that sort of thing, so that our spring and summer months were filled with produce from the garden, as well as things like shallots that my mother planted every year.

And even when we were at our beach house, which was about a hundred and fifteen miles from Portland, great baskets of fruit, and sometimes vegetables, would be sent down on the train, because produce at the beach was not as plentiful as it was in town, and fruit wasn't as good. And there in the beach house, it was sort of an idyllic existence, because we were in the center of a big meadow near the ocean. I had free rein to wander around, and practically everybody I knew went to the beach in summer. We'd go clamming and crabbing, and get into all sorts of horrible mischief.

Q: I understand that you were an exceptionally good swimmer.

A: Well, I'd swim in the ocean every day; in fact, I was considered a daredevil swimmer. People used to want to rush in and grab me out of the ocean, because I'd swim out beyond the breakers, and really into dangerous water. I never got carried away by the undertow, I always managed to get back. But people used to tear their hair out, because I was willful. I think I knew my own strength, but nobody else did.

And I used to swim in a pool every day, too. That was kind of wonderful, and there was a girl who was almost as fat as I was, and the swimming teacher pitted us against each other. Then, certain Saturday nights during the summer, they'd have a great fete, and we would have to race each other, and I always beat her and made her horribly mad. I think she went on a diet after that. We used to swim the length of the pool and back, seventy-five times, every afternoon. Which was quite a lot of exercise. Of course, that wasn't very gastronomic.

Q: Maybe not, but you must've built up one hell of an appetite.

A: That's an understatement, I can assure you. But really, looking back, we ate extraordinarily well at the beach, because of the absolute abundance of clams and oysters and crabs and salmon and trout. Matter of fact, we ate very little meat, because the meat that came down to the butcher shops there wasn't very good.

So we ate a great deal of fish and shellfish, and added to it with freshly killed chickens, and then we had wonderful hams that were shipped down to the beach from various places. Fresh meat was almost an unknown quantity in our house. But who needed it, with all that sort of thing?

Q: Were your parents both good cooks?

A: Well, of course, my mother knew an awful lot about food, because she was one of the first successful women in the hotel business in America. She understood food and liked food, and she traveled a great deal. Finally, when she found that she couldn't keep French or Italian chefs in business, she'd take them and have them train her Chinese. And that was the way she succeeded in business, to a great extent, and made her life easier. She had a pretty profound knowledge of food.

Q: I read somewhere that your father actually came west in a covered wagon.

A: That's true. The Beard family was a long trekking family. They started in the Carolinas and trekked on to Kentucky, and then into the Boonsborough trek, and into the Middle West. When my father was five years old, he left Iowa in a covered wagon, with the rest of his family, to go to Oregon. So I'm really only one generation removed from the covered wagon. Although I don't think I *look* that way.

As all trekkers did, my family had great knowledge of what the land had, and what it brought forth. I mean, they knew every kind of edible game and they knew how to care for it. They knew the wild plants and they knew the odd little things like wild asparagus and all types of wild berries.

So my father had kept this wild lore within him and he became what I call a "spotty" cook; he did certain things extremely well and he was very biased about other things. He was probably the most biased human being about cooking vegetables that I've ever known, because he carried with him the old Southern tradition and the Middle Western tradition. He felt that strong beans, for instance, should be put in with a piece of smoked jowl and cooked for about five hours; so they were so full of pork fat and smoke taste that you never tasted the beans. He also thought spinach was unfit to eat unless it was cooked for a couple of hours with a little bit of bacon.

As a result of all this, my childhood was very spotted with periods when the three of us—my mother, father, and I—never ate a meal together, because we all liked different things and cooked in different ways. We'd all be served the things we wanted at various times, which made for a very crazy family life, I can assure you. But we all ate well.

Q: When did you begin writing about food?

A: Oh, I didn't begin writing until I was about thirty-seven, thirty-eight, I guess. I'd written little things. When I was in high school, I won a *poetry* prize, believe it or not.

Q: You went to public schools in Portland, didn't you?

A: Yes, and I went to Reed College, which was one of the first progressive colleges, and got myself *very* well kicked out.

Q: Why?

A: Well, I was *too* progressive. I broke all the rules. There weren't many rules, but I broke them. I made new rules to break.

Q: Then you took off for Europe?

A: I went to Europe to study voice, and I sang quite a bit. There, again, I misbehaved, so I sort of threw *that* overboard.

Q: Where did you study?

A: London. And Italy—but I was based in London.

Q: And this was about nineteen twenty-one, twenty-two?

A: Yes, in the maddest period of Europe. And I learned everything *besides* voice. Because I happened to fall in with that incredibly mad group that was around in those days. And thank God I did; I'm tickled to death that I did. It really gave me an education. I think it made me a very much wiser, and a very much more "sophisticated"— in the best meaning of the word—and a very much more worldly human being, for which I'm very grateful.

I can remember my mother once talking about life, and saying that the greatest fault with most people was their inhibitions. And I think I got to the point where I had practically none.

Q: You stayed in Europe for about three years that first time?

A: About three years. In London, in Milan, and I was in the south of France for a while, and in Paris. Then I came back to New York and *hated* it. So I went back to the West Coast, and then came back to New York, and that's when I went to work in the theater.

Q: For Walter Hampden?

A: Yes, I went to work for Walter Hampden. I'll never forget, I was living over in Chelsea, and I wrote a very self-assured note to Mr. Hampden, because I heard he was casting *Cyrano*, and someone had told me that he liked tall people and large people. So I remember saying, "I'm large, but not colossal." Sent the letter, waited, and I didn't hear anything. And then it was Labor Day, nineteen twenty-four, and, lo and behold, there was a special delivery letter from Mr. Hampden.

We rehearsed *Cyrano* down at Greenwich House, right here in the Village, and I *was* "large, but not colossal," because there were two or three people in the cast who were much bigger than I was.

Well, we went on the road with practically a special train, because we had horses, children, stage mothers, an enormous cast, and a hell of a lot of scenery. So we could only play certain cities. It was a lot of fun. It was a very memorable trip in many ways.

Q: And you did *Othello* the following year?

A: I think so; I think *Othello* was next. I was on the stage in various productions for six or seven years.

Q: When did you get into radio?

A: In the early thirties. Doing everything from announcing to playing Daddy Warbucks to working in a four-year series of *Dorothy Dix*.

Q: In New York?

A: No, I was in Los Angeles, San Francisco, Seattle, and Portland. Strangely enough, I worked in a long series called *Covered Wagon Days*.

But I was always cooking, you know. And then I decided that I'd like to have a restaurant. I can remember planning and writing out menus, and designing. But, thank God, I just never did it.

I came back to New York again, in nineteen thirty-seven, thinking that I'd continue in radio, and hunting around for something to do in the food business. Well, nothing became of that, but I got a very interesting job teaching school, at the Buxton County Day School, over in Short Hills, New Jersey.

Q: When did you open Hors d'Oeuvre, Incorporated?

A: The very next year. I met Bill Roda, a brilliant man who was also trying to get into the food business, and we decided to open a shop on the East Side of Manhattan, where we could cater to cocktail parties in the area between Fifty-ninth Street and One Hundred Tenth, and Central Park West and the East River. We called it Hors d'Oeuvre, Incorporated, and it really flourished. We were the first people who had ever done anything like this, and we had an excellent location, on Sixty-sixth Street, right next to the Cosmopolitan Club.

We were the first people ever to sell vichyssoise in New York, outside of the Ritz, and we sold enough vichyssoise to float a leviathan during the summer, I can tell you. We were very successful until the war came, and rationing came.

Q: By that time, hadn't you published your first book, around nineteen forty?

A: Exactly right, in nineteen forty, called *Hors d'Oeuvres and Canapés*. And that began another complete change; that and the war. I wrote that, and I wrote another book, *Cook It Outdoors*, published in nineteen forty-one, and then the war caught up with me.

I was in the army for about six months. Naturally, since I was an expert on food and cooking, the army took full advantage of that fact by making me into a cryptographer—a code expert. When I got through the training school up in Pauling, New York, I wanted to be sent overseas as soon as possible. Then I found out that they wouldn't send anybody overseas who was thirty-eight or over. And I had just celebrated my thirty-eighth birthday.

I remember very vividly being told that I had my choice of going to Washington, D.C., or Presque Isle, Maine, for the remainder of the war. So I went to see Colonel Pickering, the head of the school. He told me that since I was over thirty-eight, I could get out of the service if I got a job that was necessary to the war effort. And I did.

I worked for the United Seamen's Service, supervising service clubs for the merchant marines. I was sent to clubs in Puerto Rico, Rio, Panama, Casablanca, Marseilles, quite a few places, until the end of the war. I returned to New York on a cold, grim twenty-third of December, nineteen forty-five.

Q: And started in television the next year.

A: That was it. I'd had a third book come out in the meantime, *Fowl and Game Cookery*. About two days after I arrived, I bumped into Charlotte Adams on the street, and she said, "We were wondering when you'd be back; NBC wants you to do a television show."

So that began that era. It was the first television food show, and some of the first sponsors were General Foods and Borden. Remember "Elsie," the Borden cow? Bill Baird made a wonderful Elsie, who opened her mouth and talked. It was called *Elsie Presents*, and we stayed on for two years.

Q: I remember. It was an hour-long variety show.

A: I had the cooking segment, and we went on at nine o'clock every Friday night. Of course, in those days, almost all of the television sets were in bars. And we went on just before the *fight*. So I started getting an enormous amount of fan mail from people who were in to see the fight. They kind of liked the food idea. It was great fun.

Q: You started to do a lot of magazine work about that time, too.

A: Yes, but one of the major turning points after the television show was concerned with a book called *The Fireside Cookbook*, and it was scheduled to be a very large project, heavily advertised and promoted. But the publisher told me that I would not have the standard royalties, just an outright fee. So, all my friends in the publishing business said, "You're crazy, don't do it."

I thought about it very carefully, and I reasoned: If it's going to be this big a thing, it's going to do me more good than the royalty payments could. So I took it. And, of course, it was the real turning point in my career. I became very well known across the country, which it would've taken me years to do otherwise. So I always felt that I made the wisest move I ever made when I did it.

When Beard's 1964 autobiography, *Delights and Prejudices*, was reissued in a trade paperback by Macmillan in 1990, Barbara Kafka, the distinguished food writer and restaurant consultant, who was a longtime associate of Beard, wrote a new Foreword to the book that captured his personality with particular eloquence. In part, Kafka wrote:

> Who was James Andrew Beard? He was a vast man with a brilliant mind and vast amounts of information and experiences stored in a brain that seemed to forget nothing, not a telephone number, a name, the direction through streets long unvisited, the flavors of a dish eaten last week or fifty years ago, the intonation of a singing voice on an opera stage thirty years before, a recipe once made, a bit of arcane food lore gleaned from a two-hundred-year-old book, and the birthdays and minutiae of his friends' and acquaintances' lives. . . .
>
> I miss Jim Beard, miss him terribly. Partly, that is a personal feeling, but it is one that the many who were in his classes all over America and read his books share. I miss the energy of the man, his deep rumbling laughter, the caustic comments that threw aside pretension, the immediacy of his love of the texture and taste of ingredients. . . .

That was the Jim Beard that I knew, and I miss him, too, terribly. During our weekly luncheons, we agreed that his monthly columns would continue to be targeted to the general public, rather than to the more sophisticated cookbook-buying audience, because of the overwhelmingly positive feedback I was receiving in "Letters to the

Editor." As a result, I think these columns provide an unusual window into the man's personal life. He wrote these stories in an easy, relaxed, conversational vernacular, reflecting his delightful sense of humor, his culinary idiosyncrasies, and his obvious joy in creating, preparing, and eating good simple food.

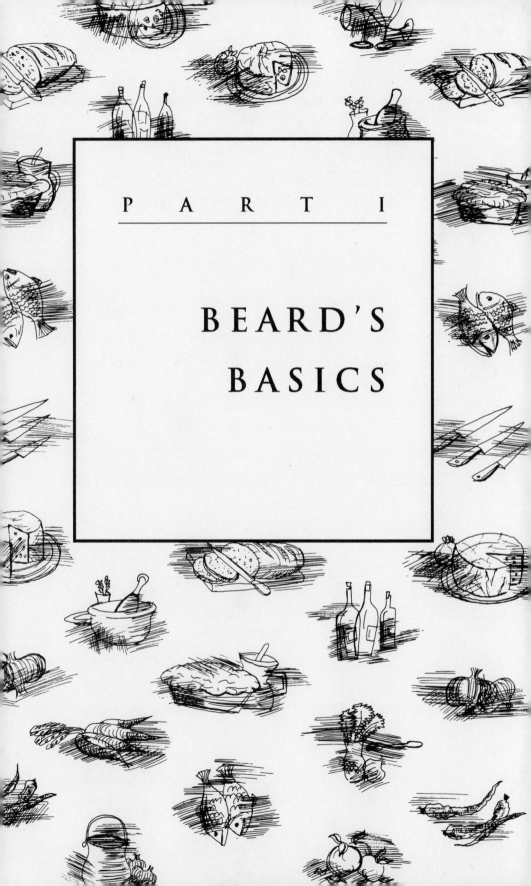

PART I

BEARD'S BASICS

CHAPTER 1

GOOD

COOKING

IS IN YOUR

HANDS

Hands were the earliest of all implements for preparing food, and they are still the most versatile, efficient, and sensitive. You can use your hands—and your hands alone—to beat, cream, fold, knead, pat, press, form, toss, tear, and pound. Because they are so extremely sensitive, the minute your hands touch or feel something, your fingers transmit to your brain messages about textures and temperatures.

If you want to test the temperature or the seasoning of a sauce or a soup or a vegetable purée, the best and simplest way is to dip your finger in. Touch your finger to your tongue and you'll know right away whether the seasoning and flavor are right or wrong. The prissy person who thinks only spoons belong in food may object, but what could be cleaner than well-washed hands? There's nothing wrong about touching the food you are preparing. In fact, there's no more rewarding and sensuous a pleasure than plunging your hands into a batter or dough and mixing or kneading away. Don't let anyone make you feel self-conscious about it. After all, we eat lots of food with our fingers. Isn't one of the most famous advertised as being finger-lickin' good? I learned to cook with my hands at a very early age, long before I used a spoon or a beater. I can remember making a quick coffee cake by first opening my hand like a big fork to mix the batter and then cupping it like a spoon to scoop the batter from the bowl. It seemed the most natural thing in the world, and it taught me the feel of a batter as nothing else could have done.

In my cooking classes I urge my students to get their hands into cake batters and soufflé mixtures, because once they get the feel of the texture and consistency this way, they never forget it. I find many people have difficulty learning to fold in beaten egg whites with a spatula and tend to overfold, but if you learn to fold them in by using the side of your hand to cut down, and the palm to fold up and over, you soon grasp the technique of quick, light folding that doesn't deflate the egg whites.

When I teach cooking, I like to structure the lessons as menus. My students learn how to time a meal so everything comes out at the right time, as well as mastering the techniques of food preparation.

So, for our very first lesson, we are going to start with a simple menu of hamburgers, green salad, and strawberry shortcake. We'll do everything with our hands, from forming the hamburger patties and testing the doneness of the meat as it cooks, to tearing and tossing the salad and making the biscuit dough for the shortcake.

Let's start with the shortcake. It will take 15 to 18 minutes to bake, during which time we'll start hamburgers and prepare the salad greens. First, preheat the oven to 450°F.

Measure 2 cups sifted flour, 1 teaspoon baking powder, ½ teaspoon salt, and 3 tablespoons sugar into a large bowl. Now put your hands in, scoop up handfuls of the ingredients, raise your hands in the air, and let the dry ingredients fall back into the bowl through your fingers. Do this several times and they will be well mixed, just as if you had sifted them together. Repeat until you are sure everything is thoroughly mixed.

Now, make a well in the center of the dry ingredients and put ¼ cup (4 tablespoons) of shortening (butter, lard, or vegetable shortening, whatever you prefer). With the tips of your fingers, crumble the shortening into the flour mixture until everything is well amalgamated and you have quite fine pieces of fat coated with flour, resembling coarse crumbs. Take ¾ cup heavy cream and work this in quickly with your hands, using just enough to make a soft, smooth, but not sticky dough, until the dough clings together. Turn the dough out onto a floured board and knead gently for 1 minute. Divide the dough into two portions, one rather larger than the other. With your hands, pat and roll each portion about ½ inch thick, making the larger piece 8 inches in diameter and the smaller one 6 to 7 inches in diameter.

Place the larger circle on a well-buttered cookie sheet and brush thoroughly with melted butter. Place the other circle on another buttered, or the same, cookie sheet and brush with melted butter. Bake for 15 to 18 minutes, or until nicely brown and cooked through.

While the shortcake is baking, wash and hull 1 quart of ripe strawberries, reserving a few of the most perfect for the top of your cake. Slice the remainder into a bowl, sugar them lightly, and set aside.

Wash and dry the salad greens. You can use romaine, Boston, or Bibb lettuce and some watercress, too, if you like its peppery taste in a salad. Discard any limp or coarse outer leaves, keeping only those that are crisp, tender, and fresh. Wash them well, shake the leaves to remove as much water as possible, then lay them on long pieces of paper toweling, roll them up so the paper absorbs any remaining moisture, put them in a plastic bag, and leave them in the refrigerator crisper drawer until you are ready to make the salad. (This can be done at least an hour ahead.)

Now for the hamburgers. A good hamburger is one of the simplest of all basic meat dishes, but even here there are one or two hand tricks that will make it taste much better.

To serve four people, take 2 pounds of chopped beef, preferably top round or chuck 75 to 80 percent lean, and divide it into 4 equal parts. Form these very lightly and gently into patties with your hands, almost tossing the meat back and forth. Do not overhandle or press the meat. Too much handling will make the patties heavy and solid, which is not what you want. The meat should just hold together. You can make the patties round or oval, thick or fairly flat, according to how you like your hamburger. If you want it rare, make them thick. If you like it medium, make thinner patties. Don't worry if they are sort of free-form rather than regular in shape. It's the taste, not the appearance, that matters most.

I happen to think pan-fried hamburgers taste better than broiled, so that is how we are going to cook them. Pat or sprinkle coarse salt and freshly ground black pepper to taste on both sides of the patties.

Now heat a film of oil in a heavy skillet. Oil is better for cooking hamburgers than butter, which tends to brown and burn at high temperatures, but if you like the flavor of butter, you can use a mixture of butter and oil.

When the fat is hot, but not smoking, put the patties in the pan and cook them briskly on one side for 4 minutes, until brown. Turn them carefully with a large spatula and cook for 4 minutes on the other side. Now press the browned surface gently with your finger and you'll find how much firmer it is than when it was uncooked. Then press the sides. These will be less firm because they have not been in direct contact with the hot pan and therefore have not cooked as much. At this point you can almost gauge how near to done the hamburgers are. Reduce the heat slightly and, for rare, give them 2 minutes more on each side. Press them again and you'll find they are rather more resistant to the touch but still slightly yielding, not hard and rocklike. Transfer them to hot plates with a spatula and serve at once. When you cut into the hamburger and find it done to your liking, remember how the patty felt when you pressed it. This is a very simple test, but it shows you how your fingers can send a message to your brain. A broiled steak can be tested in the same way.

While the hamburgers are cooking, finish the shortcake and salad. Remove the baked shortcake from the oven, transfer to a serving plate, and with a spatula or pancake turner, carefully remove the smaller circle. Cover the bottom, larger circle with the sliced and sugared strawberries, replace the smaller circle and garnish with the whole berries, lightly sugared. Set this aside to be covered with heavy cream, whipped cream, or sour cream, according to your preference.

Take the salad greens from the refrigerator and, with your hands, break them into bite-size pieces, dropping them directly into the salad bowl. Don't crush or twist them and, above all, don't cut them, which bruises and ruins salad greens.

The best salad servers I know are made of wood, and they are called salad hands because they are short and curved like hands, with fingerlike prongs. But even they will not toss a big salad as thoroughly as your own hands. When you toss greens with your hands, you'll feel when the leaves are coated and the salad properly mixed—which should always be done just before you are ready to serve it. Never let a salad turn limp in its dressing.

Let's say you have broken a large head of romaine into your bowl. Pour 6 to 8 tablespoons of good, fruity olive oil over the lettuce and then get in there with your hands and toss, toss, toss, using your hands like big forks and really tossing the greens in the air. The purpose is to give each leaf a protective coating of oil which will prevent the greens from going limp when the vinegar touches them.

Now, sprinkle the coated leaves with seasonings to taste. I like to use a teaspoon or more of coarse salt and a good ½ teaspoon of freshly ground black pepper (never use ready-ground pepper in cooking, it does not have the pungency and flavor of the freshly ground peppercorns). If you have a favorite fresh herb handy, like tarragon, chervil, or chives, you can chop and add a tablespoon of this.

Finally, just before serving the salad, add 1 to 2 tablespoons good-quality wine vinegar. I'm a miser with vinegar. I consider most people use too much and ruin their salads, so I suggest you put in 1 tablespoon first, toss well, taste a leaf, and see if you need more. It's always easier to add than to subtract. Now, I don't mean you should make a show of tossing a salad with your hands in front of guests, because then you would have to run out and wash your hands, but you can do it in the kitchen and it is well worth trying. You'll find you have a better salad.

So gather up your lovely, brown, crusty hamburgers and crisp, fresh salad, take them to the dining room, and enjoy your dinner, remembering the little lessons you have learned about testing and feeling the food as you prepare it. Next, we will move on to the extension of your hands, the most essential tools in your kitchen—knives—and you'll learn how to choose them and use them properly.

CHAPTER 2

KNIVES: THE
FINE POINTS
OF COOKING

Next to hands, the most important tool in the kitchen is a good knife. A knife can do practically all the necessary work of cutting, slicing, mincing, chopping, even scraping and pounding. Knives are the best friends a cook can have, to be treasured along with the family silver, for they are just as valuable and will last equally long if they are properly treated.

Now I don't mean that you have to rush out and buy a box of a dozen different knives. You can start out with three, perhaps, but make those good. First, and just about the most important, is what is known as a French knife, or a French cook's or chef's knife, made of either carbon steel or high-carbon stainless steel. If it's a good knife, it will be perfectly weighted, with a blade from 8 to 14 inches long, very wide at the handle and tapering to a triangle, heavy at the butt near the handle and of a more pronounced thinness at the point, with a handle that gives you a firm grip. The reason for this shape and weight is that a French knife is designed to chop, slice, and cut. The pointed end is thinner in order to slice certain things, the middle part of the blade is wider and also good for slicing, and the heavier end is best for chopping because the weight does the work for you; there is no need to expend a great deal of force to make the knife chop properly. As you get used to holding the knife, you'll find that by guiding the thin end with your left hand, you can slice mushrooms, onions, and other vegetables very finely.

The second important knife in your collection is a slicing knife, which should have a quite thin, supple blade with a rounded or pointed end. This knife is designed for slicing roast beef, turkey, a leg of lamb, a ham, or a pot roast or brisket. Properly sharpened, it will cut slices that are paper-thin, medium-thick, or very thick. This is an extremely useful knife, which no one can really get along without, and it takes the place of the old-fashioned carving set.

Last, but by no means least, there is the paring knife, which may be a little knife with a triangular blade that looks like a miniature of the French chef's knife, or a small knife with a curved scimitarlike blade.

These are the essentials. There are many other knives you can add to them. You may want to have two or three sizes of French knives, perhaps a 10-inch, 12-inch, and 14-inch, a utility knife, a boning knife with a thin, flexible blade, and a smaller boning knife for poultry, plus a fish filleting knife. All are a great help if you are really going in for cooking in a big way, but right now we are talking about the three very basic knives you need if you're just beginning to cook.

It makes no difference whether you buy a stainless-steel or a carbon-steel knife. There used to be a lot of controversy about stainless versus carbon steel, with people maintaining that it was impossible to sharpen a stainless-steel knife properly, but stainless-steel knives are quite different these days and sharpen beautifully. A stainless-steel knife that has been hollow-ground will give you good service. The secret is to keep it sharp and there are two ways to do that, either with the traditional, long, tapering, sharpening steel or with an inexpensive little gadget you can buy in any hardware store, a triangular piece of carborundum. Hold your knife at about a 20-degree angle to the carborundum and, with a quick swinging motion of your wrist and forearm, slide the blade across it. Don't lay it flat against the carborundum and scrape, just bring the knife edge down and across, maintaining the 20-degree angle, until the tip touches the bottom of the carborundum. Then repeat in an upward direction with the opposite side of the knife. You can do the same thing with a sharpening steel, but this more expensive tool will wear out before a carborundum. Another way to sharpen the knife, which you may find easier, is to lay it flat on a wood surface and, with the carborundum, make quick strokes along the edge of the blade. Turn the knife over and repeat on the other side. To be perfectly honest, providing you buy a well-designed knife of good steel and sharpen it regularly, it makes no difference whether it costs $6 or $25 [today the price range would be $20 to $75]. Don't feel you have to buy the best, unless you're a very serious cook, and then, I think, there should be no compromise. You want the very best knives you can get.

Today we're making a dinner of stuffed pork chops, ratatouille, and home-fried potatoes that will give you a chance to try out your three knives. Before we start any chopping, we are going to cook the potatoes and boil them in their jackets until they are just pierceable. Do not let them get soft. Plunge them into cold water for a minute to cool them off quickly and keep them from cooking further. Drain and set aside.

First, we're going to make the ratatouille, which is a French vegetable stew. You will need 1 eggplant, 3 or 4 smallish zucchini, 1 or 2 large onions, 4 or 5 garlic cloves, 6 or 8 fresh tomatoes (if they are not very good, it's better to use a 1-pound can of Italian plum tomatoes), and 1 or 2 green peppers. For seasoning, you will want 1 teaspoon of dried basil, or 2 or 3 tablespoons of fresh basil, if it is in season, 1 good teaspoon of freshly ground black pepper, and 2 or 3 teaspoons of salt, according to your taste. You may add a little thyme with the basil if you wish. I happen to like just the flavor of basil in ratatouille and don't enjoy mixing it with other herbs, but that's up to you.

Wash and dry the zucchini. Hold a zucchini in your left hand, tucking your nails under to grip it so that the knife won't touch the pads of your fingers. Then take your French knife and, with the point resting on the chopping board, raise the blade and then slide it down, cutting the zucchini in even slices. Cut right through the zucchini to the board, leaving the slices there in a nice pile until you need them.

Next, take the green pepper and, with your paring knife, cut around the top to remove the stem. Then, with your finger, remove all the seeds and the seed pod from the inside of the pepper. Take your slicing knife and slice the pepper across into even, thin rings. Push these into a pile.

Peel the onions with your paring knife, cut them in half with your French knife, crosswise, then put the halves on the table, flat side down, and, with the end of your French knife, cut into thin slices across the rounded side.

Now trim the top off the eggplant, cut it into slices ¾ inch thick, and then cut the slices, first lengthwise and then crosswise, into 1-

inch strips, which will give you 1-inch dice. Put the dice into a colander and sprinkle them with a small amount of salt. Press down with a plate so the salt and pressure will draw out the bitter juices.

Place the garlic cloves on your chopping board and give them a little bang with the broad side of your French knife to loosen the skin, then see how easily they will peel. If you didn't bang quite hard enough to loosen the skin, press down on the garlic with the flat of the blade until you hear a slight crunch. That means you have crushed it slightly. Now the skin will slip off easily. Either chop the garlic with your French knife, using the heavy end, or take a very sharp paring knife and slice thinly across the cloves, then cut little strips lengthwise and mince with the paring knife until you have very fine, tiny dice.

If you're using fresh tomatoes, they must be peeled and seeded. Blanch them by dropping them into boiling water for 1 minute, then remove them with a fork and, with your paring knife, loosen the skin and pull it off in long strips. With your French knife, cut a thickish slice from the top, stem end, of the tomatoes. Lay a paper towel on the chopping board, hold the tomato in your hand, cut side downward, and squeeze hard with your fingers so all the seeds and little bits of pulp surrounding the seeds come pouring out onto the towel. With your fingers, pull any remaining seeds out. Now chop the tomatoes coarsely with your French knife.

All right. Now you've cut up your eggplant, zucchini, onions, peppers, garlic, and tomatoes. Remove the plate from the eggplant and wash off the salt. Then press it down again with the plate to get rid of the excess water.

Put ¾ cup olive oil in a large heavy pot over medium to high heat. When the oil is hot (but not smoking), put in the garlic and onions. Stir them around a bit with a wooden spatula, and shake the pan until they have just become limp. Don't let them brown. Add the eggplant, zucchini, and peppers and stir them around very well so they get mixed in with the oil. Turn the heat down to just below medium, add the tomatoes, and let them blend in with the other vegetables. Add 2 teaspoons of salt, turn the heat down a little more, cover the pan, and let everything cook away for 15 to 20 minutes, stirring it once or twice to make sure nothing sticks to the bottom of the pan. Then add the basil and pepper, stir well, and cook for 5 minutes with the cover off, over low heat, so the mixture is just simmering. Now taste the ratatouille for seasoning. See if you need more salt or pepper or basil, or the sharpness of tomato. If so, add a little more canned or fresh tomato (I feel the canned Italian plum tomatoes are better than the fresh, but some people prefer to use fresh tomatoes). Now leave the cover off and let the ratatouille simmer down until it has reduced a bit—not until it is a mushy mess but just until it reaches the stage when it has recognizable bits of each vegetable, soft but not bitey, and well blended, with a beautiful overall flavor. The savory sharpness of the ratatouille will complement the fattiness of the pork chops, which you will stuff and cook while the ratatouille is simmering.

You'll be using the same knives again, except for the slicing knife. First, take your paring knife and sharpen it, because you're going to cut little pockets in the pork chops for the stuffing. These should be chops cut from the loin, ¾ inch to 1 inch thick. With the paring knife, make an incision ¾ inch from the end of the chops, halfway through the thickness, and cut as far as the bone—you don't want to make too large an incision, just a pocket to hold a stuffing of mushrooms, bread crumbs, onion, garlic, and herbs.

For the stuffing, first take 8 to 10 mushrooms, remove the stems, hold the caps on the board, with your fingertips bent back, and slice the mushrooms down very quickly with the pointed end of your French knife. When the mushrooms are sliced, switch to the back of the knife blade, where the weight is. Hold the back of the blade lightly, near the tip, with your left hand to guide it, and chop the mushrooms by working the blade in a fan-shaped pattern.

When the mushrooms are chopped, scrape them together into a little mound with your knife. Take a damp cloth and wipe the knife blade well. If you do this every time you use your knives, it will keep the blades clean and free of stains, and prolong the life of the knife.

Before you cook the mushrooms, you want to get rid of the liquid they contain—and mushrooms have a good deal. Put them in a dish towel, bring the corners of the towel together, and then twist the towel hard with your hands over a measuring cup or bowl, squeezing the mushrooms. You'll find that they will give up a lot of liquid, and that this will speed up the cooking time. Don't discard the liquid though. If you add this to a sauce or a soup, it will give great flavor. Now peel a good-sized onion, cut it in half, then in thin slices with your French knife, as you did before, and chop finely, using the back of the knife. Also peel and mince a garlic clove, in the same way as you did for the ratatouille.

Put 2 ounces (½ stick) of butter in a 9-inch skillet, let it melt, and

put in the onion, garlic, and mushrooms. Now see if you can shake
the pan and make the vegetables turn over, without stirring them
with a spoon or a spatula. Grasp the handle of the pan firmly, shake
it well, then give it a quick downward jerk so the vegetables flip up
and over by themselves. If you can master this, it's a great accom-
plishment and much easier and quicker than stirring. So, close yourself
up in the kitchen and practice shaking and turning until you have
it licked. You may get things all over the stove at first, but when you
get to the point where you can shake and turn nonchalantly, you'll
find out how much fun it is.

Don't overcook the onions and mushrooms. They should just wilt
down and blend together, because they'll get more cooking inside the
chops. Season the mixture with 1 teaspoon of thyme and ½ teaspoon
of rosemary. To get the most out of the dried herbs, put them in a
little mortar and rub them around a bit with a pestle first, or, if you
don't have a mortar, put them between the palms of your hands and
rub them well so they crunch down a little before you toss them into
the pan. Season with salt and freshly ground black pepper to taste—
the stuffing will take at least 1 teaspoon of salt and ½ to ⅔ of a
teaspoon of pepper, but you know your own salt level, so season as
you please.

Now mix in ½ to ⅔ cup bread crumbs, either the packaged kind
or bread crumbs that you have made in the blender. Stir in until the
stuffing thickens quite a bit, then add ½ cup of parsley, chopped until
fine with your French knife (don't forget to wipe the blade afterward).
Blend all this together, then take a little out with a teaspoon and taste
it to make sure it is well blended and has enough seasoning. If you
wish, you can add 3 tablespoons of red wine, sherry, or Madeira to
further enhance the flavor. If you do, let it cook for a minute or two
so that the fumes of the alcohol are volatilized by the heat.

Let the stuffing cool for just a few minutes, meanwhile wiping off
your worktable. Lay out the chops and, with a spoon or your fingers,
push the stuffing into the pockets, not overdoing it, as the stuffing
will expand in cooking. Fasten the edges together with a toothpick,
which you will remove before serving.

Put 2 ounces (½ stick) of butter and 3 tablespoons of oil in a heavy
skillet over medium to high heat. When the fat is well heated, but
not burning, brown the chops quickly on both sides until nicely
colored. This should take about 10 minutes. When they are browned,
add ½ cup of liquid to the pan—this can be red wine, white wine,

stock, or water. Adjust the heat to a simmer, cover the pan, and let the chops cook for 25 minutes, or until they are just cooked through. If they get too dry, add more liquid to the pan.

While the chops and ratatouille are cooking, you can make the home-fried potatoes. Take the potatoes you boiled in their jackets and, with your paring knife, peel off the skin. Now take either your slicing knife or a utility knife, which is similar in shape to the paring knife, with a rather large blade, and slice the potatoes ⅓ to ½ inch thick. As they have been slightly undercooked, they should not crumble. Heat 3 or 4 tablespoons of butter in a separate heavy skillet. Add the potatoes and cook very gently over medium heat, shaking the pan from time to time so that the potatoes get brown and crisp on both sides. It may be necessary, if they are very greedy potatoes, to add more butter to the pan. Season them with salt and freshly ground pepper, and cook until they are golden and crusty on the outside and soft on the inside. You can add other seasonings, if you wish, such as a little chopped onion, chopped garlic, or chopped parsley, but I think they are perfect by themselves, with nothing more than salt and pepper.

You should be able to time your meal so that the chops, potatoes, and ratatouille are all ready at the same time. Then serve them forth and enjoy your delicious dinner. If you want dessert, you might have an apple pie or apple crisp or apple charlotte, any of which are good after pork. I think you'll enjoy this symphony of flavors—the sharp, flavorful ratatouille with the succulently stuffed chops and the crisp, browned potatoes.

CHAPTER 3

GET TO KNOW

YOUR MEAT

CUTS

Years ago, when your grandmothers and mothers went to the butcher, they took with them a working knowledge of the anatomy of the animal. When they ordered a rib roast, they asked for the first four ribs. If they ordered a pot roast, they knew whether they wanted rump or an arm roast. If they bought sirloin, they knew the difference between pinbone sirloin and wedge bone sirloin. They knew where short ribs came from, and brisket, and they made delicious and succulent boiled beef. This knowledge must have been handed down from mother to daughter, like a home course in the anatomy of edible animals, and it gave them a sharpened sense of what to buy.

In my classes and in talking with people, I have discovered that no one nowadays seems to know much about the anatomic structure of meat-yielding animals, and I find this rather shocking. For economy's sake, if nothing else, it pays to know what you are buying and the best way to cook it.

Some of this lack of basic knowledge may well be due to the fact that we lived through a period of about five years when there were so many names being dreamed up by supermarket operators to identify, or misidentify, meat cuts that it's a wonder any of us knew what we were buying. There must have been a thousand retail meat-cut names that differed from city to city, and they were the most frustrating collection of names you have ever known.

Fortunately, the United States Department of Agriculture and the National Livestock and Meat Board got busy and reduced this number considerably. As a result, when I decided the other day to wander through the supermarkets to check for kinds of meat cuts and labeling, I was startled, pleased, and filled with admiration to find that not only have the cuts been uniformly labeled for easy identification, but also, in most cases, the label on the package tells not only the weight, the price per pound, and the cost of the package, but also the type and cut of meat. If the label says "beef" and it happens to be chuck, the cut is also mentioned—a blade roast, for example. I feel this is a great advance. As I made my way through the supermarket, I wondered just how many people were going to look at these labels and visualize the dishes they were going to make from the cuts. I played a little game with myself and came up with some ideas of what I would do. For instance, I saw some wonderful shank crosscuts, and shank, as I know from past experience, is a very inexpensive cut that boils beautifully and gives a lovely broth. Many French restaurants, small bistros for the most part, and some well-known restaurants, too, use shank for their pot-au-feu.

I remember making a perfectly marvelous boiled beef dish with an excellent piece of shank, and fresh vegetables. The meat, which was not overcooked when I removed it from the broth, sliced extraordinarily well and had great flavor. Shank is the meatiest cut of

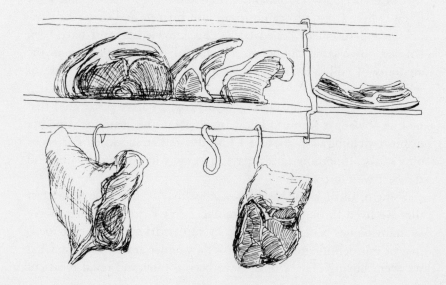

beef there is, and while it does have some tendons and gelatinous streaks running through it, the texture is pleasant and the flavor very good. Compared to the much fattier and more expensive brisket, a neighbor in the beef anatomy, it is in many ways a more desirable piece of meat. As brisket has more fat, it tenderizes more quickly, but for my choice I would be very happy with the shank. Thinking of brisket, however, recalled to me the delectable taste of a piece of brisket first seared under the broiler and then braised very gently on a bed of vegetables with some stock and wine, so that it cooked by moist heat until it was blissfully tender and full of flavor from the herbs and vegetables, and sliced beautifully.

Chuck is a part of the animal that has always baffled a great many people. It would make a perfectly beautiful braised steak, browned and then cooked with herbs and other seasonings and some liquids. The eye of the chuck is another very good cut, almost as good as an eye of the rib roast, although not quite as tender, and it can be used for all kinds of exciting dishes.

Then there are the short ribs, which come from the rib section of the animal. They take a little longer cooking and much more seasoning than some of the other cuts, but they do make a delicious finished dish.

Progressing from the front to the rear of the animal, we hardly need to discuss how to treat the tender cuts like the loin, sirloin, rib roast, and eye of the rib because most of us are well acquainted with these tender cuts used for steak and roast beef. Did you know, though, that the eye of the round, which comes from further back in the animal, can make a very good roast? It needs to be larded or barded with fat, because this is a very lean piece of meat with very little fat in it, but it has a surprisingly good texture and flavor. The bottom round is another less expensive cut that makes a very nice roast, although as a steak it is not very tender.

One section of the rear end of beef that seems to baffle people is the rump. In France and England, the rump is considered a delicate cut for steaks, and this it is. The steak will be less tender than a sirloin or porterhouse, but if the beef is prime or choice quality and correctly cooked, it really makes excellent eating. In any discussion of good pieces of meat for broiling, we must not forget the tip, a small triangular section at the end of the sirloin and the beginning of the rump, also extremely good eating. This oddly shaped piece of meat is delicate and delicious and great fun to play around with.

Another excellent steak that is often overlooked is the flank, a flat piece from the section under the sirloin, which needs to have the fat torn off before broiling. Many people think the flank should be braised, but if you buy prime or choice beef, this makes one of the best and tastiest pieces of broiled meat that you have ever tasted. Flank steak is the correct cut for London broil, and it should always be cooked quickly to the rare stage and sliced very thinly, on the diagonal.

Economical Lamb Cuts

Perhaps even more of a puzzle to the average person than the less familiar beef cuts are the inexpensive cuts of lamb. Except for loin and rib chops and that popular roast, the leg, most people are not as accustomed to lamb as they are to beef and pork. Yet there are such goodies in lamb! As far as I'm concerned, one of the most neglected cuts is the breast. I've had people say to me, "Oh, it's so fat." Well, it doesn't have to be. Nothing could be more delicious than breast of lamb that has been poached very gently, cut into pieces, breaded, sautéed, then served with a lovely sauce. Or you can prick the breast with a fork and roast it on a rack in the oven until it is crisp as crisp, with all the fat cooked out. Just salted and peppered, this is almost better than spareribs. Sometimes I partially roast the breast to draw the fat out, stuff it with a savory filling of crumbs, herbs, currants, and seasonings, tie it, and roast until it is beautifully crispy on the outside, with this pungent savory stuffing inside. How good it tastes.

If you like bones, as I do, you will find that the neck of the lamb can be one of the most rewarding parts of the animal. Have it cut into slices, brown it under the broiler, and then braise it with herbs, seasonings, and wine. This is a lot of work to eat, but well worth the trouble.

CHAPTER 4

FROM A SIMMER

TO A BOIL

Can you boil water? Or poach an egg? Do you know what it means to blanch a cauliflower or simmer a stew? Strangely enough, all these are part and parcel of the same process, which goes under the general heading of boiling.

Boiling is a relatively primitive achievement in the culinary world, but it is also a highly versatile and necessary one, because in one form or another—boiling, poaching, simmering, and blanching—it enters into nearly every recipe we prepare in one way or another. Naturally, you all know that at sea level water boils at 212°F, and that if you put a pot of water on a burner and turn the heat to high, within a very few minutes it will come to the point where you can see little bubbles form on the bottom and the seething begins. Suddenly the water will seethe and bubble furiously, like lava in the crater of a volcano—and that is boiling.

Poaching is done at what is known professionally as a feeble ebullition, which is exactly what it sounds like—a boil that is hardly a boil at all, just a faint lazy bubble that rises to the surface and sort of pops, like a carefully blown soap bubble. Fish, eggs, and similar delicate foods are often poached.

Simmering is just about the same as poaching, maybe 1 degree less active. A simmer is the steady, feeble ebullition you need when making a stew or a pot-au-feu or a pot of soup, when the surface of the liquid barely moves and the bubbles streak just below it. Often foods that have been previously prepared in one fashion or another, such as seared meat, are then set to simmer until tender and done. Simmering helps to mingle the seasonings with other ingredients, and it relaxes and tenderizes whatever you are cooking, be it a piece of meat, or a collection of vegetables, or even a mixture of fruit.

Blanching is another story entirely. Blanching, in which food is immersed in boiling water and allowed to steep or cook slightly, is actually searing with water, just as you would sear meat to seal the surface thoroughly by browning it in hot fat or under a hot broiler. Well, blanching has the same effect. It sears the surface in different degrees for different reasons. We blanch certain vegetables to make them limp, such as peppers, before they are stuffed, or cabbage, before it is chopped for certain dishes, or lettuce, before it is braised. You might briefly blanch a cauliflower for 3 or 4 minutes and then serve it shaved very finely. The blanching will remove the uncooked flavor but leave the crisp texture. You could also blanch string beans before you completely cook them, in order to keep their color bright and green.

Blanching is synonymous with parboiling, a word we have used in our cooking terminology for many years, and apart from this process of partial cooking, it also helps to remove strong odors and flavors. A ham with too much salt may be blanched, or a piece of salt pork, or bacon with a very smoky quality, before being used in a delicate dish.

Each of the processes is extremely important to the everyday round of cooking, no matter how familiar and simple it may sound. For instance, we boil an egg. Don't let anyone tell you an egg is "soft cooked" or "hard cooked." It is boiled. If you're making a soft-boiled egg for breakfast and the request is for a 3-minute egg, you boil it for 3 minutes on the dot. If you go one second over, you'll probably get a reprimand from whoever is waiting for the egg. If you are doing hard-boiled eggs, you boil them rapidly for 2 or 3 minutes, then turn the heat off, and let them rest in the hot water for another 8 or 9 minutes. If you are making an *oeuf mollet*, you bring it to a boil, boil it for 4 minutes, then remove it, put it in cold water at once, then shell it and use it as you would a poached egg.

There are many different theories about poaching eggs, but you will find, I think, that the following method is the best of all. Bring salted water with a dash or two of vinegar to a boil in a large skillet, then take your eggs and lower them into the water, not too many at a time. There are many ways to do this, but I like to use tiny cups. I drop each egg into a separate cup, lower it into the water, and then tip the egg in very quickly, so that it coagulates almost instantly and doesn't spread all over the pan. As soon as all the eggs are in the water, remove the pan from the heat at once (some people remove it before putting the eggs in) and let the eggs poach very gently in the hot water for 3 to 4 minutes, basting the tops with tablespoons of hot water, if necessary. When the eggs have set and are nicely filmed with white, remove them with a perforated lifter, such as a pancake turner, so that the water drains through. If you're going to use them right away, place them on a paper towel or dish towel to absorb the excess water before using them. If you intend to use them later on, lower them very gently into a dish of cold water so that they will stop cooking and will be easy to handle if they are going to be trimmed afterward.

Now to end this lesson, we'll have an exercise in boiling and simmering. For this I have chosen the French pot-au-feu, or pot on the fire, one of the more interesting examples of what we call a boiled dinner, and also an excellent source of stock. This old revered dish has many derivations and combinations, and I think you will agree that this version is awfully good.

I have found that in making this pot-au-feu, you get a better result if the broth is made a day ahead and then skimmed of all fat.

Put in a pot 2 large marrow bones, an onion stuck with 2 cloves, 2 well-washed leeks, a carrot, a sprig of fresh thyme or a good pinch of dried thyme, a sprig of parsley (preferably Italian parsley, and if you can buy it with the root on, use this as well as the leaves because it adds great flavor), and a whole head of garlic—not a clove, a head. Don't peel the garlic, just take off the papery outer skin and throw it whole into the pot. Add water to cover and bring to a boil, then reduce the heat, cover, and cook very slowly for several hours. Taste for salt, and add as much as you think is needed, then strain the broth, discarding the bones and vegetables, and chill overnight. Next day, skim off all the fat that has formed on the surface before adding your meats.

About 3 hours before you plan to serve the pot-au-feu, put the skimmed and melted broth in a 12-quart pot. Add 1 onion stuck with 2 cloves, a 1½-pound piece of brisket, a 3-pound piece of bottom round, and 2½ to 3 pounds of short ribs with the bone in. Tie each piece of meat so it will keep its shape during cooking. Soak 8 leeks well, removing the sand from between the leaves. Cut off the green tops and tie these in a bundle with 4 sprigs of parsley, 3 or 4 sprigs of fresh thyme, and any other fresh herbs you can get, such as tarragon, rosemary, or summer savory. If you can't get fresh herbs, add 1½ teaspoons of dried thyme and a pinch or two of other herbs to the broth.

Bring everything to a boil, then skim off the scum and any little bit of fat that rises to the surface. When meat or poultry is boiled, the chemical reaction between the food and the liquid brings forth this frothy scum, which may continue to form for 5 or 10 minutes. If you want a good finished dish, this must be skimmed off completely. After skimming, reduce the heat, cover, and simmer for about 2 hours.

Meanwhile, get your other vegetables ready. To serve eight, peel 8 small white onions, peel and quarter 8 small white turnips, and peel and quarter 12 to 14 medium-size carrots. Wash and cut in sixths a curly savoy cabbage or, if you can't get a savoy, a firm green cabbage.

After the meats have cooked for 2 hours, add the leeks and cook for 15 minutes, then add the onions, turnips, and carrots, skimming the surface every time you add anything to the pot. In a separate pan, boil 8 well-scrubbed new potatoes in their jackets.

When the vegetables are almost tender, test the meats. If they are done, remove them to a hot platter and keep warm. Add the cabbage to the pot and cook for 5 or 10 minutes more, until all the vegetables are tender. Season the broth to taste with salt and freshly ground black pepper and skim off as much fat as possible before removing the vegetables. Pour off a good part of the broth, to which the vegetables will have imparted a lovely sweet flavor, and serve this first in bowls with slices of French bread which you have sliced 1 inch thick and dried in the oven. Pass a hunk of Parmesan cheese and a grater so everyone can grate cheese directly onto his or her bowl of broth, which gives it an extra zest. Reserve some cheese on a hot platter with the vegetables. Every person should get a cut of each kind of beef, some vegetables, and a potato. Ladle the hot broth over the meats and hand around some of the traditional spicy accompaniments for this dish, such as a good mustard, coarse salt, grated fresh horseradish, and the tiny sour French pickles called cornichons, which you can buy in jars in specialty food shops. Drink a fruity red wine, such as a young Beaujolais, with your pot-au-feu. To follow, you might have some kind of apple dessert such as an apple charlotte, or crepes filled with sautéed apples, sprinkled with sugar, glazed under the broiler, and served with heavy cream.

One of the great advantages of making pot-au-feu is that you can reheat the beef in the broth the next day, or turn the cold boiled beef into something quite delicious, such as a beef hash or a beef salad.

So there you have the four related processes—boiling, poaching, simmering, and blanching—some of which we will be combining with other techniques later.

CHAPTER 5

KNOW YOUR

COOKING

TERMS

I sometimes think there is nothing quite as baffling as the cooking terms set down in most cookbooks. For instance, that ubiquitous phrase "heat and serve." Heat is a most indefinite term. It could mean heated in the oven, in a saucepan on top of the stove, over boiling water, or any number of ways. Wouldn't it be infinitely better to spell out the required process? If a vegetable had been cooked and was to be reheated, it would be easy enough to say, "Reheat for two or three minutes in a saucepan over medium to high heat, shaking the pan occasionally and adding more butter, if necessary, then transfer to a heated vegetable dish and serve." This is more direct and certainly makes better sense.

Then there is the verb *to chop*. We all know what chopping means, but there is more than one way to do it. You can use a food chopper, or a Chinese cleaver, or a large French cook's knife with a triangular blade, or any other kind of chopping device. What you use often depends on the type of food you are chopping and the sizes of pieces required for the recipe. You might use one of those double-bladed, wooden-handled choppers to chop onions or mushrooms, but if you wanted to cut a piece of meat into large cubes, you would need a cook's knife.

There are many cooking terms that people find perplexing, so I'm going to explain a few of them to you. Last chapter, we defined the differences between boiling, poaching, simmering, and blanching, all processes involving hot water or liquids. Now we'll concentrate on some of the terms that apply to meat cookery.

First, let's take lard. Many books tell you to lard less-than-tender meats that are to be roasted or braised, such as beef round, rump, or chuck, cuts without the marbling of fat that lubricates the more expensive ones. To lard, you cut firm pork fat (fatback, blanched fat salt pork, or solid pieces trimmed from a fresh ham or pork leg) into strips 4 to 6 inches long and about ¼ inch square, and push them into the hollow groove of a larding needle. For added flavor, they may be soaked first in cognac or whiskey, with perhaps some herbs. There are two or three different types of larding needles, but for interior larding the standard type is a long, grooved piece of metal with a pointed tip and a wooden handle. The needle is thrust through the length of the piece of meat several times, so that the pieces of fat, or lardoons, as they are called, will stay inside the meat when the needle is pulled out. As you pull the needle out, press your fingers against the hole in the meat, or the fat may pop out, too. This interior larding of fat not only helps to tenderize and lubricate the meat, but it also makes a rather decorative pattern that looks nice when sliced. With the new grass-fed beef, we're all going to have to learn to lard, because this meat will be much less tender and flavorful than the fine grain-fed beef we have enjoyed for years.

A word closely related to lard, and often confused with it, is *bard*. Barding is another way of using fat, on the outside rather than on the inside. To bard means to wrap a thin sheet of pork fat or other fat around a bird or piece of meat that has little fat of its own. Very often people will ask the butcher to lard beef tenderloin when they really want it barded, but he usually figures they don't know what they are talking about and bards it anyway. Barding also lubricates during the cooking process, but the meat or bird will not brown. For this you must remove the barding fat and raise the temperature for a short time before taking the meat or bird from the oven. Barding is extremely important with game birds such as wild duck and quail, which lack natural fat. You should season the bird before barding, so that the seasonings will flavor it as the fat lubricates the flesh.

Another word you often encounter in meat cookery is *corned*, as in corned beef and corned pork. Corned means that the meat has been cured by being soaked in a salt solution or brine. Corned leg of pork, sometimes called Scotch ham, or gammon in English terminology, is not as heavily treated as most cured hams are, or used to be. Our old-fashioned hams were put into a heavier brine than that used for corning, and left in for one to three weeks before being removed and lightly smoked. Nowadays, most hams—commercial ones, anyway—are given a very light cure and a very light smoking, although it is still possible to find a few companies that produce country hams with the old-fashioned flavor.

Another familiar meat which is brined and slightly corned is pastrami. This is similar to corned beef, but the seasonings are different and the beef is lightly smoked after being brined. If you have a little smoke oven, you can corn and smoke your own pastrami, which is rather fun to do.

Sear is a term often encountered in meat cookery. You sear meat by browning it very quickly with high heat, either in fat on top of the stove or under the broiler, in order to seal in the juices. Often a roast is seared at a high temperature before being cooked slowly at a lower heat. Steaks and chops are also seared, and so is the meat you will use in a stew or ragout.

Then there is the term *glaze*, to give food a glossy or glazed finish, which can be done in different ways. On top of the stove, onions and carrots may be steamed in butter, then sprinkled with a tiny bit of sugar and tossed for a few minutes until the sugar melts and carmelizes, glazing the vegetables a shiny brown. Or food covered with a sauce or grated cheese, or both, may be put under a hot broiler until the surface is brown and glazed.

A word that I find often baffles my students is *dredge*, as in "dredge with flour." I'm not sure where it originated, but it means to cover

a food with flour, cornmeal, or crumbs. You are often told to dredge pieces of chicken with flour before sautéing or frying them. An extension of this is breading or pannéing, where the chicken is first dredged in flour, then dipped in beaten egg, and, finally, rolled in bread crumbs. Dredging meat with flour makes it brown better when it is seared in fat. Breading ensures that the coating of crumbs will adhere more firmly to the food when it is cooked, also in fat.

While we are on the subject of dredging, we might as well mention an allied process, *deviling*. Foods that are deviled, among them beef bones, pig's feet, or small broiling chickens, are precooked, then rolled in crumbs, brushed with oil or butter, and broiled or baked until the crumbs are crispy, crustily brown. Very often deviled foods are served with a sauce diable, or devil's sauce, a brown sauce spiked with hot mustard, Tabasco, and pepper.

Some of the terms and processes I have mentioned are essential steps in the recipe I'm going to give you for a simple and flavorful beef stew. A stew, which in French is called a ragout, or sometimes a blanquette, is one of the easiest and most satisfactory forms of meat cookery. There's something quite exciting to the palate about a good beef or lamb stew with its savory blend of meat, vegetables, seasonings, and herbs.

To serve four, cut 2 pounds of lean beef into 1½- to 2-inch cubes, trimming off any fat. Dredge the beef cubes with 3 tablespoons of flour that has been seasoned with 2 teaspoons of salt and 1 teaspoon of finely ground black pepper, making sure that they are thoroughly coated. Melt 3 tablespoons of butter or bacon fat in a heavy skillet or Dutch oven, and when hot, but not smoking, add the beef cubes, a few at a time (don't crowd them in the pan or they will not brown properly), and toss them well until seared and browned on all sides. Transfer the browned cubes to another pot. Turn the heat down and add to the fat remaining in the pan 2 finely minced garlic cloves, 1 teaspoon thyme, and a sprig of parsley. Toss in the fat for 2 or 3 minutes, then add 1 onion peeled and stuck with 2 cloves and 1 carrot. Let them brown a little in the fat, then transfer them to the pot with the meat. And 2½ to 3 cups of beef stock or canned beef broth (or, if you must, water). There should be just enough liquid to barely cover the meat. Bring to a boil, put a piece of buttered waxed paper or foil over the pot, and cover tightly with the lid. Reduce the heat and simmer very, very gently for 1½ hours. Remove the cover and paper or foil, and test the meat for tenderness. It should be nice and tender, but if it isn't, give it a bit longer before adding your vegetables.

When you think it is tender enough, add 8 small onions and 8 small carrots, which you have glazed in a skillet with butter and a touch of sugar, and 8 small potatoes or 4 medium potatoes, halved or quartered. Cook these with the meat until done.

Remove the meat and vegetables to a hot platter and taste the sauce for seasoning, adding more salt, pepper, thyme, or garlic if needed. Should the sauce need thickening, knead butter and flour together and form into tiny balls (this is called beurre manié), drop these into the sauce, and simmer slowly until thickened. Return the meat and vegetables to the sauce just long enough to heat them through, then serve the stew on a hot platter with a garnish of chopped parsley. Have crisp French bread with your beef stew and perhaps a salad.

So there you have a recipe that combines basic cooking terms and techniques such as dredging, searing, glazing, stewing, and heating.

CHAPTER 6

COOKING

ON THE

OUTDOOR

GRILL

Since outdoor cooking began, many years ago, it has gone through so many phases that it is hard to define as a particular form of cookery. In my childhood, people improvised—or had forged—little racks to place over bonfires. This, of course, was an advance on the days when food was balanced on stones over a fire, the most primitive form of cooking. My mother had two or three racks that we used over beach bonfires, once they had burned down to good glowing coals. We grilled hamburgers and seafood and sometimes baked pancakes on the grill, and our improvised barbecue worked extremely well.

Later on, during the 1940s, when the vogue for cooking in the backyard first caught on, people built more elaborate outdoor fireplaces with towering chimneys and side ovens and fireboxes and grills. This was the era of what I choose to call the Cremation School of Cookery. Those early outdoor chefs believed the thing to do was to get a fire roaring, thrust whatever they were cooking onto the grill, and let the flames do the rest. The results were catastrophic. The high heat caused the meat to shrink and the fat to pour out; the meat, charred on the outside, was pretty rare on the inside, because if it stayed on the grill any longer it would have burned up completely. The wasted meat was something one could hardly contemplate. I've seen fine 2½-inch porterhouse steaks reduced to a mere shrivel by cremation cookery.

Gradually, people began to realize that there was an art to cooking outdoors, just as there was to cooking indoors. After the war, when they'd had a little more experience with meats and poultry and basting sauces, outdoor cooking and eating became an integral part of American living and entertainment. As these outdoor cooks learned about making fires, it became obvious that by using proper fuel, and letting it burn down to a proper degree of heat that would cook the meat gently, one could get extremely palatable results and a delicious aroma that was an overpowering stimulus to the olfactory nerve.

During the months I spent in California with Helen and Philip Brown, working on *The Complete Book of Outdoor Cookery*, I made the acquaintance of General Barton, inventor of the Barton Grill, who, after leaving the Air Force, spent many years developing what is perhaps the most accurate method of grilling over a charcoal fire that anyone has ever discovered. His methods are still standard practice for anyone who wishes to cook well alfresco.

Nowadays, we seem to be taking a more relaxed and interesting approach to outdoor cooking. People seem, for the most part, to have eschewed those big unwieldy charcoal grills and adopted the Japanese hibachi, a small and compact grill that is exceedingly efficient if you have limited space in which to cook, such as a city terrace, a porch, a tiny backyard, or even your living room fireplace. Recently, while I was in San Francisco, I used a hibachi to cook racks of lamb on a tiny terrace overlooking the bay, with rather splendid results.

It stands to reason that the first rule of outdoor cooking is to have a good cooking unit. There are some excellent commercial units on the market, ranging from little hibachis to grills with adjustable cooking surfaces that can be raised or lowered over the fire. There are also larger units that will accommodate a big piece of meat, many of them with electrically driven spits so that one can roast as well as grill. There are gas grills, electrical grills, just about every kind of unit for alfresco cooking that one could dream of.

The two main faults with most outdoor cooking are: first, people throw too much fuel on the fire; second, they leave too much fat on the meat. I'm aware of the fact that fat gives the meat its flavor, but fat melting down into the hot coals can cause a conflagration and turn your grilled meat into something quite inedible. Fuel, and I'm talking now of charcoal briquettes (or regular charcoal, if you can find it), should be used sparingly and given ample time to burn down to ash-covered coals. You may think you're losing fuel by doing this. You're not. If you thrust a pyrometer into the center of your firebed, you'd be amazed at the temperature that it would register.

When you have a bed of really dusty-white coals, and you can feel a glow of intense heat when you hold your hand over the grill, you're ready to cook. Let's say that you are going to grill some little racks of lamb. When you buy a rack of lamb, have the fat removed and the chine bone cut so that only the little ribs remain. Then take a sharp knife and run it across the bone structure at the end of the little eye of the meat, severing the remaining bit of flank. Remove this by scraping the rib bones until they are practically bereft of flesh, so you have this beautiful eye of practically fatless lamb, with well-scraped rib bones. You may marinate these little racks if you wish, but it is not necessary.

To season and flavor 4 racks of lamb, finely crush 4 good-sized garlic cloves (and by crushing I mean really reducing them to almost a liquid) in a mortar and pestle or in a heavy bowl with a mallet or crusher of some kind. Combine the garlic with 6 tablespoons peanut or olive oil and some finely chopped fresh rosemary, or dried rosemary crushed in a mortar and pestle or in the palm of your hand until it is reduced to a fine powder. (There's no pleasure in finding one of those hard, spiky little needles in your teeth as you eat the lamb.) Add 1 to 1½ teaspoons of freshly ground black pepper and mix everything together well. Then, with your hands, massage the racks with the oil mixture, rubbing it thoroughly into the meat and over the bones. It will cling to the meat only if you use the massage treatment. At the last minute, you can rub a little salt into each rack, too, or, should you be a purist, you can withhold the salt until the racks are practically done.

Lay the racks, ribs up, on the coals, and let them grill for perhaps 3 or 4 minutes. Add a little red wine to what is left of your oil mixture, and a touch more oil if need be. Then, with tongs, turn the rack on the bone side and brush the flesh side with a little of the wine-oil mixture. Let it cook with the bone side toward the heat for 5 or 6 minutes, brushing occasionally during that time and turning the rack again, if you wish, to give each side more of the heat. Cook flesh-side down for a minute, then turn to the fleshy side, brushing the meat again with the wine and oil before you do so. If you believe in last-minute salting, this would be the time to do so.

I can't give you an exact timing for grilling because I don't know your particular type of grill or how pink you like your lamb. I like mine pretty pink, therefore I take it off at an internal temperature, tested with an accurate meat thermometer, of 125° to 130°F. Tiny racks take from 12 to 15 minutes to grill to the proper state of delicious brown doneness. Turning them frequently does not hurt them, despite what people say, and it helps to color the lamb evenly. The bones may become a little charred at the ends, but this is all right. Don't worry about it.

To be absolutely certain that the lamb has reached the temperature you prefer, test the racks with a meat thermometer. If you don't have one, you can cheat by cutting into the fleshy part with a small sharp knife to see how done it is inside.

Remove the racks to a carving board or a large heated platter, and be sure your guests are ready to eat and your serving plates are warm. Lamb doesn't wait; it begins to congeal and it will do so even more rapidly on cold plates. Hold the lamb by the bones and with a very sharp carving or slicing knife carve the meat in thin slices parallel to the bone, right down to the ribs. This gives you lovely even slices much more attractive to look at and eat than if you carve the meat into little chops. Serve everyone two or three slices. After the meat is carved, divide the racks into crispy bones and serve them in a bowl or basket as an added dividend to munch on. You need no sauce except the juices that accumulate in the plates or on the platter or board, but you will need a good vegetable.

Let's say that you have some new potatoes and fresh peas. Cut a bellyband around the center of the potatoes so that you have a nice contrast between the inside and the skin, cook them until tender, and then combine them at the last minute with freshly cooked peas, quantities of butter, salt, and pepper, and a bit of raw chopped onion or chopped green onion, and you'll have a most exciting accompaniment to your lamb.

My other favorite for outdoor grilling is chicken. I like to use split broilers with the backbone or spinal column removed. A good butcher will do this for you, but if not, it isn't difficult to do yourself. Take the split chicken half with the backbone (usually it is on one side only) and feel the bone that starts at the neck and continues down the center of the back. With a very sharp French chopping knife or heavy kitchen scissors or poultry shears, cut the bone away. Now divide the chicken into two through the breast and rub them well with seasoned oil or butter. For 4 chicken halves, combine ¼ pound (1 stick) butter or ½ cup oil with a rounded teaspoon of freshly ground black pepper, 2 or 3 tablespoons of chopped parsley, 3 tablespoons of chopped fresh tarragon or powdered dried rosemary. As you are rubbing the chickens, loosen the skin around the neck end with your fingers, gently slide your hand underneath, and rub a little bit of the herby mixture on the flesh, which will lubricate and flavor it in the most marvelous way. Be sure that the skin side and the bone side are equally lubricated. This is very, very important when you are grilling chicken. You can add other things to your lubricating mixture. You can add several tablespoons of soy sauce. You can add finely chopped bacon, inserting the pieces under the skin. You can add other herbs of your choice, or lemon juice, which gives a distinctive, fresh flavor.

Before you start grilling, melt ¼ pound (1 stick) of butter, or take another ½ cup oil and combine it with a heaping teaspoon of salt, the juice of 1 lemon (or rather more, if the lemon isn't very juicy), and ¼ cup dry white wine or dry vermouth. Mix well together in a bowl and put the bowl and a basting brush close to the grill.

There are two ways to grill the chicken, either directly on the grill or in one of those large folding basket grills that lock shut, the kind that resemble the old-fashioned toaster we used over the fire years ago. Place the chicken pieces in the folding grill, quite far apart, then close and lock the grill so the chicken is held firmly.

Make a fire with 45 to 50 charcoal briquettes and let them burn down to a good bed of coals, keeping a few spares around the edges of the fire to push into the burning coals, if need be, during the grilling process. When your coals are ready, place the chickens bone-side down on the grill and cook for 12 minutes, lifting the pieces and brushing the bone side with the basting mixture once during that time. If you're using the basket grill, turn that and brush the bone side, then replace. Let the chicken cook on the bone side for 12 or perhaps 15 minutes. If there are flare-ups from the coals, spray a little water on them to douse the flames.

Turn the chicken pieces, brushing them thoroughly, so the flesh side is nearest the coals. Watch very carefully to make sure that the skin does not blister and char too much, brushing it frequently during the second part of the grilling process, which should take another 12 or 15 minutes in all for 2-pound broilers. This will give you very juicy chicken. If you want your chicken better done, grill for another 5 or 6 minutes, testing the flesh with a fork. Personally, I don't care for chickens cooked to death. I like the white meat moist and I don't care if there's a drop of pink juice at the joint of the thigh and the leg. I think this makes for much better eating.

Serve these crispy, tender chickens hot with a delicious vegetable, perhaps sautéed corn—corn cut from the cob and sautéed quickly in butter with a little tarragon or rosemary—and a huge salad of seasonal greens, to which you might add sliced tomatoes or sliced cucumbers. This, with crusty bread and a lightly chilled young Beaujolais, makes a sensationally good outdoor meal. Before serving the chicken, sever the thigh and leg joints and the wings, then put them back together tidily on the plate. That way your guests do not need to struggle with knives and forks; they may use their fingers, if they wish.

Grilling is a simple art and also one of the most intriguing of cooking methods. It used to be said that it was man's place to preside over the grill and the woman's to provide the other provender. This piece of male chauvinism has disappeared along with a lot of other old wives' tales about cooking. I know several women who are just as deft at grilling as men, for this is a process that admits of no sex distinction.

CHAPTER 7

AN EXPERIMENT
IN TASTING

Recently, we tried a most interesting experiment. We had a class in "Tasting," which was just exactly that. We tasted seasonings and foods, and discussed and compared them. People are unaware, for instance, of the difference in salt. One night, we tasted six different salts: a coarse salt that comes from France, the grains crunchy and firm, and the flaky Maldon salt that comes from England, which has, aside from its saltiness, a real flavor. We tried a very coarse rock salt, which is used mainly in kitchens for ice cream and sometimes in wine coolers. We tasted an ordinary, everyday shaker salt and kosher salt, which is semicoarse, and a very pure salt. With some of these salts, notably the kosher and Maldon salts, it was found that the quantities used were greater than those used for the more intense and highly concentrated shaker salts, or the ordinary salts that one finds on the market.

This brought forth a discussion of how most people undersalt. Many people will give a recipe and suggest the amount of salt to go in a dish, but people will pick up a dibble-dabble with their fingers, sprinkle this in, and consider it to be enough salt for an important dish, and it's not. It's one of the greatest faults in cooking, especially one of the great faults in baking, particularly in breads. People undersalt, and it leads to less palatable, certainly less assertive dishes, and certainly to a great deal of salting at table, which I consider to be rather disrespectful to the host. It's also unnecessary, most times. Very often people will salt automatically, without ever tasting the dish. It's rather silly. Salt is an important additive that establishes and emphasizes flavor, and it should be used with intelligence and discretion, but it should never be used in a miserly fashion.

Next to salt, of course, is pepper. Freshly ground pepper is the ideal one. Previously ground pepper tends to intensify in flavor, to lose its pungency, and to become much less palatable than the freshly ground variety. There are, of course, three versions of pepper on the market. We use, for the most part, black peppercorns; they may be Japanese peppers or peppers that come from Southeast Asia. Then we have white pepper, the white peppercorns with the black skin removed. They are considered by many people to be more delicate in flavor and to be more genteel to use. Why it seems necessary to use white pepper in a sauce that is a white sauce, I have never been able to find out. People are delighted to chop up black truffles and throw them into a white sauce. Why not put some good, honest, black peppercorns into a white sauce? I don't know.

Nowadays, there is a third pepper on the market that hasn't been common to all of us for nearly as long a time as black or white peppercorns. I am referring to green peppercorns, which dry into the black peppercorns, which become white peppercorns. They are soft, as compared to the others, and are a rather brilliant green. Some are preserved in water, some in a brine, and still others (which are not as good) are preserved in vinegar. A great many of them come from Madagascar. They are packed in various size cans, from about two ounces up to five ounces, and they vary a good deal in quality.

These three peppers are not interchangeable. The black and white are, but the green peppercorns require rather special usage. I think if you are interested, you might get a great deal of satisfaction out of taking some of each—the black, the white, and the green—and crushing or grinding the black and white, and chopping the green, or leaving it whole, and tasting them against each other. Don't taste without clearing your palate with a little piece of bread before tasting the others. It's very necessary. See which gives you the most satisfaction.

We are all wont to grind peppercorns and get varying degrees of coarseness. Take your pepper grinder, grind some pepper on a piece of paper, and look at the coarseness. Now, if you have several pepper grinders, as I have, try each one and see if you have varying degrees of coarseness. I'm fortunate in having two or more pepper grinders that have adjustable grinds—a very sensible idea for pepper. I also have a large grinder that has an adjustable grind, which I use in the kitchen for pepper if I'm using more than a regular pepper grinder will handle quickly. If you find that none of your grinders provides you with pepper that is as coarse as you want it, you have two or three alternatives. You may use a meat pounder, a heavy rolling pin, or a mortar and pestle, and crush the pepper to the coarseness you desire. You can also use an electric blender to grind pepper, or one of the small electric coffee grinders that are so prevalent in the market nowadays, that I, by the way, use for all sorts of spices—for peppercorns, for cinnamon, for cumin seed, for anise seed, for many types of spices. They are very efficient, and give forth a fresher, more pungent spice than the familiar little can or bottle one buys in the supermarket.

Now, for our main experiment with pepper—and this is one that I think you may enjoy playing with, especially if you're entertaining a group of people (so that you will not have any waste)—we bought 3 flank steaks. If you have a feeling that this is going to overwhelm your budget or be too much meat for you to eat at once, you might buy 1, or 1½, and divide it into 3 pieces. Trim the excess fat and any tendons that occur on the flank steak. A flank, as you know, is a steak that comes from the end of the rib and the sirloin, and is quite flat. It used to be considered a steak that had to be braised,

very often stuffed, and given long, moist cooking, but flank steaks from good cattle make for delicious eating when broiled and broiled quickly.

So, you have your flank steaks. One good-sized steak of about 2 pounds will serve four people very well, and 1½ or 2 steaks will serve six to eight amply. If you want to play with this and have an experiment for guests, you could have six to eight people and experiment with this steak *au poivre*.

A steak takes about 3 to 4 minutes on each side, broiled fairly close to the broiling unit, and turned once. Gauge the other things you are going to do for dinner accordingly, so that your steaks can come out blissfully rare and ready to serve with whatever else you're having. About 15 minutes before you're ready to broil your steak, or steaks, grind enough of the white peppercorns and the black peppercorns, or crush them, to give you about a tablespoon of each. Then cut enough of the green peppercorns, that have been drained, to give you approximately the same quantity of coarsely cut green peppercorns. Season each of the pieces of meat with a different kind of peppercorn. Press them into the respective pieces of meat to be broiled, along with some coarse salt. This should be crushed in with the heel of your hand, and you should press it in on both sides, so that there is an infiltration and crust of the peppercorns and salt at the time you cook the steak in the broiler. Let them rest for about 10 or 15 minutes to absorb some of the pepper flavor. Have your broiler hot. Have your other food ready to serve, and have hot plates. Now, take your steaks and place them on a rack in the broiling pan, and broil them for at least 3 to 4 minutes, each side, and brush them as you turn them with a tiny bit of butter, if you wish. When they are broiled on both sides, remove them to a carving board or boards, and place a pat of salted butter on each one. Now, remember these steaks have been peppered and salted before cooking—and don't tell me that they're going to pull the juices out, because they aren't.

Then, with a very sharp knife, cut thin, sparsely diagonal slices of the steaks and give each person two or three slices of each one, separate from each other, perhaps, by whatever vegetables you are serving, and, if you want to be very scientific about it, have little memorandums so your guests know which is which. Taste these steaks with the vegetables, or perhaps some bread, and see what the difference is in these three peppers. It's extraordinary, and you may do the same thing with lamb chops or chicken.

I don't feel as grim about the possibility of using freshly ground pepper at the table as I do about salting at the table. There is a great difference of opinion with people as to what degree of peppering they wish. I find that I'm a very heavy pepper eater with certain things. On broiled meats, for instance, I like a great deal of pepper, and on scrambled eggs or fried eggs, I like an enormous quantity of freshly ground pepper, and with potatoes. I think that pepper enhances certain other vegetables, notably yellow turnips, and gives them a more rounded flavoring and contrast. So, I think you've got to experiment with pepper and see how you stand with certain dishes.

There may be dishes you always thought were dull that you'll find very rewarding and very, very worthwhile if you add freshly ground pepper. I'm a great believer in playing with pepper. Now, mind you, this has nothing to do with the other peppers and chilies and sauces made with peppers that we use as condiments. It has nothing to do with Tabasco, which is a sauce made from Tabasco peppers, a variety of chili; it has nothing to do with cayenne pepper; it has nothing to do with tiny green peppers in vinegar, which are used sometimes, or the crushed red pepper pods that the Italians are so fond of as additives to certain dishes. This applies only to the peppercorns—green, black, and white—that we use on our tables every day, and usually three times a day, to enhance and to give added flavor to many, many dishes we serve.

CHAPTER 8

FRYING

I don't think there is any food in this country more popular than French fries. They are served with hamburgers, with steaks, with chicken, with eggs, and with practically anything else on the menu. Children scream for them and adults are equally addicted. They can come crisp and cooked to perfection, or they can come flabby and miserable. Either way they are eaten slathered with catsup, mustard, and even mayonnaise.

They are only one of the many fried foods Americans dote on— we are probably the world's greatest consumer of things fried—and by fried I mean deep-fried, because cooking in a skillet with only a small amount of fat, what many people call frying, is really sautéing. We deep-fry fish, we deep-fry vegetables, and, unfortunately, in diners and greasy spoons we deep-fry bacon, a dreadful morsel to put in one's mouth. It is the quick and easy way to cook, and the newest of all the cooking processes. In this country, however, it has had a long history.

A breakfast specialty in New England used to be doughnuts and crullers, which, of course, are deep-fried. And there was also that old by-product of bread baking, "dough gobs." These were made by tearing off chunks of risen dough and dropping them into hot lard.

They came out crisp and crinkly and were anointed with fresh maple syrup. Many a family filled itself on dough gobs before setting out on a morning of accomplishments. In the South, around New Orleans, there were the fascinating calas, really deep-fried rice croquettes, that were hawked through the streets with the cry *"Calas tout chaud."* How they were kept *tout chaud* I will never understand. Elsewhere in the South there were fried pies, which were mounds of pastry filled with fruit and securely sealed around the edges. These were dropped into hot fat and cooked to a flaky brown finish, a nice change from the usual baked pie. I can remember my first experience with fried pies on a bus trip to the South. A man climbed aboard with a large basket of lunch which included these little pies. He shared them with everyone around him. They were still warm, juicy and crisp, and I succumbed to their charm at once.

In the days before kitchen thermometers, frying used to be a hit-or-miss proposition. One heated the fat—and it was usually lard or beef fat—and tossed a piece of bread into it to see if it browned quickly. If it did (in about thirty seconds), the fat was ready for frying. But this wasn't foolproof. It was a guessing game that sometimes worked and sometimes didn't. Nowadays we have deep-frying thermometers and French friers with thermostatic controls. Anyone can make perfect fried foods if he wants.

We have a variety of fats to choose among for deep-frying. We still have lard, favored by earlier generations, and very good for frying. We have vegetable fats, such as Crisco. And we have beef fat. This has to be rendered but is worth the trouble, because the flavor of beef lurks in the fat. Potatoes fried in beef fat make one of the choicest dishes imaginable. There was a speakeasy in New York that built its reputation on potato chips fried in this way and served at the cocktail hour.

Then we have a selection of oils. Olive oil is used by many Italians and French for deep-frying. Peanut oil is almost universally used— by the Chinese, the French, the Americans, and the English. Corn oil is also popular.

If you reuse fat or oil, strain it through cheesecloth after each frying and store it in a cool place. To clarify it, following a second or third fry, cook a couple of potatoes in it. If this doesn't work, it is time to begin afresh. I generally get three or four fries out of a container of whatever oil or fat I am using, although I find that beef fat is less durable than oil. When I am through frying, I try to conserve as much of the remaining oil or fat as I can. You can use the same oil to cook different foods without risk of transferring flavors. However, it is a good idea to keep a separate supply for fish.

There is a wide choice of frying equipment available: proper French fryers fitted with a basket that sinks into the boiling oil, making it convenient to transfer the contents to absorbent paper; heavy iron pots that can be used in conjunction with a basket; or electric skillets especially designed for deep-frying. The Chinese use a wok for this purpose and it works very well. For people who like to fry in open fat, there are innumerable skimmers and strainers. No fancy equipment is really needed. As long as you have a solid container to hold the fat and a good skimmer or basket, you are in business.

It is essential to have a shallow pan lined with absorbent paper on hand when you are frying so you can allow the cooked food to drain of any excess fat. If you are frying a large quantity of food, it will be necessary to do it in batches. In this event you may want to heat the oven to 200° to 250°F, so that you can slip a pan of cooked and drained food in to keep warm. If it is something like doughnuts or crullers that do not require warming, simply place on racks to cool.

There are several ways to prepare food for frying. Potatoes, naturally, are fried in their peeled state, usually cut into long sticks that range in thickness anywhere from the McDonald's size of ¼ inch to the 1-inch giants you find in some restaurants. In one restaurant in New York, the long Idaho potatoes are cut into wedges with the skin left on and fried that way, an interesting variation. Many foods, such as vegetables, are floured before frying. Thin strips of unpeeled zucchini, for example, almost matchstick in size, when floured and dipped for just a moment into hot fat come out brown, crisp, and delicious. Chicken, too, is dipped in seasoned flour before frying. Doughnuts and crullers get coated with a certain amount of flour, which helps them to brown quickly, since they are rolled out and cut on a floured board. Then there are the fried foods that are done in various and sundry batters—egg batter, buttermilk batter, or beer batter. Onion rings are prepared this way, and the famous Japanese shrimp dish tempura. Finally, some things like croquettes are treated to several steps before frying, being dipped in flour, then in an egg mixture, and rolled in crumbs.

Here are a few recipes you can use to practice your frying techniques. Let's begin with everyone's favorite, potatoes.

FRENCH FRIES

For six persons you will need at least 6 good-sized potatoes. Peel them and then slice in any of the following ways: Cut straight across the potato in thin slices or on the diagonal; or cut the potato lengthwise into slices of any size that you want—from ¼ inch to ¾ inch—and then cut each slice to make long sticks of uniform thickness.

Now there are three ways to handle the prepared potatoes. They can be fried at once in deep hot fat (375°F), lowering a few at a time in the basket. Do not overcrowd or the temperature of the fat will drop, and the potatoes will be soggy and greasy instead of crisp. Let them cook until they are a deep golden color. They will turn themselves in the bubbling fat. Once they are cooked they should be placed on absorbent paper. Check the temperature of the fat between fryings. If you are cooking a large quantity of potatoes, put each batch in a 250°F oven to keep warm until all of them are done.

This is the second method: Place the prepared potatoes in cold or ice water and let them rest for several hours. Then remove them and dry thoroughly. I find that a large bath towel is the best thing for drying. Spread out the towel, lay the potatoes on it, and roll it up until the water is absorbed. Then proceed to cook the potatoes as described in the first method.

A third method often used is this: Take either the freshly cut potatoes or the soaked and dried potatoes and deep-fry them in deep fat heated to only about 325°F, until they are just barely seared and lightly colored. Remove them at once to absorbent paper and let them rest. When you are ready to serve, plunge them into very hot fat— about 365°F—for a few moments. They will turn crisp in a hurry. The advantage of this double-cooking method is that there is less frying time and the potatoes come out crisper.

There is another style of fried potatoes that I am fond of these days, and it requires shredding. I put mine through the shredding attachment of the Cuisinart food processor. These little strings of potatoes need only be lowered into hot fat (375°F) for a few seconds to become delicately crisp and lovely in flavor. They can be served in a great bird's nest of a mound on a heated dish or used as a garnish for a roast.

Onion rings are another much-sought-after fried food, especially with steak and roast beef, and just because people love fried onions. I garnered a recipe years ago from an old fellow columnist of mine,

Cecily Brownstone, and it is as fine a one as I have ever had. These onions are wonderful with steaks or chops cooked over charcoal. Prepare them in the kitchen and rush them along when the meat is ready. They are even good as an hors d'oeuvre to be served with drinks, if you have someone to take the trouble to cook them and keep them coming out of the kitchen.

CECILY BROWNSTONE'S FRIED ONION RINGS

Beat together 1 egg and 1 cup of buttermilk. Then stir in 1 cup of flour and ½ teaspoon each of salt and baking soda.

Cut 3 or 4 large onions into ¼-inch slices and break up into rings. Soak in ice water 2 hours, adding more ice if needed. Remove, dry thoroughly, dip in batter, and fry in deep fat a few at a time at 375°F. Remove from the fat when nicely browned and drain on absorbent paper. Keep warm in the oven till ready to use.

Lest you think that the only fried foods worth having are potatoes and onions, let me introduce you to an Italian dish called Fritto Misto, literally "mixed fry," which consists of a combination of meats, fish, vegetables, and sometimes sweets, all deep-fried. The one given here—using fish and vegetables—is one with an interesting batter made with beer, which, in addition to being a leavener, seems to make everything cooked in it rather tender and crisp. It is very much like the batter the Japanese use for tempura.

FRITTO MISTO

First prepare the batter, and it is best made several hours ahead of time. Combine ¾ cup of flour with 2 egg yolks (reserve the whites), 1½ teaspoons of salt, 2 tablespoons of oil, ¾ cup of beer at room temperature, and a grind or two of black pepper. Stir well until it is free of lumps, and let it rest for about 2 hours. Just before you start the frying, beat the 2 egg whites—you have already used the yolks— until they are stiff but not dry. Fold them gently but firmly into the batter. Meanwhile, in a deep fryer you should heat the oil of your choice to 375°F. Also heat the oven to 250°F, and have some baking sheets lined with absorbent paper.

We did this dish in a recent class of mine with great success, and this is the selection of things we fried: Rex sole, filleted and cut into pieces about ¾ inch wide to make what are sometimes called goujonettes; artichoke bottoms, cooked until tender, cleaned of the choke and cut into halves; raw string beans, raw asparagus tips, and cauli-flower flowerettes, blanched for 1 minute in boiling water; eggplant, cut into "fingers"; mushroom caps; and zucchini, cut into very thin strips and rolled in flour.

All of the ingredients were dipped in the batter, except for the zucchini, and then deep-fried. It took about 25 minutes to do the entire job. After the fish and vegetables were drained, they were handsomely arranged on a large silver tray and presented as a first course.

You can vary the ingredients for Fritto Misto in any way you wish. For vegetables, you might use spring onions, onion rings, cucumber strips, or any seasonal items. For the fish, you might choose among scallops, crab legs, or shrimp—either the jumbo ones or the more modest size. Do not cook the fish beforehand, since it will get ample cooking in the fat. A Fritto Misto can be served as a first course or a main course.

Fried foods can be as exciting as anything in the cooking repertory if done properly, and they are fun to work with besides. Get busy with your fryer and see how creative you can be.

CHAPTER 9

SOME LIKE IT

HOT

Have you ever, when walking down a street in your neighborhood, suddenly found your nostrils quivering as they pick up the fragrance of tomato and garlic and oregano? "Ah," you say to yourself, "our neighbors must be having spaghetti and meatballs tonight."

Or you might be going along the corridor of your apartment house and smell curry issuing from one door, at the next the wonderful aroma of frying chicken, and a little further on, more than a hint of corned beef and cabbage cooking. Mouth watering, you might open your own door and sniff that spicy mixture of soy and garlic and fresh ginger and grated orange that means you'll soon be eating teriyaki steak or teriyaki chicken.

It's wonderful what our noses tell us. In Texas, Arizona, or lower California you seem to be enveloped in a heady cloud of chili. Within three or four blocks you may smell six or more different versions, for among the legion of chili peppers each has a different pungence and a different quality of hotness or mildness or sweetness. There are very few aromas, or bouquets, if you will, that can touch the smooth, velvety bouquet of a good chili. There's no other bouquet of cooking food that has quite that penetrating provocativeness. It smells rich, yet it doesn't taste rich. It smells complicated, but it really isn't. It smells divinely good and arouses the most urgent longings. When you just can't stand it any longer, you rush into the nearest chili joint and have a bowl of canned chili with beans that gives you a momentary satisfaction, even though it has about as much good chili powder in it as you could put under the nail of your little finger. But no matter—it does something marvelous to your soul.

I know one famous New York hostess who used to entertain with great pomp and ceremony when she had a large household staff. Now, rather than do something less impressive, she has switched her tactics and delights her friends with one of the world's greatest chili recipes, which she serves in her beautiful Spode bowls with Georgian silver spoons. To enter her house and be greeted by that wondrous, unctious, appetizing aroma, a tantalizing overture to dinner, sets all your taste buds working overtime.

It's funny how you can meet up with chili in the most unexpected places, like encountering a childhood friend in some odd corner of the world. I shall never forget one time sitting down to dinner in a famous American restaurant in Paris, a place that prided itself on its American dishes, and finding on the menu "Chili con Carne," followed by (and I'm translating the French for you) "a sort of cassoulet with chili peppers." Well, a chili is as far from a cassoulet as an Orange Julius is from a Romanée-Conti. I'm sure any Frenchman who ordered the restaurant's excellent chili would be pretty puzzled by that description.

There's a great joy and satisfaction about making chili, playing around with it, putting good meat and good flavors together—and I don't mean buying a chili brick in a Texas store, adding a pound of hamburger, and turning out something mediocre. I'm talking about a well-made chili, brought forth with pride and served with beans on the side, or rice, or even pasta. That can be divinely good.

Everyone seems to have his or her own little rules about chili. Some still grind the chili peppers in the Mexican *metate*, a lava-stone mortar. Others soak the peppers in liquid and then scrape the pulp from the skin. Certain cooks combine several different chili peppers—in fact, some dishes are said to have as many as twenty-three or twenty-four chilies represented in the combination. Most of us just use chili powder, which is a mixture of chilis plus other herbs and spices, and here it is important to pick as good a chili powder as you can find. Some are mild, and a poor excuse for anything that might be called chili. Others come in varying degrees of sweetness and hotness. One or two spice firms produce a sweet as well as a hot chili powder, which is a very good idea because that way you can get the balance you want without adding other fiery ingredients such as cayenne or Tabasco. There used to be a great spice company in Denver, the Spray Spice Company, that made extraordinary chili powders, and there are still places around the country where one can get them freshly made, skillfully blended and very, very good. I think the best way is to start with the finest chili powder your local markets have to offer and suit your mixture to your own palate, combining it with the classic additives, like ground cumin and oregano. Oregano happens not to be on my list of favorite flavors, classic though it may be. I prefer to add thyme, or a little rosemary, or sometimes sage, according to my mood.

There are more controversies and opinions about what goes into a good chili than there are about any other food. Some people feel chili must have tomato in it. Others say chili should be made with beef broth, or with beer, while others just toss in some water. Well, I have made exellent chili with beer, with tomato purée or cooked-down tomatoes, and with a rich beef broth. Once, when I experimented and made my chili with part pork and part beef, I used both beef broth and pork broth. I don't really think it matters, you should use what is most appealing to your taste.

Then there's the battle between the beaners and the nonbeaners, a battle that will be waged for as long as we eat chili. Beaners believe that chili must be cooked with kidney beans or pinto beans, as well as the meat. I do not subscribe to this. I think beans are marvelous *with* chili. I like refried beans, those that have been cooked, mashed, and recooked very slowly (classically, with lard) until they become crispy on the outside and smooth and soft on the inside, like perfectly mashed potatoes. And I like red kidney beans or pinto beans, but they must be cooked separately and served with chili, along with rice. Then, although this may sound like heresy, I think that pasta and chili are extremely friendly. The combination of the two, in the Italian manner, perhaps with some Parmesan cheese sprinkled on top to give a lift, is absolutely dreamy.

One doesn't have to be too much of a purist. I've experienced all kinds of variations on the straight line of chili that have been very successful. Ground nuts—either ground toasted hazelnuts or peanuts or cashews—added to chili as a thickener, an enrichment, and for a difference in flavor and texture can be quite delicious. I remember once having poached chicken with nut-thickened chili spooned over it and rice and beans on the side. It had a hauntingly different quality, the quality of a great sauce. A grating of bitter chocolate tossed into the chili, on the lines of the Mexican *mole*, to give body and smooth out the flavors is something else that is much to my liking.

Chili couldn't be easier to make. I have a recipe I use over and over again that is simple, flavorful, and as authentic as any chili recipe can be. Just serve it with a bowl of beans and a bowl of rice or, if you'd rather, with good crackers or tortillas and perhaps a relish like *salsa fria*, that cold sauce of chopped-up tomatoes and onion and a spicy touch of chili pepper.

First, take about ½ pound of well-chilled suet (beef kidney fat; if you can't get suet, use rendered beef fat or beef drippings) and chop it very finely, either by hand or in the food processor. If you are using the processor, it is easier if you freeze the suet. Chop 2 very large onions, add them to the skillet, and sauté them very gently, adding the rest of the suet or fat as the onions start to melt down. Cook very slowly until the suet is rendered to a liquid and the onion has practically melted into the fat.

For your meat you will need 3 pounds of top round or rump of beef, sliced ½ inch thick and then cut into ½-inch dice. As you dice the meat, trim off and discard most of the fat. Add the meat to the onions in the skillet along with finely chopped garlic cloves—2 to 4, according to taste. Let the meat brown well and blend with the onion, garlic, and fat. Don't rush it. Just shake the pan thoroughly so everything mixes together. When it is well browned and blended, add a minimum of 3 tablespoons of chili powder, 1 tablespoon of ground cumin or cumin seeds, and a healthy dash of Tabasco. Cover the mixture with boiling beef broth or tomato purée or warm beer, whatever liquid you prefer. Cover the skillet and simmer at the lowest possible heat for 2 to 2½ hours, stirring occasionally. As you stir, taste and correct the seasoning, for you and you alone can tell how you want your chili. You may want more chili powder, more Tabasco, or perhaps some finely chopped jalapeño chili pepper to make it hotter—and, of course, you'll want to add salt according to taste.

You can either serve the chili at once, or you can let it cool, chill it overnight, and then remove the excess fat from the top and reheat it the next day. In this way, it has a chance to mellow, and if you can stand the wait, it's preferable.

You can take this basic chili and vary it by changing the flavoring slightly, or thicken it by mixing in ground nuts or cornmeal.

Here's another version of chili, this time made with ground beef. This one makes a wonderful hot and spicy topping for hamburgers and the Coney Island red hots I'm going to tell you about later.

Sauté 4 finely chopped large onions and 4 finely chopped garlic cloves in ¼ pound suet (beef kidney fat). Add 3 pounds finely ground lean beef, preferably round steak, and brown quickly, until all the pink has disappeared. Then add 1 teaspoon oregano, ⅓ to ½ cup chili powder, 2 dashes of Tabasco, 3 tablespoons tomato paste, and 1½ cups of warm beer. Cover and simmer for 45 minutes. Uncover, taste, and correct the seasoning, adding salt and whatever you think it needs. Add more liquid if necessary. Cook the chili down for another 15 minutes. Serve garnished with finely chopped fresh coriander, sold in Spanish-American markets as *cilantro*, or with finely chopped parsley. You can vary this by adding whole-kernel corn or ground nuts during the last 15 minutes of cooking time.

A touch of chili does a great deal to enhance a number of other dishes and it proves you to be an imaginative cook without really stretching your imagination too far. For instance, for breakfast you might put poached eggs or fried eggs on toasted English muffins or corn muffins and spoon your chili over them, adding perhaps a little chopped cilantro or shredded Monterey Jack cheese. With good coffee, toast, and guava jelly and cream cheese this makes a great Sunday breakfast for guests.

I once made a batch of chili and suddenly found myself inundated with a group of about eighteen people I had to feed. I hadn't the faintest idea what to give them and my batch of chili was only enough for about six, but I decided to make an experiment—and it worked. First I chopped 3 very large onions and about 6 garlic cloves and sautéed them in a very large skillet in olive oil. As they softened I added chili powder, sage, rosemary, tomatoes, sherry wine (for some unknown reason), and about a cup of chopped parsley. I let this all cook down well for about 25 to 30 minutes, until the flavors were well blended, then I dumped my lovely chili in and let it cook for about 10 minutes more. I served this forth in my best soup bowls, with toast, grated Parmesan cheese, and sour cream to dollop on, and it was one of the greatest soups I have ever served, a tremendous success. Quince paste, which I always keep in the larder, and cream cheese finished off this very good supper for eighteen people.

Another way to stretch a batch of chili is to put a layer of cooked rice in a deep 9-inch casserole—you'll need between 2 and 4 cups of rice—add some shredded Monterey Jack cheese and a few black olives, and then fill it up with chili. Sprinkle a few sesame seeds on top, put it in a 350°F oven for 25 minutes, take it out, sprinkle the top lightly with shredded Monterey Jack, and return it to the oven just long enough to melt the cheese. Serve very hot with refried beans or kidney beans and some pickled jalapeño peppers if you can eat the really hot ones, otherwise you might have a *salsa fria* that has a cooling, refreshing quality and hot tortillas.

You want to make a good taco? Easy as pie. Either buy your taco shells or make them by frying tortillas in hot fat until they are golden. When they are ready to be filled, put some shredded lettuce in the bottom, then add some Monterey Jack cheese, a bit of chopped chili pepper, a good helping of beans, fill with hot chili, put more lettuce on top and a few sesame seeds. Eat at once, with plenty of napkins handy because the tacos will dribble and drip, but that doesn't matter because they taste like heaven. Or make yourself a delicious chili burger. Make your hamburger, put it on a toasted and buttered bun, give it a slice of tomato and either a slice or two of onion or some chopped onion, then spoon chili over it to your heart's content, top it with the second half of the toasted bun, and put just a dab of chili on top for color and some chopped cilantro for authentic flavor. With a glass of Mexican beer you couldn't have a more appetizing lunch or supper. A chili burger is one of the high points of the burger family.

While we are talking of the many uses of chili, let us not forget a classic of American eating that goes back as long as I can re-member—the Coney Island red hot. While it is called Coney Island, I have a feeling that this chili-laden frankfurter really originated in Chicago, but I may be wrong. The Coney Island red hot grew into a national chain, though not one as prevalent and publicized as McDonald's or Burger King, the great hamburger chains. Over the past sixty years, in the more offbeat section of most important cities, almost in the tenderloin section in some places, there would be a store called the Coney Island Red Hot with a great steaming frankfurter dripping with chili painted on the window. The chili recipe of whoever started Coney Island red-hots was made not with cubed meat but with ground meat, as so much chili is, and it was not too thick, but beautifully seasoned, hot, and flavorful. The store was not, as a rule, decorated with any sense or style; it had just stools, chairs, and a few tables, and usually you would order one or two red-hots per person and carry them home in a sack, or eat them on the street, unless you decided to sit there and have just one Coney Island red hot with a glass of beer. The rolls were rather thin and the franks frankly mediocre, but with a lavishment of really good chili and quantities of chopped onion they were one of the greatest junk foods—and still are—that I have ever known. If you've never tasted this part of the American junk food culture, hunt around until you find a Coney Island Red Hot store [now defunct]. Or, if you want to make your own, use the ground-beef chili recipe I gave you, heat it up a bit more with some hot chili pepper, and serve it on hot dogs with loads of chopped onion. Eat it with a glass of beer or even a Coke, and you'll have something extraordinarily good, something that satisfies the longing for a pungent taste in your mouth. Even after you've brushed your teeth and gone to bed, there will be just a hint of that marvelous chili flavor left somewhere on your palate so that you wake up in the morning with the thought that you had a satisfying chili experience the night before.

I remember when I was a child in Portland, Oregon, there were two Coney Island Red Hot joints in my particular bailiwick, one right next to the streetcar I would take home at night and another a couple of streets away. At one-thirty or two in the morning, you'd find there a mixture of what were then called hoboes, fashionable people in evening clothes, and just plain lovers of Coney Island red hots, all indulging their consuming passion. It was great fun. Strangely enough, no one has ever taken credit for inventing this most American of foods. It just seems to have come about naturally.

I adore chili. It is so universal, so homely, so much a part of our traditions, and it comes very close to being one of the most popular of all our national dishes.

COOKING
WITH WINE

One of the phrases I loathe the most is "gourmet cooking." What gourmet cooking is I will never know. There is fabulous cooking, good cooking, mediocre cooking, and bad cooking, and I'm convinced that some people can never rise above bad, probably because they don't really like to cook. It is the urge to get into the kitchen and the delight of making something work out according to a recipe or your own thinking that makes for good cooking.

One of the things that enhances good cooking is a good wine. There is no such thing as "cooking wine." During the late unlamented period of prohibition, fancy grocers sold a cooking wine with so much salt in it, it was unusable, and certainly undrinkable. I doubt if anyone ever made a fortune out of it. There's a French saying, "The better the wine, the better the dish." That does not, of course, mean that one should take a bottle of Lafite '59 and use it for making a *coq au vin*. It does mean that one cooks with wines that are flavorful and full-bodied, whether they be from America, France, Italy, Spain, or wherever. The whole purpose of cooking with wine is to add flavor to a dish, either by putting it in the food as it cooks or using it in a marinade to infuse meat or game with wine flavor, and the wine should be one you would like to drink. I very often use a wine for cooking and serve the same wine at table. Naturally, I don't do this with the rare wines I serve on special occasions, but for a simple, ordinary dinner it is very pleasant. In most cases, you will not use more than a cup in the recipe, which leaves an ample amount in the bottle for two people. If not, you can have an extra bottle handy. So pick your wines for the kitchen with the same care that you pick them for your cellar.

Just about every type of wine lends itself to cooking, including sherry, port, and Madeira. We all know that dry white wine enhances a chicken sauté or a fish, or fish dish, and gives a zest and a tartness it wouldn't have otherwise, and that a full-bodied red wine can do wondrous things to a stew or braised dish, a brown sauce, or a dessert like pears poached in wine. The sweet wines, like the French sauternes, are luscious with fruit and other desserts.

Because wine is used as a flavor, the most important thing to remember is that the alcohol should cook out, leaving only the taste of the wine. Somewhere in the cooking process the wine must reach the boiling point and stay there for a minute or two to evaporate the alcohol, otherwise the dish will have a disagreeable, harsh, and rather bitter overtone. If a recipe calls for a small amount of wine, that's what it is supposed to have. That isn't being stingy or economical, but giving the wine its proper place in the combination of ingredients, so you get just the right degree of flavor. So if a recipe lists 2 tablespoons of wine, or ½ cup, don't pour in more and drown everything. Nor do you have to add wine to every dish you cook. Keep it for the dishes where it really counts.

Very often people who start to cook with wine do so with a degree of caution. There used to be a misguided group who would add a drop of sherry to a soup just before it was served, not realizing that it should have cooked in the soup for a few minutes to take away the rawness. Properly used, sherry can give a great distinction to a cream soup or a bisque or a thick soup, though you wouldn't put it in vegetable soup or clam chowder. Canned soups benefit enormously from a touch of sherry. Say you are fixing a meal for an unexpected guest and all you have is canned soup. You combine two different soups to enhance the quality and maybe give the impression that you made the soup yourself. So taste it, add a tablespoon of good dry Spanish sherry for each serving, cook the soup for a few moments, then taste it and see if you have added enough to take it out of the realm of canned soup. Usually 1 tablespoon per cup of soup will change the quality and give a sort of dressed-up flavor.

In colonial American recipes, and a great many French and Portuguese recipes, you'll find a wine that I consider is one of the most valuable for cooking—Madeira. Madeira is a fortified wine from the island of the same name, and in the eighteenth century it was the standard wine in this country, drunk in inordinate quantities. All of the great names in the history of our country had cellars of fine Madeira. Firms like S.S. Pierce of Boston had their Madeira shipped around the continent in casks to age it properly before selling it to their New England customers. There are two kinds of Madeira, one very dry and suitable for brown sauces and soups, the other sweeter and better for desserts. One of the most famous French sauces, *sauce Madère* or Madeira sauce, is a brown sauce flavored with Madeira and truffles and served with beef and poultry. In the days when thick luscious turtle soup was a popular item on menus in this country, it was Madeira that gave the soup its rich flavor. Today, if I am doing a sautéed chicken, I very often add a little Madeira to the pan and let it cook down and add its beautiful flavor to the bird. Or I may sauté kidneys very quickly, then deglaze the pan with a little Madeira, blending it with cream and maybe some chopped mushrooms. I use Madeira in a brown sauce for roast chicken or turkey and add a touch to the stuffing for my Thanksgiving or Christmas bird.

Wine figures in cooking so many ways, from the simple, fast sauté to the stew or daube, for which the meat is marinated in red wine for twenty-four hours and then slowly simmered in the marinade until it is richly flavored, tender to the bite, and exciting to the palate. Red wine is the essence of such great dishes as *boeuf à la bourguignonne*, where the red wine of Burgundy comes into play, and also *coq au vin rouge* from Burgundy or the Auvergne, cooked with the red wine of either region. In the classic version of coq au vin, the chicken is slowly simmered in red wine, as much as a bottle, but I have evolved my own quick way of doing this dish, which I find works better with the very tender chickens we get these days.

First you make a brown sauce. Melt 3 tablespoons butter in a heavy saucepan, add 3 finely chopped shallots or green onions, and sauté until limp and golden. Stir in 2 cups dry red wine and two 10½-ounce cans beef bouillon (not consommé), and bring to a boil. Season with a couple of pinches of dried thyme and cook over high heat until the liquid is reduced almost by half. Work 4 tablespoons soft butter and 4 tablespoons flour to a paste with your fingers, then roll into tiny balls. Drop these little balls, a few at a time, into the boiling liquid and cook, stirring constantly with a wooden spatula or a whisk, until the sauce is thickened to your liking. Don't add all the balls at once, as they take a little time to break up and thicken the liquid. When thickened, season to taste with salt and freshly ground black pepper, then strain the sauce into another pan. Butter a piece of waxed paper and lay it on top of the sauce to prevent a skin forming, and set aside until ready to use.

Heat 2 tablespoons butter and 1 tablespoon oil in a heavy skillet, add 18 peeled small white onions, and sauté them until lightly browned, then sprinkle with 2 teaspoons sugar and cook, tossing, until the sugar caramelizes and gives them a nice glaze. Set aside while making the chicken.

For this I use 2 broiling chickens, split, with the backs removed. Rub them well with salt, pepper, melted butter or oil, and paprika (which gives them a nice color) and put them on the rack of a broiling pan that has been rubbed with melted butter so the skin won't stick. Broil them 4 inches from the heat, bone side up, for 12 to 14 minutes, basting once or twice with melted butter, then turn them, brush the skin side with butter, and broil for another 12 to 14 minutes, again basting once or twice.

While the chickens are cooking, cook ¼ pound salt pork (cut in fine dice) in a heavy skillet until the fat has melted and the pork is brown and crisp, then add 18 firm white mushroom caps and toss them in the fat with the pork until lightly browned.

Now comes the time to assemble the dish. The chickens are cut into serving pieces—legs and thighs, breasts and wings—and they then go into a casserole with the glazed onions, the salt pork and mushroom caps, and the brown sauce, and the whole thing is gently heated together over medium heat until it reaches serving temperature, then served forth with boiled rice. In this way the chicken is never overcooked and stays tender, moist, and juicy, and the onions and mushrooms retain their crispness.

That's just one way to use red wine in cooking. It is, of course, an essential part of many marinated dishes. Venison may be marinated in red wine with flavoring herbs and vegetables, then cooked, with the strained marinade used for sauce. If a leg of lamb is marinated this way, then wiped dry, roasted, and served with a sauce made from the marinade, it is known as "mock venison." There's a similar dish from Spain done with a pork roast, usually a fresh ham, that is marinated for a week, then roasted and served with a sauce made from the marinade, pine nuts, and currants or raisins. This gives a delightfully different zest to "drunken pork," the name of the dish in translation. In certain parts of France, pork is cooked this way and called "mock wild boar." In both cases, the long soaking in the marinade gives the lamb or pork a very pleasant, slightly gamy flavor, not strong enough to turn off those who are not lovers of game, but just enough to give a distinctive quality that the fresh meat never has.

Then, of course, red wine rinses the pan in which foods are sautéed on top of the stove, like steak *au poivre*. After the steak is removed, the red wine is added to the pan, stirred around to loosen all the little bits and pieces of browned goodness lurking on the bottom, allowed to cook down, and then poured over the steak as a natural sauce. The same procedure is followed for sautés of chicken, or other meats such as beef scallops.

A few fish dishes feature red wine, notably those from Bordeaux and Provence, where the wines of the region are used. These are, however, the exception rather than the rule, although I do remember with great pleasure a famous recipe very often served at the now departed Café de Paris, a whole salmon poached in a white wine court bouillon and served in red wine aspic.

White wine enhances many cooked foods, of course, from fish and

seafood to chicken, veal, and pig's feet, often poached in a white wine
court bouillon. It is used in chicken sautés, for braising chickens and
small birds.The Alsatian equivalent of the Burgundian *coq au vin,*
for instance, is made with the white wine of the region and very
good it is, served with homemade noodles. Then there are the lovely
braised veal dishes, such as the *blanquette,* or white stew, where white
wine gives the veal a totally different flavor from those where red
wine is the braising medium. Veal, which more than most other
meats takes its flavor from the seasonings it is cooked with, thus can
be given two entirely different qualities, depending on the wine.

Of the few cheese dishes where wine is used, the most famous is
the Swiss fondue, correctly made with a dry white Swiss wine and
with kirsch, the white brandy distilled from cherries. The Gruyère
cheese melts in and blends with the wine to a thick softness, and as
it thickens, interestingly enough, one adds a little kirsch, which thins
it out and breaks up the rather stringy thickness of the cheese and
wine mixture. No doubt you have made fondue a hundred times,
but maybe you have never been aware of the difference in texture
produced by the distilled alcohol. It is a very interesting process, for
it happens in no other dish I know.

For Chicken Calandria, as this dish has been called, you will need
a 4- or 5-pound roasting chicken. Have it cut up as if you were going
to make fried chicken—legs and thighs, the breast cut in 2 or 3 pieces,
the back (very good pickings) and ribs, the gizzard and heart. Heat
⅓ cup olive oil or peanut oil, or a combination of the two, in a heavy
12-inch sauté pan or skillet. Roll the chicken pieces in white water-
ground cornmeal and, when the oil is very hot, sear them slightly,
turning often until they are nicely browned. Then reduce the heat,
add 3 medium onions, finely chopped, and 3 or 4 cloves of garlic,
also finely chopped. Mix well with the chicken, then add 1 cup good
red wine, preferably a fine Cabernet Sauvignon or Pinot Noir from
California, as this is a Mexican-Californian dish, 1 teaspoon salt, 1
teaspoon freshly ground black pepper, a pinch of mace, and either 4
or 5 leaves finely chopped fresh coriander [cilantro], if you can get
it, or ½ teaspoon oregano. Cover the pan and simmer gently for ½
hour, turning the chicken pieces once or twice during that time.
Meanwhile, toast 1 cup blanched almonds in a 350°F oven until
delicately browned, and also toast, on a separate baking sheet, 1
teaspoon sesame seeds. Remove the cover and add to the chicken the
toasted almonds, 1 cup small pitted green olives, 4 tablespoons sweet
chili powder, if you can find it, otherwise 2 tablespoons regular chili

powder, and the toasted sesame seeds. If your wine has cooked away, add another ½ cup. Just let the chicken blend with the seasonings and cook for a few minutes, then serve at once with rice, or polenta or hot tortillas.

There's another way of preparing this dish, which gives it an entirely different texture. Proceed as for the first recipe, but add 3 cups boiling water along with the red wine. Reduce heat and simmer for 1 hour. Remove the cover, add the almonds, olives, chili powder, and sesame seeds, and simmer another 20 minutes to ½ hour. At this point, mix ¼ cup of white cornmeal with a little cold water, add to the pan, and stir until the cornmeal thickens the liquid, stirring all the time to prevent the cornmeal sticking to the bottom of the pan and burning. This version is better if cooled, refrigerated, and reheated and served the next day. It is really more of a strew, and the chicken is very well cooked. Though it has a wonderful flavor, I think I prefer the first version, which is really more of a sauté, where the chicken is not cooked quite as much.

You might finish your meal with Pears in Red Wine, a light and pleasant fruit dessert. Any pears will do, from the very ripe Bartletts to the very hard, green winter pears—these will, of course, take much longer to cook. Make a syrup by boiling together for a few minutes 1½ cups of sugar and 2½ cups of good red wine. Taste to see if it is sweet enough for your taste. If not, add more sugar and cook until dissolved.

Meanwhile, peel, halve, and core 6 pears—a little melon ball cutter is good for coring, or you may use a teaspoon. Add the pear halves to the syrup, bring it just to a boil, then reduce the heat to a simmer and poach the pears very slowly until they are just pierceable with a fork. This can take anywhere from 20 minutes for ripe Bartlett pears to 1½ hours for very hard winter pears. They should hold their shape and not be mushy. Let the pears cool in the syrup and serve chilled with heavy cream. The addition of a slice of orange or lemon and perhaps a couple of cloves to the syrup makes a very interesting flavor variation.

Cooking with wines is fun and fascinating, for you can experiment constantly. Try doing your favorite wine dishes with different wines—Californian, French, Spanish, Italian, German. Each will give a different quality to the dish. It's also interesting to compare the flavor of a dish cooked with a certain wine with the wine itself, as you drink it at the table—you will learn a good deal about wine that way for it is a very subtle tasting experience.

SHOPPING THE
SAN FRANCISCO
MARKETS

One of the most exciting things about traveling is the opportunity it affords the palate-conscious person, the food sensualist, to discover what the markets in the various and sundry cities of our country have to offer. There are many places where one can shop wondrously well. One of them is San Francisco, a cosmopolitan many-languaged, many-cuisined city, where I gave demonstrations and cooking classes. I wanted to indulge in much saladry in my classes, so my first shopping foray was to the produce markets.

Here I found a glorious array of artichokes, from babies no bigger than two thumbs to enormous ones the size of a dog's head. I saw tiny cymling or pattypan squash of tender green, ready to be cooked and eaten whole, or blanched and used in a salad, and small, firm yellow crooknecks. There was asparagus of every stature, from the noble jumbo to the slender stalks of wild asparagus, and onions of all hues, types, and uses—for chopping, for purées and sauces, for salads, sandwiches, and French-frying. In the kitchen, it is well to remember that one onion is for one purpose, another for something else. The enormous Spanish onions make heavenly sandwiches and juicy French-fried onion rings. The small white onions are perfect for onions Monegasque. Red Italian onions, thinly sliced, lend a special pungent sweetness to salads, in combination with cucumber, with mushrooms, and with crisp greens. The ordinary run-of-the-mill yellow onions are our basic standby and invaluable ally. Sliced or chopped, and sautéed, they lend flavor to a stew, to calf's liver Venetian style, to Lyonnaise potatoes, or any of those other gutsy dishes that enhance a menu.

Huge, firm white heads of garlic brought visions of a smooth and creamy garlic purée, chicken sautéed with whole garlic cloves, garlic-redolent sauces like the Provençal *aïoli*, and blanched crushed garlic mixed with cream and butter and introduced into a purée of potatoes for one of the most delicate and sublime dishes in the whole repertoire of that stalwart vegetable.

Fruits are another of the joys of the San Francisco markets. I was entranced by the giant strawberries with the stems left on, like little handles, to make it easier to dip the berries in sugar, kirsch, and cream. I rejoiced to see piles of the little-known blood oranges, heavy with wine-red juice, sweet to the palate, a complete departure from the everyday orange, and great heaps of avocados, ripe and yielding to the touch, ready to be made into a mousse, into an ice cream, or tossed into a *salade composée*. Nearby were red-cheeked peaches, nestled in their own glossy leaves. In just a few weeks there would be others in the market—the white peaches, tender of skin and even more tender of flesh, and succulent, sun-ripened apricots, incomparable in color and flavor.

One day I visited a New East food store and found dozens of whole spices, some that one seldom sees, ready to be ground and release their exotic fragrance. There were various kinds of lentils and perhaps six different types of rice, the makings of many a delicious Arab or Italian dish.

One morning I went marketing in Chinatown, wandering among all those mysterious and fascinating shops that sell the ingredients for the many-flavored dishes of the Chinese cuisine. I saw beautiful fresh-killed chickens and ducks, plump pieces of ginger root, unusual vegetables, and the most exquisite seafood—bass, snapper, sole, crab, shrimp, skate wings—in picturesque juxtaposition to dried oysters, dried scallops, dried shrimp. Here were strange sausages (not as familiar to me as those in the neighboring Italian markets, like cotechino and big fat mortadella, a bologna-like sausage liberally larded with fat pork).

At a vegetable stand I bought a bunch of Chinese parsley, or fresh coriander, known to the Spanish-speaking population as cilantro, that herb with the peculiar, persuasive perfume that shocks the nostrils

and palates of some and stimulates those of others in the most gloriously sensual way. It is a constant fascination to note the subtle
differences in texture and flavor of foods from different countries.
Contrast the jicama, a Mexican tuber akin to the sweet potato with
another kind of tuber, the Oriental water chestnut, crisp and nutty
to the tongue. Or the delicate, feathery leaf of Chinese parsley with
the flat-leafed Italian parsley, deceptively similar in appearance but
worlds apart in taste, and both of them with our customary curly
parsley, another taste again. Startling similarities are common in the
food world. Shopping for Chinese ham, one discovers it comes from
Virginia, the flavor and texture of Smithfield ham being close to that
of China. One wonders which came first, and decides it must have
been the Chinese. Perhaps some long-ago voyager flattered his palate
by reproducing that taste and texture here.

Such cultural interchanges in food make me long to prepare a
United Nations of a meal, one which would bring together all those
distinctive tastes—a venture that might turn out well, and then again,
might not. It is by shopping with one's eyes and tasting with one's
palate that we are inspired to try new and exciting combinations and
offbeat marriages of ingredients. To merge the joys of sight with the
joys of the other senses is the greatest of all achievements in cooking.

Shopping for the raw materials for a simmering stockpot, I walked
into a supermarket and found, as well as all the vegetables and
flavoring herbs I needed, a butchery department with a great collection
of meats and bones. I bought beef marrow bones, veal bones, a chicken,
leeks, carrots, onions, turnips—all the essential flavors and essences
that, aided by salt, yield a wonderful base for soups, sauces, and many
classic recipes. It intrigues me to guide the flavoring by adding more
onion or garlic or parsley, balancing the almost overpowering authority of the turnip against the sweetness of the carrot and onion,
the subtle strength of the leek and the pungency of the thyme and

bay leaf, and melding them all into a rich and powerful stock that can be used to enhance perhaps a dozen different dishes.

With such lovely vegetables and fish in the markets, we are going to make a cold summer dish of poached salmon, cold leeks, potatoes and fresh peas, hard-boiled eggs, and crisply tender greens with an unctuously garlicky sauce, *aïoli*.

For six servings, buy a thick 4½-pound piece of steelhead or chinook salmon—you'll want some left over. Also buy 12 leeks, 3 pounds of tiny new potatoes, 4 pounds of green peas, a head of garlic, a cucumber, parsley and lemons, fruity olive oil, and a variety of lettuce—romaine, Bibb, and if you can find it, the beautiful ruby salad lettuce. Eggs, I assume, you have. If not, buy a dozen.

First make a court bouillon for poaching the salmon. Put in a fish cooker, or pot of a suitable size and shape to accommodate the salmon, 3 quarts water, 1 cup white wine, 6 peppercorns, 3 sprigs parsley, a medium onion stuck with 2 cloves, 1½ tablespoons salt, 1 to 2 teaspoons thyme, 1 bay leaf, and 2 slices of lemon. Bring to a boil, reduce the heat, and simmer 35 minutes.

Now measure your piece of salmon at the thickest point, from back to belly. Let's say it measures 3½ inches. Wrap the salmon in cheesecloth, leaving two long ends so that it can be easily lifted from the pot, put on a rack in the pot, and gently lower the salmon onto it. Let the simmering liquid return to a boil, then turn the heat down and simmer for 10 minutes per measured inch, or 35 minutes in all.

The minute it is done, remove it from the court bouillon, take off the cheesecloth, wrap in foil or plastic wrap, and allow to cool at room temperature. If you are serving the salmon the next day, it may be put in the refrigerator after it is thoroughly cooled, but frankly I prefer to serve it the same evening so that it can stay at room temperature until serving time. The icy embrace of the refrigerator does nothing for the flavor and texture.

While the salmon is poaching, prepare the accompaniments. Hard-boil 6 eggs. Wash the leeks well, cut off the root ends and some of the green part, then soak them in cold water for a while. Poach them in salted water until they are just tender-crisp, about 30 to 35 minutes, adding a bit of lemon juice to the water to help draw out any sand that might still be lurking between the leaves.

Cut a little bellyband around the potato skin with a paring knife and boil the potatoes rapidly in salted water until just pierceable, then cool them out of the water. If the peas are really fresh, young and tender, shell them and serve them raw. They taste wonderful that way. If they are not, blanch them for about 5 minutes in boiling, salted water until barely done, then cool.

So far, everything is simple. Your *aïoli* is another matter. It's easy to make if you have a food processor, not so easy if you make it by hand. With a food processor, put in the container 1 good fat clove of garlic (or 2 cloves, if they are small) for each person. Add 2 whole eggs. Process until the garlic is completely crushed and the eggs blended with it. Then pour in, gradually, letting the machine run all the while, 2 cups fruity olive oil, or enough to make a very thick emulsion, like a stiff mayonnaise. Taste, add salt to your palate's content, a squeeze or two of lemon juice, and a few grinds of fresh black pepper, and there you have your *aïoli*.

If you don't have a food processor, you have to work. Chop or slice the garlic very finely, then crush it thoroughly in a large mortar with the pestle. With the pestle, crush and work 3 or 4 egg yolks into the garlic until well blended. Very gradually add some of the oil, crushing and stirring constantly with the pestle, until the mixture starts to become a thick and luscious emulsion. I warn you, this isn't easy. It takes time, patience, and a strong right arm. Season with salt, lemon, a tiny touch of vinegar, if you like, and keep grinding and crushing until you have worked in 1½ cups or more of oil and produced an *aïoli* that is stiff, garlicky, and aromatic.

Now to assemble and garnish your dish. Peel and seed the cucumber and cut in paper-thin slices. Remove the skin from the salmon and arrange it in the center of your most beautiful platter. Lay a few slices of cucumber on top and a few slices of lemon around it. Make an attractive arrangement of the leeks, potatoes, shelled and quartered hard-boiled eggs, peas, and the rest of the cucumber around the salmon. Garnish with parsley sprigs and a few choice lettuce leaves. Serve the *aïoli* in a handsome bowl, or if you had a lovely big stone mortar to make it in, leave it in the mortar. Eat crunchy French bread with this and drink plenty of chilled white wine, and you'll have a meal that is sheer bliss.

Marketing is an experience as soul-satisfying as eating, and the greatest spur to imaginative cooking I can think of. I shall never cease to adore the joys a marketplace has to offer, and I shall never stop heading straight for the markets, wherever I happen to be.

PART II

PREPARING AND COOKING A TO Z

CHAPTER 12

THE APPLE OF
HIS EYE

Small wonder that the apple has received such fame and acclaim over the centuries. After all, this was the legendary fruit that tempted Eve in the Garden of Eden. That wily serpent knew well what it was doing, for the apple, with its luscious color and sensuous curving form, is perhaps the most tempting of all fruits, promising delight to the senses and palate.

I was lucky enough to grow up in apple country. Oregon's Hood River Valley and Washington's Yakima Valley were noted for their superb apples. I well remember the many Yale and Harvard graduates who came out and set themselves up as gentlemen-farmers to raise apples or pears. They worked with the dedication and zeal of the true hobbyist. The late Lucius Beebe, the famous raconteur, political writer, social arbiter, and railroad buff, owned such a place in the Hood River Valley. He showered his friends at Christmas with boxes of beautiful Spitzenburgs, Northern Spies, or Winter Bananas of huge proportion and heavenly color. Each apple was individually wrapped in a different color of tissue and encased in a separate box, so exquisite that the recipients seldom shared the fruit but kept it for their private pleasure.

In my family each member had one or two favorites and there

were apples aplenty to satisfy all. First came the very early Gravensteins and Transparents. The Gravenstein, a green apple with reddish
and pinkish streaks, crisp and tart, was one of the greatest. It could
reach enormous proportions and gave off a marvelous perfume. Alas,
while it was perfect for eating and cooking, it had one serious fault
in the eyes of the commercial growers: It was quite tender and bruised
easily, and thus was banished from the market. (Occasionally, if you
visit a country orchard, you will be able to buy Gravensteins, but
that's about the extent of their availability.) In our garden we had
three magnificent trees of Gravensteins, from which we picked
throughout the summer and into the early fall. After that they became
much too ripe to eat, but they made delicious applesauce and a glorious
jelly because their delicate skin was full of pectin.

Following the Gravensteins and Transparents we had a parade of
other apples such as the Northern Spy, excellent for cooking, and the
Spitzenburg, wondrously brittle to the bite and flowery on the palate—rapturous eating. The Spitzenburg was enormous—almost the
size of a small child's head—and it baked like no other. For many
years the Northern Pacific advertised their famous baked apples,
which were mostly Spitzenburgs, baked until the sugary top was crisp
and the flesh soft, unctuous, and full of flavor. Every home cook
aspired to this same mastery, but few succeeded.

Then there were the amusingly named Winter Bananas, large
yellow apples shaped rather like the Delicious, and also the king-size
Rambeau, which was my father's favorite. Fortunately, a family friend
owned a tree in Portland that produced Rambeaus. I remember it
was a rule that a certain part of the crop was set aside for my father
because of his passionate devotion to this particular apple. It was, in
my opinion, a good apple, but not worth all the fuss he made.

Oddly enough, when I was visiting a friend in Pennsylvania, we
went to see a neighboring farmer who raised odd varieties of apples
and pears. I'm sure most of his flourishing business was due to the
nostalgic smell and taste memories of his customers. When the farmer
mentioned that he sold Rambeaus, it was like a bolt from the past.
I purchased a good quantity to see if I could relive my childhood and
taste again the fruit that had received so much praise from my father.
Well, it was just another apple, pretty enough and beautifully shaped,
but without the glamour my father had invested it with, and a taste
hardly worth remembering.

Not so with others. Two or three years ago I had the wondrously perfumed, tender-skinned Gravensteins, and they brought back many happy days and happy feasts of succulent dumplings, deep-dish pies, baked apples, and apple crisps.

Some apples have created a great tradition. The Pippin, praised in song and story throughout England and Scotland, was carried into most English colonies in the heyday of the British Empire. I think the first time I tasted the famous Cox's Orange Pippin was in Germany, and I thought then that no other apple could possibly rival its crisp texture, tangy flesh, and glorious bouquet, which permeated a room or cellar with an exciting, winy odor. Then there is the famous French russet apple, the Canadien. I'm not sure where it actually originated, but I'm certain the French enjoyed it long before the apple became a feature of international commerce.

I could go on discussing varieties of apples that I loved, recalling their bouquet, flavor, the snap of the skin, and the crunch of the flesh, which all blended together in one remarkable eating experience—but most of them are now things of the past. In the days of my childhood apples were grown in great profusion and tremendous variety in all the great apple states. In 1910 the New York Horticultural Society published a two-volume set of books, elaborately illustrated with color photographs, that described the many varieties of apples grown in New York State. It is astounding and saddening to look at it now and see the range of long-forgotten apples once produced in that one state alone. Today we are limited to the five or six that have proved most amenable to picking and to scientific cold storage and controlled-atmosphere storage which prolong their edibility and life for many months, from fall to early summer. One may have Golden Delicious or Red Delicious practically all year, but what they gain in longevity, they lose in flavor. The growers have chosen them and other varieties because they have long shelf life, they hold up well, and they are good to look at—irrespective of how they taste.

On the East Coast we have a fairly good cooking apple, the slightly tart Greening, but it is by no means an eating apple. It does, however, make a good pie, good kuchen, and good applesauce. In the last few years we have also imported an excellent apple from Australia and New Zealand called Granny Smith.

A good ripe apple picked at its peak is so marvelous as a dessert or as a between-meals snack, peeled, and enjoyed with a piece of cheese. It can be just as remarkable when cooked. Sliced thinly and

sautéed quickly in butter with a sprinkling of sugar, apples have an éclat that perfectly complements certain rich meats, such as pork, ham, even venison. Apple dumplings, pastry-wrapped and baked in the oven in a heavy syrup, or steamed inside a suet crust, are a very special thing.

Then there are the other aspects of apples. Driving through the countryside in the fall, especially in Pennsylvania and parts of Vermont, one becomes aware of a heady apple odor in the air—not apples on the branch, but apples being pressed for cider. If you can get this glorious potable freshly made, before it has been processed to stop fermentation, you will have a rare and refreshing treat. And who could forget apple candy and other confections, like the homemade candied apples of Halloween?

If you can find a source for good fruit, there are many apple dishes that can be savored throughout the year, from a simple but sensational baked apple, served warm with thick cream for dessert or with light cream for breakfast, to a magnificent Polish baked pudding called *Sharlotka*, made with apples, pumpernickel bread, wine, currant jelly, served smothered with chilly yogurt, and consumed quickly before the yogurt has a chance to melt.

Fried apple rings are a great American delicacy, dating back to when early settlers planted apple trees in Pennsylvania, Ohio, and Indiana, and then, following the Oregon Trail, in Oregon, California, and Washington. In those days the pioneers who headed west depended on cured and salted meats for their survival, and they always looked for ways to relieve the saltiness of their diet with a fresh tart or sweet-and-sour flavor. Fried apples served with bacon, ham, or sausage, or cooked in bacon fat and eaten with pancakes or other hot breads, were a great favorite then, as they are now. Italian sausages and fried apples have a great kinship, and a platter of apple rings with a roast of pork or fresh ham can't be beaten.

During the great fall apple season, take a weekend off to scour the countryside and shop the farmers' markets for some freshly picked apples. It surely will be worth the trip.

CHAPTER 13

BAKING YOUR

OWN BREAD

Of all the kitchen procedures, probably the most exciting and gratifying is making bread. If you've only known the commercial breads—the oversweet white supermarket bread, whole-wheat bread, and some of the so-called health breads, for example—you have no idea what making your own bread is going to do for you. To knead by hand, to shape a loaf, and to smell that wonderful, yeasty aroma as it bakes is a soul-satisfying, emotionally fulfilling experience, as sensual as eating. Once you've started, you're hooked for life. You'll never stop making bread.

Bread, in one form or another, is one of our oldest foods, and in many countries and civilizations it has been the staff of life. Bread, cheese, wine, three of our greatest foods, have kept body and soul together over long periods of time—and can you think of a better combination?

You all remember, I'm sure, the story of how King Alfred of England forgot the battle while baking cakes on a hot stone, but did you know the "cakes" were actually loaves of unleavened bread? Unleavened breads are very old, very historic. The Egyptians baked them, and the flat bread common throughout the Middle East, pita, is probably the ancestor of those early breads. Pita, which is split open and filled with food, originally grilled meats pulled off the skewer, serves as plate, knife, and fork in one. In India, certain breads are baked in the big clay tandoor ovens, the same ovens used for tandoori chicken, and oddly enough, in parts of Russia one still finds a flat bread closely resembling that made in the tandoor oven.

These days, bread making is not the tremendous undertaking it once was. Our grandmothers and great-grandmothers would bake enough bread to last the family for a week, so old recipes are quite likely to call for a bushel of flour and quantities of yeast, salt, and sometimes milk and butter, enough to scare off anyone with only a tiny, modern kitchen. Don't let that bother you. You can easily make just one or two loaves, wherever you live, whenever you feel like it. It's not a long-drawn-out process. You can make bread by hand, you can make it in an electric mixer with a dough hook, or you can make it in a food processor. The satisfaction you get from making, baking, and eating your loaves more than makes up for the little time expended.

There's nothing in the least complicated about making a good loaf of bread. Let's start with the simplest of all, a white loaf, one that I make constantly. All you need is flour, water, yeast, salt, and a little sugar to start the fermentation of the yeast.

The first essential for good bread is good flour. The finest flour is unbleached, which makes a sturdier loaf, and my preference is for hard-wheat flour, which isn't as easy to come by as other flours but can be found in some health-food stores or ordered by mail from mills in different parts of the country. If you don't want to go to all that trouble, I recommend that you look in your supermarket or grocery store for an unbleached all-purpose flour. Since people in this country have taken up bread making again, the demand for un- bleached flours has grown to such an extent that you can find them almost anywhere.

Yeast is a vital factor in bread. There are two types of yeast. One is a fresh yeast, which comes in ½-ounce, 1-ounce, and 1-pound cakes. The other is the familiar active dry granular yeast found in all su- permarkets, in individual packages and in 8- or 12-ounce jars. If you buy the soft fresh cake yeast, the water in which you dissolve it should not be more than 90° to 95°F, the temperature of fairly warm tap water. Water over 95°F can kill the active yeast cells and your dough will not rise. If you have a meat thermometer that registers from 0°F you can test the heat of the water very easily. Granular yeast, on the other hand, may be dissolved in water of a higher temperature, from 110° to 115°F. It's a good idea to memorize that little table, because often people experiment with bread and don't remember about it and then are surprised to find that their dough will not rise. So always be sure to check the water temperature.

Now as I mentioned before, a little bit of sugar helps the yeast to start working and fermenting, which is needed to make bread rise. If you're using fresh yeast, crumble it into a measuring cup, add 1 tablespoon of sugar for a half-ounce yeast cake, and mix them together with a spoon or fork until the mixture becomes quite soft and runny, like a darkish, syrupy liquid. Then add ½ cup of warm water. Let it stand for a few minutes and it will begin to bubble and foam. This is called proofing—it proves that the yeast is active. If you're using dry yeast, add it to the ½ cup warm water with the 1 tablespoon sugar, stir lightly, and let it stand until it begins to foam and work. Once proofed, the yeast should be used very soon.

The next important ingredient in bread making is salt. Most people do not add enough salt to flavor the bread. My feeling is that you should use 1 tablespoon of salt for every 3¾ to 4 cups (approximately 1 pound) of flour. Less makes the bread rather flat-tasting, more makes it oversalty, but you must gauge to suit your own palate.

You also need a good big bowl for mixing and a bowl for rising. The bowl for rising should be lightly greased with 2 tablespoons of butter or oil to make it easier to extract the dough from the bowl after rising. Another necessity, of course, is bread pans. The recipe I'm giving you is enough for one pan measuring 8 × 5 × 3 inches, or two smaller pans measuring 6 × 4 × 3 inches. With some pans, the top will brown but the sides will not. This is because of the material of which they are made. The best bread pans, available from kitchen equipment stores such as Williams-Sonoma, are made of black sheet iron and measure 8 × 5 × 4 inches. They bake magnificently and the loaf will come out crisp and brown on all sides.

Well, having absorbed all that information, let's get down to making our loaf of white bread. You will need 1 package active dry yeast or 1 half-ounce yeast cake, 1½ to 2 cups of warm water (110° to 115°F for dry yeast, not above 95°F for fresh yeast), 1 tablespoon of granulated sugar, 1 tablespoon of salt, and 3¾ to 4 cups of unbleached all-purpose flour. The last measure is approximate because flours differ and you may need ¼ cup, maybe ½ cup, more than the lower measure to make the proper dough.

Combine the yeast, sugar, and then the water as previously directed. Stir well and set aside to proof. Meanwhile, measure 3¾ cups of unsifted flour into a 2- or 3-quart bowl, setting aside some additional flour for kneading. Add the 1 tablespoon salt to the flour and blend well. Then add approximately ¾ cup of the warm water and stir with a wooden spoon or with your hands to make a mixture that is thick and sticky. Now look at the yeast. If the little bubbles appear and the mixture has swelled a bit, the yeast has proofed and may be added to the flour. Add the yeast mixture and stir until all the ingredients are well blended and thick enough to form a ball. If you have a very stiff dough, add a tiny bit more water. Then, with your hands, scoop the dough out onto a lightly floured pastry board, marble slab, or countertop and begin to knead. Kneading is extremely important because it distributes the fermented yeast cells through the dough, and they start to work on it and make it rise.

There are several ways to knead. As I have large hands, I find a one-handed method is most satisfactory. If, however, you have small hands, you'll probably find it better to use them both. Sprinkle the dough very lightly with flour and dust your hands with some of the flour from the board. Now push the heel of your hand, or hands, down into the dough and away from you, almost as if you were rolling it out. Fold the dough over, toward you, giving it a quarter turn, and again push it out with the heel of your hand. Continue the sequence of pushing, folding, and turning until it becomes a rhythmic pattern. Keep on kneading until the dough no longer feels sticky to the touch, but smooth and elastic. You may have to knead a little more flour into the dough to banish the stickiness, because flours differ a great deal and the humidity of the room also affects the bread.

The way to tell whether or not your bread has been kneaded enough (although it may interest you to know that it is practically impossible to overknead bread) is to poke the dough with your finger. If it has been kneaded enough, it will spring back. Then, if you look at the ball of dough, you will notice little blisters or breaks on the surface. Both of these are indications that the dough has been kneaded sufficiently.

Sometimes, as a change from the kneading, you might pick up the bread dough and slam it down on the board, giving it a real whack, then pull it together and continue kneading, or give it several slams down.

When the dough is smooth and elastic and springs back when touched with your finger, it can be put in your previously greased bowl. Turn it around several times, so that the surface gets a little film of the butter or oil, cover bowl and dough with a towel or a piece of plastic wrap, and put it in a warm, draft-free place to rise until double the bulk, which will take from 1 to 2 hours.

If you are using a mixer with a dough hook, rather than using your hands, here's how you go about it. Put the ingredients into the mixer bowl and mix with dough hook until they form a ball. This will take about 4 minutes, which is equivalent to kneading by hand for 10 to 15 minutes. What I like to do, if I'm using the machine, is to remove the dough after 2 or 3 minutes, and then continue kneading by hand to give a good finish.

If you are mixing your dough in a food processor, you cannot put in as much flour as you would if you were making the dough in a mixer or by hand—the machine will not accommodate it. With a food processor, you cannot [normally] use over 3 cups of flour, so you have to adjust the other ingredients accordingly. Again, finish the kneading by hand.

When the dough in the greased bowl has doubled in bulk, test it by plunging two fingers into the dough. If the dough retains the finger marks, it has risen to the proper point for further manipulation. Now you are faced with a decision. If you would like a loaf that is finer in texture and probably better in flavor, let the dough rise a second time in the greased bowl. If, on the other hand, you are anxious to finish the loaf quickly, punch the dough with your fist so that it deflates completely (this is called knocking down), take it out of the bowl, put it on a floured board, and either with a rolling pin or your hands, roll or pat the dough out into a square about 1 inch thick. Let it rise, covered with a bowl or towel, for about 5 minutes. The exertion of being punched down and rolled or patted out will have tightened the dough up a bit, so it needs this time to rest before you go on with the next step, shaping it and putting it into the pans.

However, if you want a better-textured loaf, after punching the dough down with your fist, remove it from the bowl, give it two or three kneads, shape it back into a ball, replace it in the buttered bowl, cover it, and let it rise again until double in bulk. After this, proceed exactly as for the shortcut loaf, rolling or patting the dough and letting it rest before shaping. The only difference is that the dough gets one extra rising.

While the dough rests, take one 8 × 5 × 3-inch bread pan or two 6 × 4 × 3-inch bread pans and grease well with butter or oil. If you are using two pans, cut your square of dough in half. Start rolling the dough with your hands into a fat sausage shape, and as

you roll it over, pinch and press down with your thumbs, pressing the upper edge against the lower part of the dough. As you do this, roll in a little bit of the dough from the side so that you get a well-rolled, well-shaped loaf. When you finish rolling, pinch the final edge very well and turn the loaf so that side is to the bottom, then pop the loaf or loaves, seam side down, into the greased pan or pans. With your fingers, adjust the dough in the pans so the loaves fit well, and press down lightly. Now, with a razor blade, make three slashes, about ½ inch deep, across the top of each loaf. Cover the pans with a towel or plastic wrap, put them in a warm, draft-free place, and let them rise until the dough has come just above the edge of the pan and has formed a loaf shape. This will take from 30 minutes to 1½ hours.

Preheat the oven to 400°F. Put 1 egg white and 1 tablespoon of cold water in a small bowl and beat slightly with a fork. When the bread has risen above the rim of the pan, brush the surface of the bread with the egg mixture, not pressing, but just skimming lightly over it with the brush. Then pop the bread onto the shelf in the center of the preheated oven. If you are baking two loaves, don't place the pans parallel, but slightly separated.

Bake the loaves for 10 minutes, then reduce the heat to 350°F and continue baking for about 30 to 35 minutes. To see if they are done, remove them from the pans and test with your knuckles. Grasp the bottom of the bread pan with a heavy pot holder, take another pot holder in your other hand, and invert the pan so the loaf comes out onto the pot holder covering your palm. Tap the bottom of the loaf with your knuckles. If it is baked, it will have a deep, hollow sound.

With some pans, the top will brown beautifully, but the sides will not. In this case, slip the loaves back into the oven *without* the pans for about 4 or 5 minutes so the bottom and sides will get brown and crisp.

When the loaves are ready to be taken from the oven, put them on a wire rack and let them cool thoroughly. I know it's a great temptation to slice the warm bread, but you get a very poor, doughy texture, not the full flavor and good texture of bread that has just cooled. So, resist temptation and let your loaf cool. Then you can slice it and eat it with good sweet butter and maybe a little jam and experience one of the greatest rewards of cooking—your very own home-baked bread.

CHAPTER 14

GLORIOUS
BREAKFASTS

My first experience of great, groaning breakfast boards came about through an aunt who had a sheep ranch in eastern Oregon. At that time, because of the great distances between ranches, there was an unwritten law that you left your door unlatched. If your friends were riding or driving at night and needed a place to stop over, they could walk into the house, they knew where the bedrooms were, and they would stay overnight, often without the host even knowing they were there.

Between feeding the family, the crew who were working on the ranch, and these drop-in guests, the cook never knew quite how many to prepare breakfast for in the morning. Breakfast often lasted until almost lunchtime, and it was quite a production. In those days, the cooks were mostly Chinese, and damn good, so good that anyone would be happy to have them in a restaurant today. Breakfasts were extraordinarily lavish, for very hearty appetites. There would be home-cured ham and bacon, eggs by the carload, more or less cooked as you wanted, always chops and steaks, sometimes chicken or quail, and quantities of hot, fluffy, baking-powder biscuits, sometimes corn bread and always a sweet bread of some kind, a raised coffee cake or a quick coffee cake, a gingerbread or an applesauce or jam cake. In the summertime, there would be a blackberry-jam cake and huckleberry cake. The ranch owners took pride in always having homemade jams, jellies, and preserves and fruits in season. In winter, there would be stewed figs, prunes, peaches, apricots and other dried fruits, or home-canned peaches, pears, cherries, and apricots, for that was a time when everyone canned fruits in enormous quantities.

These luxurious, leisurely feasts were a time for a jovial exchange of pleasantries and a good deal of local gossip between a mixed assemblage of people—some of whom had been up since dawn doing chores, others who had just dropped in and stayed overnight—and the constant change of characters around the table made for very interesting conversation.

This was my introduction to huge, convivial breakfasts and I adored it. Later, when I was studying in England and visited country houses outside London, I was equally fascinated by the enormous buffets that were set out at breakfast time on the sideboard, kept warm in silver serving dishes heated with hot water. A day started with a jolly whirl of lifting lids and deciding what one wanted for breakfast. The choice was usually staggering—deviled kidneys, various kinds of smoked fish such as kippers, Yarmouth bloaters, Arbroath smokies from Scotland, and smoked haddock, sometimes little lamb chops, a cold roast or a ham from which you could cut a slice or two, and always wonderful Irish or Wiltshire bacon, boiled eggs, and perhaps curried eggs or kedgeree—a glorious array of savory dishes to keep one going until lunchtime. One aspect of breakfast I found rather curious. The British always make their toast ahead of time and leave it sitting in a toast rack until it gets stone cold. Hot toast seems not to enter into the British breakfast style, so you have to learn to like your toast cold and crisp, or forget about it—actually, slathered with butter and good, dark Seville-orange marmalade, aged in the wood until it was dark and delicious, the cold toast was quite acceptable. Sometimes fruit, in the form of a fruit compote, a dish of prunes, an orange or grapefruit, entered into the breakfast, but it was not considered of great importance.

We in the United States have gone through various eras of breakfasts, and you'll find that tastes differ according to the part of the country you are in. In more rural areas, people still indulge in ham or bacon and eggs, pancakes, hashed brown potatoes, hot breads, and fruits, washed down with strong black coffee. For city dwellers, a glass of orange juice and a cup of coffee seems to suffice, and many a late riser or hurried commuter merely gulps down coffee and eats not a thing. Still, there are those of us who like to sit down comfortably with a pot of tea and a piece of toast or an English muffin and some fruit, and relax over the morning paper.

The meager breakfasts most people eat these days are rather saddening when you consider that we used to be a nation of hearty breakfasters who, I'm certain, ate more ham and bacon than any country in the world and quantities of pork sausages, in links or patties. However, I have never taken to the idea of having a stack of pancakes and sausages on the same plate and pouring maple syrup over the whole thing. If one has sausages with pancakes or waffles, one should have it separately, not degrade the sausage by smothering it in syrup or honey.

Instead of the hearty, leisurely breakfasts of old, we now have a new institution and new word—brunch. Brunch, which is essentially a late breakfast to which guests are bidden as they would be to lunch, is one of those contractions that fall disagreeably upon the ear. If you are going to invite people to a noontime meal, either call it a late breakfast or an early lunch, not a brunch. And do give some thought to what you serve. One time I was invited to a late breakfast consisting of coffee or tea and seventeen different kinds of sweets—coffee cakes, sponge cakes, chocolate cakes, jam tarts, nothing but sweets. Was this late breakfast? I suppose to those who adore pastries and desserts more than any other part of a meal this would be sheer heaven, but for someone whose taste buds prefer savory things it was indeed a nasty shock.

There are many good, savory dishes you can serve at a late breakfast, from broiled chicken with bacon to interesting fresh or smoked fish things, such as beautifully sautéed trout or smelts or fresh sardines with crisp watercress, lemon, and crunchy homemade whole-grain

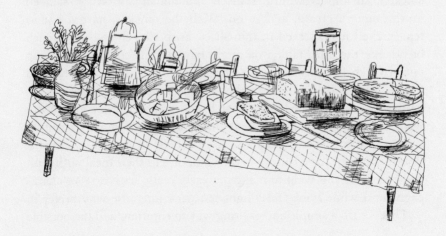

toast or finnan haddie poached in milk, with plenty of butter and chopped parsley, crisp toast or hot biscuits. Then there are all those fascinating egg dishes, such as omelets, fritatas, eggs à la tripe, and poached eggs served in various styles. My great friend Rudolph Stanish, who has made a career of omelets, does delicious variations like chili omelet, a curried shrimp omelet—even a fine herbs omelet can make an ample and thoroughly enjoyable breakfast with perhaps sausage cakes or link sausage and good fruit to start with. Or, with the advent of the electric pasta machine, it would be rather fun to serve your own tender, thin fresh pasta sauced in any way you choose, perhaps tossed *alla carbonara* with bits of shredded Virginia ham, raw eggs, butter, and grated Parmesan cheese, or simply with olive oil, lemon juice, and cheese. Have sliced tomatoes or hot asparagus, in season, and croissants or brioches to go with it.

One of my favorite late-breakfast menus is perfectly grilled kidneys *en brochette,* cooked just to the pinky stage, with sautéed potatoes and fresh asparagus, toasted homemade bread or English muffins, and, in season, luscious fresh raspberries with *crème fraîche* or heavy cream afterward.

If you are looking for a way to entertain a large group of forty or fifty, you might give a Sunday late-breakfast buffet, with a choice of different dishes to cater to a variety of tastes, having setups on three tables so the guests can wander around and choose at will. One table might have smoked salmon, smoked sturgeon, smoked eel, pickled herring, crisp Swedish and Norwegian rye breads, good pumpernickel, thinly sliced onions and cream cheese, and perhaps a platter of scrambled eggs. At another table, have one member of the family making omelets to order with a choice of fillings such as curried chicken, shrimp Newburg, spinach and hollandaise sauce, sautéed mushrooms in cream, and so on. With the omelets, have a hot or tepid baked ham, served in thin slices, crisp French rolls or French bread. For the third table, you might have a more conservative setup with two chafing dishes holding frizzled chipped beef and creamed oysters, plus patty shells and baked potatoes. Serve the oysters in the patty shells, the chipped beef in the baked potatoes. Some guests will want to sample the food on all three tables, others may want to concentrate on one. I would also have a table of fruits and cheeses. People can then have fruit to begin with, or end their meal with fruit and cheese. If you want to make the party really festive, serve champagne and white wine and a light red wine for those who prefer it.

This is such a simple and exciting way to entertain and the possible repertoire of suitable dishes is so enormous that one need never serve the same thing twice. Here, to start you off, are three easy dishes that would be delicious for your late breakfast or early lunch (brunch).

First, the British kedgeree, a dish of rice, fish, and curry sauce that is usually made with fresh, canned, or smoked salmon, but might also be done with kippered cod or salmon or sablefish. Make a curry-flavored béchamel sauce by melting 3 tablespoons butter in a heavy saucepan, adding 2 teaspoons good curry powder, and cooking it in the butter for 2 minutes, stirring (this takes away the raw taste of the curry powder) before mixing in 3 tablespoons all-purpose flour. Cook this roux, stirring with a wooden spatula, for 2 or 3 minutes, or until frothy, then gradually stir in 1½ cups hot milk, making sure there are no lumps. Cook over medium heat, stirring, until the sauce is smooth and thickened. Simmer for 3 or 4 minutes, then season to taste with salt and pepper. Mix 1 pound flaked cooked salmon or canned or smoked salmon into the sauce. Cook 1 cup long-grain rice according to your favorite method, which will give you 3 cups cooked rice. Arrange the hot rice on a platter and surround with the salmon and sauce. Garnish with sliced hard-boiled eggs and chopped parsley. This will serve four. With the kedgeree, have hot biscuits and grilled tomatoes or cooked asparagus.

Roast beef hash is a very American dish, hearty enough for a late breakfast and a good way to use up your leftover roast beef. For this you will need 2½ cups diced cold roast beef with some of the fat, 1½ cups finely diced boiled potatoes, and 2 small onions or 1 medium onion, finely chopped. Melt 5 tablespoons beef drippings or 3 table-spoons butter and 2 tablespoons oil in a heavy skillet, add the onion, and sauté until just transparent; do not brown. Add the potatoes and cook them over medium heat until lightly browned and crisp at the edges. Add the beef, season to taste with salt, freshly ground black pepper, and a little dried thyme. Blend the beef and vegetables well, then cook down until the beef is brown and the hash crisp on the bottom. For a richer hash, add ½ cup heavy cream, raise the heat a little, and let the cream cook out so it forms a crust on the bottom. You can serve poached or fried eggs on top of the hash, if you like. Garnish with a good sprinkling of chopped parsley and serve with a salad of thinly sliced onions and tomatoes with vinaigrette dressing or shredded fresh vegetables with yogurt dressing, hot homemade rolls, and strawberry or raspberry preserves. Serves four.

The third dish, clam tart, is what most people would call a *quiche*, a term I find overused. I prefer the word *tart*. For this you will need a partially baked 9-inch pie shell. Line a 9-inch pie pan with your favorite pie pastry, prick the bottom of the dough well with a fork, line the shell with foil, and then weight it down with raw rice or beans—this prevents it puffing up during cooking. Bake the shell in a 425°F oven for 14 to 16 minutes, until bottom is set and edges lightly browned. Remove pan from the oven, take out the foil and rice or beans, and brush the bottom of the shell with beaten egg yolk or Dijon mustard, which seals it and prevents the crust from becoming soggy when the filling is added. Return to the oven for 2 minutes to set the glaze on the shell.

While the shell is baking, cook 4 thick slices of good bacon in a skillet until crisp, remove and drain on paper towels, then crumble the bacon. Pour out most of the fat from the pan, leaving about 1 tablespoon. Sauté 2 tablespoons finely chopped onion in the bacon fat until soft, but not browned. Drain an 8-ounce can minced clams, reserving the juice. Spread the bacon, clams, and onion evenly in the partially baked pastry shell. Lightly beat 4 eggs and combine with the reserved clam juice and 1 cup heavy cream. Season to taste with salt, freshly ground black pepper, and a little grated nutmeg, plus several drops of Tabasco if you like a slight spiciness. I think it improves the flavor. Pour the custard mixture over the clams and bake the tart in a 350°F oven for about 30 minutes, until the custard is just set. If you wish, sprinkle the top of the custard with a little grated Parmesan cheese before baking. Serve this tart, which is enough for four to six, with a tossed green salad and chilled white wine. Fruit and cheese make a nice follow-up.

CHAPTER 15

COBBLERS:

A BUCKLE IS A

SLUMP IS A

GRUNT

When the Bicentennial occurred, it was fascinating to reconstruct and re-create some of the foods our ancestors knew and loved. In each of the thirteen colonies, food was a very different thing. Some settlers lived extraordinarily well and some lived extremely simply. Our New England forebears were not as skilled at certain pastries as were the colonists in the southern parts of Virginia and Maryland, where servants were plentiful and living more luxurious. Although before and after the Revolution great delicacies and exquisite cooking could be found in areas where the wealthier and more aristocratic people lived, much early American cooking tended to be solid and satisfying rather than elegant, and it was from these simple traditions that many of our great regional dishes came.

I was reminded of this recently when I had dinner at a lovely old turn-of-the-century farmhouse in Oregon, high on a hill overlooking Young's Bay. For dessert our hostess had made three enormous cobblers, which made me immediately think of New England and Pennsylvania. I remarked, "Oh, I see we have a buckle, a grunt, and a slump," at which the guests looked distinctly puzzled. So I explained. "If you go by New England nomenclature, we have one of each—a gooseberry buckle, a wild blackberry slump, and a blueberry grunt— although nowadays they have all become known as cobblers."

Oozing with luscious fruit and juice, topped with a crispy, golden, baking-powder crust, and served with a veritable vessel of whipped cream, a quart at least, the cobblers were so delicious that after eight or ten people had feasted on them, there wasn't much left, though some guests, exhibiting great strength of character, had only one helping.

Because of shortages of certain foods back in the 1700s and early 1800s, desserts were essentially functional, utilizing whatever was at hand. Although there were mills, fine flour was not always in great supply. Neither was sugar, which came from the West Indies, so maple syrup was frequently the sweetener. However, fruits were always plentiful in season: strawberries and raspberries, apples from the trees that had been brought from Europe and planted here, and wild berries that grew in profusion—blackberries, blueberries, huckleberries, snowberries, and cranberries. Those early desserts like the buckle, the grunt, the slump, the cobbler, and the pandowdy were all simple ways to use these fruits and to bring much-desired sweetness to a family meal.

Today, we have all those ingredients that our ancestors lacked, and we use a rich biscuit mix or biscuit dough to make these unsophisticated dishes more palatable and interesting. So now, let's put together a modern version of a cobbler, a slump, or a grunt—pick your name.

Let us say we have 2 quarts of gooseberries, from which we've removed the little tails. Arrange them in a 12 × 14-inch baking dish and add 2 to 3 cups of sugar, depending on the tartness of the berries. Crush the berries ever so lightly with a potato masher or wooden mallet to break the skin, so the juices will run into the sugar and create a syrup. Add a few grains of salt; that's very important.

Now let's proceed with the crust. Measure 3 even cups of all-purpose flour, using a dry measuring cup. Always use the metal measuring cups for dry ingredients because you can level off the top with a knife and get a very accurate measure, which you can't do with the glass or ceramic cups designed for liquid measuring. I notice in my classes that this seems to be one of the most difficult things for students to adapt themselves to. Even experienced cooks will put flour in a liquid measure or liquid in a dry measure. Actually, weighing is the only really accurate and dependable way of measuring dry ingredients, but as yet we Americans seem loath to adopt the scale, though we will have to, when the metric system finally catches up with us.

To the 3 cups of flour, add 6 tablespoons of sweet butter and cut it in very finely with a knife, or work it in with your fingers. Our ancestors probably used pork or beef drippings as shortening, but we have plenty of butter, which has a nicer flavor. Sweet butter, in case you didn't know, is unsalted butter, and it is much more delicate in taste than salt butter and, therefore, preferable.

After the butter is worked in, add ¼ teaspoon of salt and ½ cup of sugar or, if you prefer, 4 tablespoons of maple syrup; then measure in 2 teaspoons of baking powder. Early cooks probably used baking soda and cream of tartar for leavening, but baking powder, which can be measured evenly, is much more acceptable. Mix the dough thoroughly with two forks or with your hands so that the baking powder is thoroughly incorporated with the flour-butter mixture. The dough should feel crumbly. At this point, add enough milk or half-and-half or, if you want greater richness and delicacy, heavy cream, to make a very soft dough. Depending on the flour, it will take from ¾ cup to 1¼ cups of liquid to give you a soft, workable dough. It shouldn't be firm like a pie crust—just a soft, tender, workable dough. When you have worked in the liquid, pat or roll the pastry to a size that will fit the top of the baking dish, then roll it around the rolling pin and unroll over your fruit mixture. Drape the dough carefully over the top and brush it with a little milk or cream or, for a beautifully deep color, 1 egg yolk mixed with 1 tablespoon of milk or cream. Make a few little slits in the dough with the point of a knife to allow the steam to escape, and bake in a 425°F oven for 10 minutes. Then turn the heat down to 350°F, and continue baking until the fruit is cooked through and the cobbler crisply brown on top.

In place of gooseberries, you can use various other berries (except for strawberries, which don't cook nearly as well in a cobbler as other

fruits; they lose a certain quality and are better for a shortcake than a cobbler or slump). Raspberries cook extremely well, but as you would need 1½ to 2 quarts of them, at present prices they are better forgotten, unless you're feeling extremely lavish or are lucky enough to live in a part of the country where they are cheap. Wild or cultivated blueberries and blackberries are very good. With cultivated blackberries, it's interesting to use 1 cup of finely shredded or chopped apples to each pint of blackberries. It gives a nice blend of flavors and a certain body to the syrup during the cooking.

Apricots in season, merely split, pitted, and sugared, are delicious. If you crack a few of the pits and put the kernels in, it adds a lovely bitter-almond flavor. Peeled and sliced peaches make a superb grunt, and so do apples—peeled, thinly sliced, and sugared, with a touch of nutmeg, if you like it, or just plenty of butter and a little vanilla, which is more to my taste. Red pie cherries, pitted or not, are another good choice. They need a goodly amount of sugar, and you have to taste them to know exactly how much.

If you want to make a smaller buckle or grunt, I have another dough that is equally effective and even simpler. This time, we'll make an apple grunt.

Peel 5 or 6 tart apples, cut them in sixths, and arrange them in a well-buttered, deep 9 × 5 × 3-inch bread pan. Fill the pan with apples, dotting them with butter—about 4 tablespoons in all—and sprinkling them with ½ to ¾ cup of sugar, depending on your personal taste and the tartness of the apples. Personally, I like very little sugar with this type of apple, because, as it cooks down, the natural sweetness comes through.

The crust is simplicity itself because it is made with self-rising flour (very common in the South and other parts of the country), which contains its own leavening, probably baking powder, baking soda, and cream of tartar. Mix 1¼ cups of self-rising flour with a pinch of salt and, if you wish, 1 or 2 teaspoons of sugar; then whip 1 cup of heavy cream and fold this into the flour. Either drop it on your apples by spoonfuls or pat it out. Dropping is much easier and also gives a slightly rough texture to the topping, delicious to eat.

Bake the grunt in a 400°F oven for 5 or 10 minutes; then reduce the heat to 325°F, and continue baking for 45 minutes to an hour, until the crust is deep brown and the apples have bubbled up around the edges. Let the grunt cool slightly before eating, with additional whipped cream, if you're feeling luxurious. This is a very different and interesting type of dough and one that I'm sure you will enjoy.

It can be used for other fruits, but it makes such an unusual apple dessert that I would give that first preference.

Of course, pies in the early days were not the same as the pies of today. As a matter of fact, they were probably better than most of the shallow pies we have, because they were deep-dish affairs baked in an oval pie dish about 3 inches deep, with a broad lip around the rim. The crust was much firmer, so the pies were quite a bit more serviceable, shall we say, than those we are used to. After baking, the crust was often removed, cut into wedges, and then replaced around the sides of the dish. The pie was served with these wedges of crust rising almost like the petals of a flower from among the fruit. Sometimes cream was poured into the center, and sometimes the apples were removed and puréed before the pie was served, which made a very handsome presentation.

If you would like to try this early-American, or Anglo-American, version of apple pie, you need the traditional British oval pie dish, which is about 9 inches long and 6 inches wide, with a broad lip around the edge to hold the crust. Some of the better kitchen-equipment shops sell these dishes. There's also a little holder that is put in the center to prop up the crust. Some of these have a blackbird on top and are known as pie birds; others are just plain practical types made of white earthenware. Of course, you can always improvise a holder out of an inverted egg cup or demitasse, or some similar object that comes slightly above the edge of the dish.

For the pastry, carefully measure 1¾ cups of all-purpose flour into a bowl. Cut 4 ounces (1 stick) of butter into very small pieces, and add to the flour with ½ teaspoon of salt and 1 tablespoon of sugar. Cut the butter into the flour or work it in well with your fingers until the mixture is quite flaky and about the consistency of cornmeal. Add 1 whole egg and mix it in very quickly with a fork or with your fingers. If the pastry is too dry to form a ball, add 1 or 2 tablespoons of ice water, just enough to make it hold together. Knead for just about a minute, then wrap in waxed paper and chill for about 30 minutes.

Meanwhile, butter the pie dish well. Peel and slice paper-thin 6 to 8 tart apples. Greenings are good, so are Pippins and Granny Smiths. Failing those, you might use Golden Delicious. Set the holder in the center of the dish and build the apples up around it in layers, dotting each layer with butter and sprinkling it with 2 or 3 tablespoons of sugar. The apples should come just to the top of the dish at the sides, slightly higher in the center.

Roll out the chilled pastry between two sheets of waxed paper. Roll one side, then flip the pastry over, lift up the waxed paper to loosen it from the pastry, replace, and continue rolling. Roll and turn until the pastry is large enough to fit over the pie dish and drape over the edge. Trim the pastry edges, roll the trimmings out, and cut a strip about ½ inch wide and long enough to fit around the lip of the dish. Lay the strip around the rim and moisten with water; then carefully peel one sheet of waxed paper from the large piece of pastry—running your hand under the other to loosen it—and quickly flop the pastry over the pie dish, adjusting it so that it is even all around. Remove the second piece of waxed paper. Press the crust firmly against the strip on top of the lip with your fingers or on the back of a fork. Trim off any excess of top crust from around the edge. Make a hole in the center of the crust just over the holder, to provide a steam vent. Brush the crust with 1 egg yolk mixed with 1 tablespoon of water or cream. Bake the pie in a 450°F oven for 10 minutes, then reduce the heat to 325°F, and continue baking for another 35 to 40 minutes, watching very carefully. If the crust seems to be getting too brown, drape a piece of cooking parchment or foil over it. Remove the pie from the oven and let it cool slightly.

To serve, cut the crust into wedges and serve the apple filling with a wedge of crust on top. Accompany this with whipped cream, if you like.

This early American pie makes a good companion to our slumps, buckles, and grunts, which over the years grew in favor with the country, spreading from the eastern seaboard through the Middle West and over the Oregon Trail to all parts of the land. These traditional desserts are well worth a place on your menus and provide a delicious change from what we usually eat today.

CHAPTER 16

THE DELIGHTS
OF COLD FOOD

I have always loved cold food. Sometimes I think I really enjoy roast beef more the second day, thinly sliced and eaten with a salad. If I have roasted a chicken to a perfect golden crispness of skin and moistness of flesh, I prefer to let it cool at room temperature until it is just tepid and have it with a salad or vegetables—especially asparagus, when it is in season. More than once I have taken a piece of cold steak left over from dinner the night before, sliced it, and eaten it on toast for breakfast.

Meat, poultry, and fish, cooled until they have mellowed and absorbed the seasonings and flavorings with which they were cooked, can be much more sensually satisfying to the palate than if they were taken from the oven and gobbled down hot. There are exceptions, naturally. A deliciously pink and rare little rack of lamb eaten minutes after roasting is one of my favorite meals. Yet that, too, can be as good cold.

Never be afraid to have leftovers. They can give you many happy meals. I often deliberately buy more meat than I need for dinner for just this reason. Beef, veal, and pork are so good cold. To me, one of the most unsung of all culinary delights is a cold roast loin of pork served with a mustard mayonnaise heavily scented with green peppercorns, or perhaps a cold fresh ham that has been stuffed before roasting with various flavorings, served in thin slices that display the colorful mosaic of the stuffing. In my book, cold veal comes a close second to pork for summer dining alfresco, especially that unbelievably glorious combination of veal with tuna and a touch of anchovy the Italians call *vitello tonnato*. Thin slices of this cold veal, masked with tuna-flavored sauce or mayonnaise, and served with a rice salad dressed with a vinaigrette, and possibly mixed with tiny crisp pieces of vegetable, are a triumph. Just plain veal with a mustard mayonnaise, or a veal salad, can be something to purr about.

The important thing about planning a meal of cold food, whether it be for consumption at home or on a picnic, is to have an interesting contrast of flavors. You might accompany cold meat or a cold fowl like poached Rock Cornish hens with a crisp green salad, and give it a garnish of raw or dressed vegetable. You can find fresh Rock Cornish hens weighing one pound or slightly over in the markets these days. Poach them in chicken broth, let them cool until tepid, then arrange them on a serving platter surrounded by a collection of vegetables that have been sliced or shredded in the food processor and marinated in a vinaigrette sauce, then topped with finely chopped dill (we used paper-thin slices of carrot, seeded and sliced cucumber, and julienne of celery). Mask the hens with a combination of ⅔ cup homemade mayonnaise and ⅓ cup yogurt and add some cherry tomatoes for color. You might start your meal with a cold tomato bisque and homemade bread. The ring of Roquefort mousse filled with a watercress on our buffet table is a good flavor contrast to the chicken and marinated vegetables, and you'll find a recipe for it later on in this article. With this menu of predominantly cold foods, it would be fun to end with a hot but light dessert, such as a fruit soufflé. For wine, offer a choice of two—a chilled white wine from Alsace and a light, fruity red Côte du Rhône.

Another good progression of contrasts would be to start with a refreshing salad of seafood, celery, and greens, then have cold roast beef with mustard mayonnaise, accompanying it with the pepperiness of watercress or the bitterness of arugula or the crisp, sweet crunchiness of raw snow peas, a kaleidoscope of flavors to pique your palate and tickle your taste buds. Or you could have something as rustically simple as a good salami or any hearty sausage, cut into thin rounds, with green onions and radishes, a loaf of homemade bread with sweet butter, a hunk of cheese, and a bottle of wine, for an informal lunch in the garden with all the earmarks of a picnic.

Cold fish has many guises. On a weekend, tempt your appetite with a leisurely, Scandinavian-style breakfast of cured or smoked fish—good herring with cream cheese and crisp bread or rye bread, or the classic American combination of bagels and lox with cream cheese, thinly sliced onion, and capers. It's a nice breakaway from the usual routine. As a first course for luncheon or dinner, think in terms of thin slices of delicately smoked salmon with capers, olive oil, a little chopped onion, and freshly ground pepper, or the unctuous richness of fillets of smoked eel served with a mound of dilled cucumbers and good black bread and butter. Probably as perfect a cold fish dish as one can ask for is a poached striped bass with a sauce *gribiche* perfumed with finely chopped herbs, or mayonnaise colored green by the leaves of spinach, parsley, and tarragon and faintly tinged with garlic. Or your luncheon might be built around a big platter of South American *seviche*, strips of sole or tiny bay scallops "cooked" in a lime juice marinade, then combined with olive oil, chopped green onions, parsley and canned green chilies, salt, pepper, and spicy Tabasco, a dish guaranteed to revitalize the most jaded of hot-weather appetites. In the salmon season, the Scandinavian *gravad laks*, raw salmon cured with salt, sugar, and dill, served with a dill-flavored sweet mustard sauce is another winner.

Summer menus need not only contrasts of flavor, but also contrasts of temperature. After cocktails in the garden, hand around demitasses of strong, rich, steaming chicken consommé to lead into a cold supper. Serve just enough of the hot soup to give the palate a welcome jolt before switching back to the cool tenderness of tiny roast squab served tepid with a variety of salads—a rice salad, a mushroom salad, a bowl of crisp watercress—and a well-chilled white wine or lightly chilled Beaujolais or California Zinfandel. That is divine feasting. Or you might start a dinner with an unctuous cold avocado and yogurt soup, then bring on a cooled roast chicken, and instead of the customary salad, a big bowl of peas, quickly cooked and tossed with butter and served good and hot. For dessert, have fresh fruits, with or without heavy cream, and some crisp homemade cookies for that touch of sweetness people often crave at the end of a meal. In summer, I always like to keep a cookie jar filled with lemon cookies or *tuiles* to serve with fruit.

I have always adored picnics and the planning and preparing of wonderful, appetizing meals to carry to the beach or mountains, or enjoy in the car at the side of the road if I am traveling from one place to another. How much more satisfactory it is to indulge in the pleasures of your own packed lunch than to depend on the grim

mercies of the fast-food stand or the local diner when hunger grips. I make it habit always to carry a basket or hamper stocked with the civilized amenities for eating en route, a little case of my best crystal glasses and huge old-fashioned damask napkins that you can practically envelop yourself in.

I have two favorite picnic menus. One is crisply broiled, herb-scented chicken with a package of onion sandwiches (thin slices of onion sprinkled with salt between slices of homemade bread spread with sweet butter) and firm, ripe tomatoes that have been peeled and encased separately in plastic wrap. For the tomatoes, I like to take along in a plastic bag a little bunch of fresh basil picked from the garden and a screw-topped bottle of vinaigrette sauce. Or I might take crunchy little hearts of romaine or tender Bibb lettuce. Cheese and fruit—I lean more toward fruit—and macaroons or other good crisp, chewy cookies complete the meal. Everything gets packed into an insulated bag or ice chest, along with a couple of bottles of chilled white wine or, if I am in a festive mood, champagne.

My other picnic menu is a little more extravagant, because it requires a marinated fillet of beef. I make a teriyaki marinade with ½ cup soy sauce, ½ cup peanut oil, 4 or 5 finely chopped garlic cloves, a little grated orange rind, a touch of Madeira, and a good deal of freshly ground black pepper, and leave the fillet in the marinade for 12 to 24 hours, turning it several times. I then roast it very quickly in a 450° to 500°F oven for 25 to 30 minutes, basting it occasionally with the marinade. I like to do this in the morning and let it cool a bit at room temperature, not in the refrigerator, so it still retains a little of the warmth of the oven. As accompaniments for the rare beef, I like a French potato salad, crisp French bread, and cherry tomatoes, or perhaps firm whole cucumbers that can be sliced in spears at the picnic spot, picked up with fingers and dipped into a dill-flavored yogurt sauce. For the dip, I combine 1 cup plain yogurt with 4 tablespoons chopped fresh dill, a touch of salt, and freshly ground black pepper. This is lovely with cucumbers or cherry tomatoes or any other crudités I might take along. To finish, I might have cheese and more French bread, or perhaps apricot sherbet or fresh raspberry ice cream kept firm and cold in containers that have been well insulated and packed in dry ice. A slightly cooled Beaujolais is the wine I would choose to go with the beef fillet.

If, like many people, you have always taken a dim view of cold food, just give it a whirl. Think up menus based on the foods you like best, and I guarantee you will soon be as hooked as I am.

Now, here is the recipe for a Roquefort mousse that can be filled with seafood salad instead of watercress if you want to serve it as a first course or a luncheon entree.

Soften 1 envelope unflavored gelatin in ¼ cup strained lemon juice, then add 1 cup boiling water and stir until the gelatin is completely dissolved. Put into a mixing bowl ¼ pound Roquefort cheese that has been left at room temperature for 1 hour to soften, and mash until smooth with a fork or wooden spoon. Peel and grate enough cucumber to make 1 cup, then wrap it in a dish towel and squeeze out all the moisture that might stop the mousse from setting properly. Combine the cucumber, cheese, 4 tablespoons finely chopped parsley, 2 tablespoons finely chopped canned pimiento, 1 tablespoon finely chopped capers, 1 teaspoon grated onion, 1 teaspoon salt, and ½ teaspoon freshly ground black pepper. Mix well, taste for seasoning, and add more pepper, if needed—you will probably not need more salt because of the sharpness of the cheese. (If you have a food processor, use it to mash the cheese and combine with the other ingredients.)

Combine the cheese mixture with the gelatin and mix until smooth. Chill in the refrigerator for 20 minutes, or until slightly thickened— it should be thick enough to support the air bubbles in the whipped cream you will be adding.

Whip 1 cup heavy cream in a chilled bowl with a whisk or electric hand beater until it has doubled in volume and holds soft peaks when the beater is lifted. Remove the chilled cheese mixture from the refrigerator and lightly but thoroughly fold the whipped cream into it.

Brush the inside of a 6-cup ring mold with vegetable oil, turn upside down to drain off the excess oil, then pour the mousse mixture into the coated mold. Cover with plastic wrap and chill in the refrigerator for 4 hours, until the surface is firm when pressed with a finger. Unmold the mousse onto a platter, then return to the refrigerator to firm up. When ready to serve, fill the center with watercress, or with 2 to 2½ cups seafood salad, and sprinkle the salad with a little chopped parsley. As the mousse is very rich, make the seafood salad with a tarragon-flavored vinaigrette dressing rather than with a mayonnaise. This makes six to eight servings.

CHAPTER 17

IN PRAISE OF CORNED BEEF

We've all heard of the biblical land of milk and honey, but I think America will go down in history as the land of corn bread, chili, and beef. The steer, the animal that provides beef, has been perfected in this country. Nursed, nurtured, pampered, and fattened, it produces the world's finest beef, which visitors from France, Italy, and other countries are immediately urged to taste.

Beef is not all steak and standing rib roasts, although you might think it from the menus of some restaurants. There are other delicacies we think of as particularly American, and one of them is salt beef, better known as corned beef, a staple in this country for well over two hundred years. One of our great traditional dishes is the New England boiled dinner of corned beef and vegetables, although there is a good deal of evidence to prove that the original New England boiled dinner was made not with salt beef but with salt cod and that the other famous New England dish, a sort of post-boiled dinner called red flannel hash, was a hash of fish chopped with the leftover vegetables. According to many authorities, after corned beef had taken over the central role in the boiled dinner, the New Englanders made a vegetable hash of the chopped leftover beets, carrots, turnips, potatoes, and cabbage, cooked with a little bit of beef fat until nice and crispy, and served it with thin slices of cold corned beef. This seems very logical, for in those days beef was not so plentiful that people could afford to chop it up for the next day's hash. In this, it is very much like the hash the British call "bubble and squeak," a dish of chopped fried potatoes, cabbage, and onion served on Monday after Sunday's dinner of roast beef.

The boiled dinner is a beautiful sight, if properly arranged on a platter. There lies the glistening slab of luscious beef, with its entourage of appropriate vegetables—carrots, turnips, onions, beets, potatoes boiled in their jackets, wedges of green cabbage, and sometimes leeks, rutabaga, or parsnips. Traditionally, all the vegetables, except the beets, were cooked with the meat. Beets were usually cooked separately, so as not to color the water and tinge the other vegetables with an unbecoming blush. With mustards, pickles, and good bread and butter this was a lavish and a memorable feast. Nowadays, with our less hearty appetites, we are more apt to serve a simpler version of the boiled dinner, just corned beef and cabbage, a piece of boiled or steamed corned beef with separately cooked cabbage and potatoes. It rarely extends beyond that, although you certainly could, if you so desired, put some carrot, onion, and garlic in with the beef.

Lately, too, we have discovered that the corned beef cooks just as well, if not better, when steamed in the oven in very little water rather than being cooked on top of the stove in a great kettle of water. I am all for this method, and it is the one I am going to give you for my version of corned beef.

First, you need to buy a good piece of corned beef brisket, about 6 pounds. Brisket is by far the best cut for corned beef because it is thin, well fatted on both sides, has a delicious flavor, and carves into lovely even slices. Six pounds of meat will give you plenty for a dinner for six, with enough left over to make hash and corned beef sandwiches.

Wash the meat well, trim off excess fat, and place it in a flat baking pan. Add water to come almost to the top of the meat, to the fat line, a few crushed peppercorns, a bay leaf, and 2 or 3 garlic cloves. Drape a piece of foil over the pan, put it in a 325° to 350°F oven, and let the meat cook very slowly for about 3 to 3½ hours, or until tender when tested with a knife. The internal temperature, tested with a meat thermometer, should register 140°F. Cooked this way, the corned beef comes out firmer and easier to slice than when cooked on top of the stove. It also gives you the opportunity to use the burners of your range to cook separately whatever vegetables you may want to have with your meat.

What do you do with leftover corned beef? Lots of things. First, there are probably more sandwiches with corned beef than any other meat I can think of, beginning with the plain, pure, and simple one of corned beef and bread. There is a great controversy as to whether or not the bread should be buttered. I think it should. Take the cooked corned beef and trim off practically every bit of fat. Put it into a dish or a pan, put foil on the top, and then cover it with a plate or board and weight it down with canned goods (tomatoes, peaches, any of the heavier cans will do) or with weights from the kitchen scale, if you happen to have one of that type. If the meat is weighted as it cools, it will have a firmer texture and slice perfectly. Slice it against the grain in thin diagonal slices. Spread good rye bread or pumpernickel or even a fine white bread with butter and mustard to make a frame for the lustrous pinkish slices. The bread should not be too thick, the corned beef should be thin, and the butter and mustard plentiful. Trim the sandwich so it looks attractive. Good pickles are a must with a sandwich of this kind.

Then there is the very famous Reuben sandwich that started in a New York delicatessen and has become an international favorite. Originally, if my memory serves, the Reuben was made with rather thickly sliced pumpernickel, lots of corned beef, Russian dressing, cole slaw, Swiss cheese, and sometimes sliced turkey—and a great delicacy it was. Now the sandwich has changed its character and makeup completely and comes forth as toasted rye bread with corned beef, Swiss or Gruyère cheese, and sauerkraut, very often served quite hot.

Recently, I had a quite different and most delicious version of the Reuben, one that showed some intelligent thinking in the kitchen. Lightly toasted slices of rye bread spread with a touch of butter were covered with a goodly portion of sauerkraut that had been cooked down with bacon fat, white wine, and plenty of garlic and pepper. Thin slices of corned beef were laid on the sauerkraut and covered with thin slices of Gruyère cheese, then the open-face sandwich was popped under the broiler to melt the cheese and crisp the edges of the bread. The sandwich, dressed with tomatoes, was rushed to the table on a hot plate.

Another good approach, if you are giving a cocktail party, is to make tiny toasted Reuben sandwiches of corned beef, Swiss cheese, and sauerkraut on cocktail rye and serve them as a hot hors d'oeuvre.

Of course, I'd be the last to criticize if you decided just to settle for a plate of that lovely, juicy, flavorful corned beef with a good potato salad or cole slaw, or even a vegetable salad of note. By "of note" I mean a salad of impeccably cooked vegetables, still firm to the bite, drained and dressed with a vinaigrette sauce. Add some mustard and pickles and nothing could be better.

Cold corned beef is the making of another simple but wondrous dish—corned beef hash. For hash, you should leave a little bit of fat on the meat. Dice or finely cut the meat by hand or in a food processor—don't put it through a meat grinder.

You will need some firm, waxy cold potatoes that have been cooked in their jackets. Peel, chop, or dice them very finely. I like my hash to be about 60 percent meat to 40 percent potatoes. Some like more potatoes and some less, but to me a 60-40 balance makes for a delicious hash. To this add finely chopped onion to your taste. I would say about one-third or one-half as much onion as potato, or, for 2 pounds corned beef and 6 cold potatoes, about 1 good-sized onion, but please yourself.

Mix the chopped meat, potato, and onion together very well and season with a touch of nutmeg and freshly ground black pepper, but hold back on the salt until the hash has cooked a bit. Cooking often brings out the salt remaining in the beef, so wait, taste, and add salt as needed.

Melt 6 tablespoons beef fat, or butter and oil (with a heavier accent on butter than on oil), in a heavy iron or stainless steel skillet. Add your hash mixture and press it down rather heavily with a spatula. Let simmer over medium heat until it develops a crust on the bottom that can be loosened with the spatula. Turn the hash with a spatula to see if it has begun to form a crust, then press it down again. Some people add a little boiling water, which enables the crust to form more quickly, or a little cream, and let it cook down. When the bottom is crusty, shake your pan and loosen the crust with a spatula, and very carefully either turn the hash out onto a platter, crusty side up, or fold it over as you would an omelet, and slide it onto the platter.

Traditionally, corned beef hash is served with poached eggs on top, but it's just as good with fried eggs or with a dish of perfectly scrambled eggs. You can also add a little finely chopped green pepper to your hash mixture, which makes it much more pungent.

As good as commercial corned beef can be, your own corned beef will be even better. This is not the horrible, messy job you may imagine, and fairly easy to do. You will need a big container of enameled metal or glass, or a heavy earthenware crock. Whatever you use, it must be big enough to hold the meat and enough brine to completely cover it and come about 2 or 3 inches above the meat in the crock.

Buy 2 pieces of fresh beef brisket or flanken, weighing 8 to 10 pounds in all. Wipe well with a damp cloth and give the meat a number of very deep piercing jabs with a big fork so that it will absorb the brine. Put the meat in the crock.

To make the brine, you will need for each gallon of water 2 cups of rock salt or curing salt, 2 cups of dark brown sugar, 1½ teaspoons of bicarbonate of soda, and 4 teaspoons of saltpeter, which is sold in drugstores as potassium nitrate. Add any spices you want, such as crushed allspice or peppercorns, blades of mace, and several cloves of garlic. Mix all these ingredients with 1 quart of lukewarm water, and when they are well blended and dissolved add the rest of the water. Pour this brine over the beef in the crock, making sure it is well covered, and let it soak for 8 to 10 days. If you leave it for 10 to 12 days, it will be more matured and slightly saltier, and will have a finer flavor and texture when cooked. You may possibly have to add a little more brine during this period, to make sure that the meat remains submerged.

This corning formula and technique also works beautifully for pieces of pork, pig's feet, and fresh tongue. It's a valuable recipe to hold on to.

When the beef has corned sufficiently, remove it from the crock, rinse it in cold water, and then cook either in a covered pan in the oven, as directed before, or by putting it in a kettle of cold water, bringing it to a boil, and simmering it for 1 hour. Then drain off the salty water, replace with fresh boiling water to cover the meat, and simmer until the corned beef is tender, about a further 2½ to 3 hours.

As good as corned beef is, there is a sizable faction who sing the praises of pastrami. Pastrami, originally a Romanian dish that became very popular in Jewish delicatessens in Europe and then in this country, is also a cured cut of beef brisket or flanken, but it is more highly spiced, smoked, and usually rolled in coarsely ground pepper and spices. Although pastrami can be a pretty delicious morsel, if I had to take sides and choose the one that I would eat for the rest of my life, I am sure I would choose good corned beef, although I'll probably be damned by a number of people for making that statement. Corned beef is much more versatile, and it has a lovely homely quality that even the finest pastrami can't touch.

The best pastrami I've ever eaten was one I made myself. I'm going to give you the recipe, because if you live in a place where you hanker for but you can't get good pastrami, it's easy enough to make your own. You must have some sort of smoker to do it properly, but there are so many different little smokers on the market now that it is hardly a problem.

For the pastrami, you will need 4 or 5 pieces of beef brisket, about 20 pounds in all. Combine 2 cups of kosher salt, ½ cup of sugar, 4 teaspoons of saltpeter, ½ cup ground ginger, ½ cup crushed pepper, and 5 or 6 cloves of crushed garlic. Sprinkle this mixture evenly over the surface of the meat, on both sides. Put this meat in a flat pan, cover with foil, and weight down with a plate or board and canned goods. Refrigerate for 20 days. Remove from the pan and dry in the air, suspended in front of a fan, for 2 hours, then put in your smoker and smoke at 150° to 175°F for 24 hours. To cook, simmer the smoked pastrami in water to cover for 3 to 4 hours, or until tender. After cooking, you can rub the outside with cracked pepper and spices, if you wish. You can also treat a beef tongue this way, and that's delicious, too.

Corned beef and pastrami make a wonderful couple. Where would we food lovers be without them?

CHAPTER 18

ECONOMICAL,

VERSATILE

CRÊPES

One of the most sustaining and popular foods throughout our early history was pancakes, or hotcakes, or flapjacks. Every miner, every prospector, every pioneer who trekked across the land, practically every child, could mix up a mess of flapjack batter. This typical American food, as basic as any we know, can be infinitely satisfying. Pancakes are sometimes light as a feather, at other times pretty leaden; nevertheless, a pancake properly baked and properly accompanied by syrup and sausages or bacon is a deliciously tasty and economical dish.

I'm not going to lead you across the plains or into the Yukon with this lesson, but I am going to give you a recipe for a pancake or crêpe batter which is at one and the same time as basic as 1-2-3, and one of the great tests of cooking ability. We use the French word *crêpe* for the type of thin, unleavened (save for the eggs) pancake that can be used as the base for many different dishes, both savory and sweet. Crêpes can be served as an hors d'oeuvre, as a main dish, as a dessert— and they're a pretty good breakfast dish, too, if you so choose. You should have no trouble making crêpes, provided you have a good recipe for the batter and take a little care mastering the baking technique, which is rather different from the usual way of making pancakes.

First, assemble your equipment. You'll need a mixing bowl; a wire whisk or a wooden spatula; a thin-bladed, supple spatula with a blade about an inch wide and 8 inches long—not a big pancake turner, but a narrow metal spatula; and a suitable pan, about 6 or 7 inches in diameter. Now, this can be the classic French iron crêpe pan, about 1 inch or 1½ inches deep, or a Teflon-lined omelet pan with rounded sides; it can be a griddle (although this is not very convenient); it can be an iron skillet 7 inches or 8 inches in diameter, or almost any heavy frying pan of suitable shape and material. I use a Teflon-lined cast-aluminum omelet pan for crêpes most of the time and it works beautifully.

If you can, make your crêpe batter two or three hours ahead of time and let it rest. The reason for this is that you will be making a nice, smooth batter of flour, eggs, liquid, salt, and a little melted butter or oil, and by letting it rest, you enable the flour to expand and absorb the liquid so that you get a better blend of ingredients. A batter that has been allowed to stand cooks better than a newly made batter, because it has settled and ripened slightly. It does not start to work as a yeast batter would, unless it has stood for a day or so, but it will undergo a smoothing and enriching process which benefits the crêpes.

For a basic crêpe batter, which will be enough for 16 to 18 crêpes, break 3 eggs into your bowl, and with a wire whisk or wooden spatula, break up the yolks and whites and mix them up well. Season with a good pinch of salt and, if you are making savory crêpes, mix in 1 cup of milk or 1 cup of beer. Beer gives a nice, light quality to the crêpes and a taste that blends well with the savory filling, but I would not use it for dessert crêpes. Here, milk is preferable. Blend together very well and then stir in, with a whisk, ⅞ cup of all-purpose flour (that's 1 cup, less 2 tablespoons), and as you stir, mix in 2 tablespoons melted butter or 2 tablespoons oil—corn oil, peanut oil, or olive oil. Blend until the batter takes on the consistency of very heavy cream, which is what you need for baking. Depending upon the dampness or dryness of the flour, you may need another ¼ cup or more of liquid, but this you must decide for yourself. If you know what heavy cream or thick cream looks like, you can pretty well tell when you mix the batter whether it has the proper consistency. I find that I seldom need to put in more than a cup of liquid, but there are times when I may add a few more spoonfuls.

If you are making dessert crêpes, follow the same recipe, using milk rather than beer, and sweeten and flavor your batter with 3 tablespoons of sugar and 2 tablespoons of cognac or 1 tablespoon of vanilla extract or grated lemon rind (just the zest, the yellow part of the skin). After mixing it well, let the batter rest for 2 to 3 hours.

When you are ready to bake the crêpes, put your pan on medium to medium-high heat and have near at hand the flexible metal spatula, a small pan of melted butter, a pastry brush, and a plate on which to stack the baked crêpes (you can stack them with waxed paper between, if you plan to use them later on or the next day).

The secret of a perfect crêpe is to make it *thin* and *tender*. When your pan is good and hot, brush it well with the melted butter, which should sizzle slightly. (If you have let the pan get too hot, the butter will brown and burn a bit, which you don't want. In this case, wipe it out with paper towels, cool the pan slightly by waving it in the air, and start again.) When the butter sizzles, take about 3 tablespoons or a little less than ¼ cup of the batter in a small ladle and pour it into the hot pan with your left hand. Holding the handle of the pan with your other hand, tilt the pan so the batter quickly swirls around and runs all over the bottom and around the inside edge of the pan. Put it back on the heat to bake on one side, which will take 3 or 4 minutes, maybe less. You can tell when it is baked by shaking the pan. The crêpe will move slightly on the surface. Now, if you are a hardy soul, tip and shake the pan so that the crêpe hangs over the front edge of the pan a little. Pick it up quickly with your fingers and turn it over. If you have had flapjack training in your earlier years, you may flip the crêpe to turn it over, if you prefer. Or, if you can't flip, and are afraid of burning your fingers, run the spatula very

carefully around the edge of the crêpe, slide it underneath, and then, very quickly, lift and turn it over. This method can be efficient or it can be destructive, if you aren't careful. Should you break or cut into the crêpe with the spatula, you've just got to smooth it back with your fingers after turning, hoping it will hold together. I find turning it with your hands or flipping is much safer and much more professional. When the other side has baked, turn the crêpe onto the plate, either by picking it up with your fingers, as before, or by reversing the pan over the plate quickly so the crêpe falls out.

The amount of batter will yield up to 18 crêpes, depending on the diameter of the pan and the thickness of the crêpes, and that is enough for a main course for six. For dessert, it will serve eight or more, and for an hors d'oeuvre, probably twelve. However, you alone know the appetites of your guests, so bake accordingly. You may want to make more than one batch. Just stack them with a piece of waxed paper between each crêpe, and if you want to freeze them, wrap them in foil.

It's a lot of fun to make crêpes, and if you've never done it before, I suggest that you take some time to practice until you become deft at turning the crêpe, sliding it out of the pan, and getting it back in again all in one piece. Remember, the crêpe should not overbake. If the edges become girdled with brown, your crêpe will be too crisp and you'll have difficulty rolling it. Crêpes should be rather pale so that they remain supple and roll easily. Don't worry if each one is not a thing of beauty. The filling and the sauce will take care of the looks.

So now, having made all those crêpes, you want to know: "What am I going to do with them?" That's a very good question. You can make a variety of fillings. One of the best ways is to poach and cut up a chicken, which will be mixed with a velouté sauce.

Buy a small whole chicken weighing about 3 pounds, wipe it well with a cut lemon, and place it in a deep 4-quart kettle with a small onion, a piece of celery, a clove of garlic, a carrot, a sprig of parsley, 1 tablespoon of salt, 2 grinds of black pepper, and enough water to cover two-thirds of the chicken. Add the giblets, too, the gizzard, the heart, the neck, and the liver. They all help to give the broth flavor. Bring to a boil on fairly high heat and skim off any scum that rises to the surface, then turn the heat down to low or medium-low, cover the pan, and let the chicken poach—not boil, but poach, with the feeblest movement of the liquid—for 40 to 45 minutes, or until it is just cooked through. Uncover, remove the chicken, and cook the broth down over fairly high heat, uncovered, for 5 to 6 minutes. Taste for seasoning and see if you need more salt and pepper. The broth should have a full, rich, chicken flavor.

When the chicken is cool enough to handle, remove the skin and then, with a paring knife or small knife, cut through the white meat and see if you can cut it all off the breastbone in one piece. You should be able to, if you learned our knife lesson earlier. Cut the white meat into ½-inch to ¾-inch cubes, remove the dark meat from the legs and thighs, and cut that into cubes, too. If there are tidbits of meat left on the bones, pull these off in little shreds and put them with the rest of the chicken. You can cut up and add the giblets, too, if you like.

Now, strain the chicken broth, which you'll use for the sauce, and measure 1¼ cups of it.

Melt 3 tablespoons butter in a saucepan of enameled cast iron or stainless steel, or one with a Teflon lining (don't use aluminum or black iron, as you are going to enrich your sauce with egg yolks later on), and blend in 3 level tablespoons flour. Cook, stirring, until the mixture turns golden and bubbles a little, then add a touch of salt, some freshly ground pepper, a bit of freshly grated nutmeg, and the 1¼ cups of chicken broth. Cook, stirring well, until the mixture thickens, then let it bubble and simmer for a few minutes, stirring from time to time, until it has become quite thick. You now have a basic béchamel sauce, which should have a good, well-seasoned flavor, with a chicken overtone. Taste to see if it needs more seasoning. You may also want to add another little pat of butter, stirring it in well, to make the sauce richer.

Take the pan from the heat and let it stand on the stove, close to the burner, while you blend, in a measuring cup, 2 egg yolks and ½ cup heavy cream, which will be the enrichment that turns your béchamel into a sauce velouté. Take about ⅓ cup of the still-hot béchamel sauce and stir it into the egg-cream mixture in the measuring cup. Now stir this back into the sauce in the pan, replace over medium heat, and cook, stirring until it begins to thicken a little bit. Do not, under any circumstances, let it come to a boil, or you'll have scrambled eggs instead of a lovely sauce velouté.

Mix the cut-up chicken into the sauce and place over very low heat until it is thoroughly warmed through.

Butter an 8 × 11-inch baking dish. Take your crêpes and spread them flat on a board or counter, place some of the chicken mixture on each one, in the center, fairly near the lower edge, roll the crêpe up carefully, and place it in the buttered baking dish, seam side down.

Continue until you have used up the crêpes and most of the chicken,
tucking the crêpes together so they don't unroll. For a main course,
allow two crêpes a person, or three if you have hungry people to
feed. Put the remaining chicken and sauce back on the heat, stir in
another ¼ cup heavy cream, and let it warm through. Pour this over
the rolled crêpes in the baking dish, and sprinkle with a little grated
Parmesan cheese.

Just before you are about ready to serve, put the dish in a preheated
375°F oven until the crêpes are heated through. Serve them on hot
plates with a vegetable such as broccoli with lemon butter, or cauliflower, or have a good salad and some crisp French bread.

This is only one of many different dishes you can make with the
basic sauce and basic crêpe recipes. You can mix cooked shrimp or
crabmeat into the sauce, in which case you'd make it with milk rather
than chicken broth, or with fish stock if you have any on hand. You
can use flaked salmon or tuna, adding a touch of curry to the sauce
if you like (cook the curry powder with the butter and flour, or it
will have a harsh, raw taste). You could put diced ham in the sauce
and a little sherry. Or, if you have a special vegetable, such as mushrooms, you might slice and sauté them and put them in the sauce.

I'll now tell you briefly about filling your dessert crêpes. The
simplest way is to spread them with your favorite preserves, like
raspberry or damson plum, roll them, and then place them in a
buttered skillet or a crêpe suzette pan, over medium to high heat,
and let them heat through. Sprinkle them lightly with sugar, heat
and ignite ½ cup bourbon or Cognac or rum, and pour it flaming
over the crêpes. Shake the pan until the flames die down, and serve.
What could be simpler?

Or you might make a banana filling, a special favorite of mine.
Slice 6 peeled bananas very, very thinly, and sauté them very quickly
in 6 tablespoons butter, shaking the pan and stirring them. Add ½
cup brown sugar, let it melt into the butter and caramelize, then pour
½ cup warmed rum into the pan, light it, and flame the bananas.
Roll this lovely banana mixture into the crêpes, spooning some of it
over the top. Enhance the crêpes with whipped cream if you like, or
with a good bottled chocolate sauce from a specialty shop, heated
through, and you'll have a perfectly fantastic, spectacular, and very
easy dessert.

CHAPTER 19

HOW TO
ENJOY DIETING

It seems to me that most people who are put on a diet by their doctor feel and act as is they have been given a prison sentence. Sometimes it is the fault of the doctor, who makes it sound like the grimmest kind of self-denial, but more often it is the attitude of the dieter. Dieting is not the most pleasant thing in the world to face, but it is no prison sentence, and it can be an adventure if you look on it as something new and different—a breakaway from the habits that have been formed during a lifetime—more creative than destructive. It is really a matter of thinking before you eat—thinking about calories, chemical content of foods, and pleasant ways to overcome the prohibitions. You are starting out on a whole new world of eating, and if you have any imagination whatsoever, you can have fun doing it.

For close to a year I have been on a salt-free, fairly low-calorie diet. I have not suffered or felt martyred because certain things have been denied me, and certainly I have not lost my taste for good food. It's foolish to go through life bemoaning the fact that you can't have this or that. Twaddle! You can omit certain foods and still enjoy eating. Going without salt is the thing dieters seem to dread more than anything else, but I can assure you that I've been to dinner parties where the entire meal was cooked without the addition of

any salt, just intelligently flavored, and practically no one added salt
to a dish, regardless of whether they were allowed it, which is just
about the greatest compliment anyone serving a salt-free menu can
ask for. There will always be people who feel they must salt a dish
before they even taste it, and I think it would be a good lesson if
they were put on a salt-free diet for a time. To be sure, you miss salt
in certain things you eat, but you have to compensate by looking for
foods where it really won't be missed.

To me, the one food that salt-free cooking makes difficult is bread.
Bread without salt is rather dull unless it is spiked up with fresh
herbs or garlic mixed into the dough. Just plain salt-free bread dis-
courages you from eating much of it, which is probably a good idea
for anyone on a diet, anyway. It does toast quite well, and you can
put things on the toast that give it a bit of zest. Then, of course, there
is cheese, which depends so much on salt for the maturing process
and flavor. Cheese is high on the taboo list for those on a salt-free
diet, or a low-calorie diet, for it is high in calories, too. There are
salt-free cheeses on the market, but except for a salt-free mozzarella
that is very good in certain dishes, I have yet to find one to take the
place of a fine aged Gruyère or Cheddar or Parmesan, or to touch a
good Camembert or Brie. You can make a fresh, natural, saltless
cheese by lining a strainer or a perforated mold, like the one used
for *coeur à la crème*, with cheesecloth, pouring in yogurt and letting
it drip until all the liquid whey has drained out. In texture it is rather
like cream cheese without the cream; the flavor is tart, and it works
pretty successfully in sauces and things like that.

Let's consider a few more things that are taboo. Butter, of course,
for some kinds of diets. Low-sodium folk can have a certain amount
of salt-free margarine, and you'll find if you start using it that it
becomes something to which you can easily adjust your palate. Salt-
free margarine is bland, with a nice color, and while it is not butter,
it is not to be sneered at by any manner or means. Most stores keep
salt-free margarine in the freezer and so should you, except for the
small amount you are currently using. Naturally, oils are not to be
used too profusely, but there is one point I would like to bring up
about oil. Most diet treatises push corn oil, cottonseed oil, and safflower
oil, but don't forget that you can also have olive oil which, considering
the small amount you use, is a great boon in texture and flavor. If
you have been an olive oil addict all your life as I have, it will give
you a certain warm satisfaction to be able to have a little bit on a
salad or a vegetable or to do a light sauté. That is something to be

thankful for. Then, the low-calorie or salt-free dieter will not have a great deal of milk, except for small amounts of skim milk, and certainly a minimum of heavy cream. Yogurt, I find, is an excellent substitute for cream and one of the dieter's very good friends because it mixes well with vegetables, makes an interesting salad dressing, and with the addition of garlic and fresh herbs and spices can be the base for low-calorie sauces.

If you have to keep a strict watch on your sodium intake, you'll have to avoid celery, which is very high in sodium, beets, spinach, chard, dandelion greens, and frozen and canned vegetables (unless they are specially packed), but there is very little else in the vegetable line that is verboten.

Most shellfish are very high in sodium, although low in calories, but apart from canned tuna, salmon, and sardines—all taboos because of their salt content—there are quite a few fish that can be included in your regimen. Lean meat, preferably broiled, roasted, or poached, is all right, of course.

A salt-free diet is your opportunity to delve into flavors you may not have explored before. I find my very best seasoning friends are garlic, shallots, onions, lemon, lime, orange, chives, tarragon, and other fresh herbs such as sage, thyme, rosemary, and mint, wine vinegar, and Madeira. I love the smell and taste of mint and, as smell is part of your appreciation of food and so doubly important on a diet, I find I use it more often than before. The wonderful dried mint sold in Middle Eastern shops has a pungency and flavor almost equal to the fresh, and it is a delightful additive to many dishes heretofore not thought of as being palatable with mint. I have used mint in tomato sauce, on fish with lemon juice and freshly ground black pepper and garlic, on chicken and vegetables, and in vegetable purées. It is a very friendly herb. So, of course, is garlic, possibly the best of all stand-ins for salt. A combination of finely chopped garlic, coarsely ground pepper, and lemon juice can do wonders for almost any dish that is unsalted or tastes flat for other reasons. Onion has the same quality, and I am using it more than I ever did. A little Madeira is a great help, too, because the flavor is rich and almost immoral—and we need to feel we are being immoral within the bounds of our permitted diet.

A baked potato once or twice a week is another great joy, and not even an indulgence for the low-calorie dieter, as it only has about ninety calories. I learned years ago to appreciate the wonderful earthy flavor of baked potato without butter or salt, just freshly ground black pepper. It may surprise you to find how much better and fluffier it is—the butter flattens the fluffiness down, as does sour cream, even yogurt. A well-baked, crisp-skinned potato needs nothing more than pepper to excite the palate, though you could, if you wanted, add a few chopped chives or a little chopped onion or garlic. I wouldn't.

I have also changed my whole pattern of salad eating. I no longer toss a salad with dressing. Now I just arrange endive or leaves of lettuce attractively on a plate, put one or two dressings in small bowls, and let everyone pick up the greens and dip them in the dressing like finger food. One of the dressings I like is a mixture of 3 table-spoons yogurt, 1 tablespoon salt-free mustard (which is available in most stores), a few drops of olive oil, and a few drops of wine vinegar, usually sherry wine vinegar. You can vary this by adding fresh or dried tarragon, rosemary, or basil, and it makes a most flavorful and interesting dressing for salad greens or a composed salad, and a good sauce for hot vegetables.

Freshly squeezed lemon juice is enormously beneficial to your diet dishes—a piece of broiled veal, for instance, or broiled chicken. You can marinate the chicken in lemon juice, white wine, garlic, shredded fresh ginger, and a tiny bit of olive oil, broil it, and eat it hot or cold. Or you can baste a roast chicken with oil, lemon juice, white wine, and ginger, tarragon, or rosemary. Roast it at 400°F for 25 minutes on one side, 25 minutes on the other, and 20 to 25 minutes breast up (that's for a 3-pound chicken), basting it the while.

Another of my favorite diet dishes is fish, either broiled or braised in a 425°F oven on a bed of chopped shallots or onions with some white wine, allowing 10 minutes for each inch of fish measured at the thickest point. With freshly ground pepper and lemon juice this is a most attractive meal at any time. Or I may poach the fish in water and a bit of white wine with lemon juice, several lemon slices, pepper, and perhaps tarragon, thyme, or parsley, again following the rule of 10 minutes cooking time per inch. Don't overcook fish; this is one of the errors too many people make. I serve it hot with lemon juice and chopped parsley, or cold with the yogurt-mustard dressing as a sauce.

A good meat cut for dieters is what is called a paillard of veal, a thin cutlet sliced from the leg, like scaloppine, about 4 or 5 inches in diameter, pounded well and broiled very quickly close to the heat on a broiler pan that has been heated so that the meat practically chars where it hits the grids of the pan. It should cook in a matter of minutes, no more than 3 or 4. Brushed with a tiny bit of margarine or oil and served with plenty of lemon and freshly ground pepper, which makes a delicious saucing for the veal, this is a most satisfactory dish.

If you are put on a diet, you should ask your doctor what your alcoholic intake can be. I am allowed more spirits than wine, for particular reasons, but on so many diets you may take two or three glasses of wine a day if you are so inclined. Of course, you can use wine in cooking, because the alcohol and calories are burned off by heat—and the same thing goes for spirits. Even if you can't drink Cognac, bourbon, kirsch, or other spirits, you can certainly flavor your food with them. To have a bit of kirsch or framboise or Cognac or bourbon with poached or raw fruit gives it a lot more glamour. Don't add the raw spirit, though. Heat it first to remove the alcohol and let it cool.

You might be interested to know that I have always been a great Perrier water addict, and when I was in the hospital a year ago, my doctor had the Perrier water analyzed and found it contains no natural sodium, so it is a very safe drink for a salt-free diet. If you consume it in great quantities, as I do, you will find that the refreshing flavor and effervescence assuage the desire for other kinds of drinks, which

is a great help if you have to cut down on wine and spirits. In fact, the "in" drink at New York business luncheons these days seems to be a glass of Perrier water with a slice of lemon, so you'll be right in fashion.

That covers dieting at home, but what, you might ask, does one do when invited out for dinner? Well, if you are going to a friend's home, the polite thing is to say that you are on a salt-free diet or low-calorie diet, and if they really want to see you, they will ask what you are allowed to eat. Simply tell them what you can have and make it something easy, so all your friend has to do is hold the salt on your portion of fish or meat, or cook something that isn't rich and high in calories. As for restaurant dining, for the most part you are better off going to those where you are well known. In New York, I can go to Quo Vadis, Trattoria de Alfredo, The Coach House, or to most any of my regular haunts. At Windows on the World or The Four Seasons, for instance, they wouldn't dream of letting me have anything with salt in it. If you have a few favorite restaurants, tell the owner about your diet, and he will probably be very glad to see that the food you are served complies with your diet.

Once in a while, if you feel an overpowering desire to have a pastry or a chocolate mousse or something that is adverse to your diet, don't feel you have to resist. Order it, enjoy it, and don't let your conscience bother you. Recently I went to a dinner cooked by one of the greatest chefs in France, and I said to myself, "Who cares! I'm going to enjoy this," and I did. I made up for it the next day by cutting down on calories, but I think that is the way one should approach a diet. Be faithful on a regular basis, but if you want to break the rule once in a while, do it grandly and with no regrets.

CHAPTER 20

GAME

For a great many people in this huge country, shooting, cooking, and eating game is a way of life. On my travels, I find that more and more of my friends have freezers stocked with game that they have shot or bought. In Europe, the list of game that is eaten is much wider, and to some of us, rather shocking, but in this country, at least, the game we are most interested in is venison, pheasant, wild duck, and quail. Succulent quail are so addictive that while most people can eat two at a sitting, I have known some who ate six. Quail can be prepared in a variety of ways. My friend Prentice Hale in San Francisco removes the breasts from the birds, sautés them gently in butter with salt and pepper and a little lemon juice, and serves them for breakfast with bacon, toast or rolls, and plenty of hot coffee— and a magnificent breakfast it is. Another way to cook these birds is to flatten them, wrap them in a piece of bacon, put them on a piece of buttered bread, and roast them in a very hot oven (450°F) for 20 to 25 minutes, until the bacon fat has lubricated the breast and the juices have descended into the bread that has become toasted in the heat of the oven. Or the birds can be barded well with fatback and roasted on a rack in a shallow baking dish in a 425°F oven for about 22 minutes. They should be basted once or twice with melted butter, combined, if you wish, with some white wine, and the barding fat can be removed for the last 4 or 5 minutes of roasting. Roast two quail per person and a few extra to have left over, because they are very good cold. Quail can also be sautéed whole and quickly in butter or oil, or in clarified butter. Put a few juniper berries inside each bird and at the end of the cooking time add a little gin to the pan and flambé the quail. Gin, as you know, has juniper as one of the aromatics. It is grossly overlooked as a spirit with which to flambé game, for the little touch of juniper it brings to the meat is just delicious. Serve sautéed quail on pieces of crisp buttered toast with the pan juices spooned over them. They need no other seasoning than salt and pepper.

If you don't have a chance to go out and shoot your own quail, there are many quail farms, like the one run by a friend of mine in New Jersey (from which you can buy them by mail), or they may be found in better butcher shops and frozen in many markets.

The French, by the way, have a nice way of roasting quail. After seasoning and larding them, they wrap each bird in vine leaves. Or, if you are a devotee of the grill, you can split and broil them very quickly over charcoal so they don't get overcooked and dry, but retain a tender moistness.

When I was growing up in Oregon, quail were rather a luxury to us, but wild duck were there in plenty, and we usually had quite a number hanging in the cellar. Plucking a duck is something I learned at an early age—and there was more than one way to do this. Some people believed in plucking them dry with the fingers, others plunged them into boiling water and then plucked them, and still others gave them a coating of melted paraffin to pull off the feathers. Only this morning, as I was thinking about this article, I found in a catalog a triumph of the modern imagination that would make the ideal gift for a duck hunter—an electric duck plucker that also plucks quail and pheasant. It is expensive but, heavens, if I were plucking ducks as much as I used to, I would buy one like a shot.

Roasting wild ducks has always been a subject of controversy. There are those who feel that a duck should be cooked very, very briefly, barely heated through, and eaten as raw and bloody as possible. Others (my father was one) like their duck cooked 1½ to 2 hours, until extremely well done. I can remember some rather spectacular duck feasts in my young days. Sometimes the ducks were seasoned with a sprig of rosemary and a few juniper berries, put 3 on a spit, rubbed with olive oil, and revolved over a charcoal fire for about 25 to 30 minutes and then flamed with Cognac. They were marvelously good, pink but not bloody, and tender as butter. We would often stuff teal, the tiny duck that comes mostly from the West, with a small piece of onion, a piece of orange rind, and a few juniper berries, bard them with bacon, and roast them very quickly in a 400°F oven for about 25 minutes.

When you roast wild duck, gauge a half duck per person, unless they are pretty small, in which case you'll need one duck per person, and see that you bring them to room temperature before roasting. When you plan your menu, there are certain things I think go very well with duck. I love mashed turnips, especially yellow turnips, or a combination of half mashed potatoes and half mashed yellow turnips with plenty of butter and freshly ground black pepper. Applesauce mixed with freshly grated horseradish to taste (I like mine pretty peppy) is an excellent accompaniment, and of course you'll have a beautiful red wine, either a great California or French wine—that's a marriage that might have been made in heaven. I personally like a fine Bordeaux, a Château Latour or Château Palmer or Château Haut-Brion, or perhaps a St.-Émilion, such as a Château Cheval Blanc. Or you could have a Rhône red, a Hermitage or Gigondas, or an excellent California Cabernet Sauvignon.

My friend Mary Hambert's duck has a stuffing. For 4 wild ducks, combine 1 cup chopped onion, 1 cup finely chopped parsley, 1 teaspoon thyme, ¼ teaspoon sage, 4 cups dried bread crumbs or prepared stuffing mixture, 1 teaspoon salt, 1 teaspoon freshly ground black pepper, and ½ to ¾ cup melted butter. Mix well in a bowl to make

a rather moist stuffing, stuff the ducks, and tie a piece of salt pork over each breast. Place them on a rack in a roasting pan and roast in a 350°F oven for 45 minutes to an hour. Some people like them better done than others, and because of the stuffing they take a little longer to cook. (If you are roasting teal or very small ducks, 30 minutes is enough roasting time.) For well-done duck, give them a little bit longer. Baste the ducks well with melted butter several times during the cooking period. These ducks are delicious served with just the pan juices poured over them, the mashed turnips or turnips and potatoes, and horseradish applesauce—or you could have peas, if you can get good ones. Peas and duck have a great affinity for each other.

Duck is best cooked in simple ways that enhance the natural wild and gamy flavor. Perhaps the simplest way is to split the ducks and broil them over charcoal or in the electric or gas broiler. They will take about 18 minutes, 9 minutes on each side, to become pinkly rare, and they should be brushed with butter from time to time. Season them with salt and pepper or put a little rosemary on the ducks so that it cooks in and flavors them. If you wish, when you remove the ducks to a platter for serving, you can flame them with gin or Cognac. Baked yellow squash is very good with broiled ducks.

Next to duck, pheasant is probably the most delicious and popular of the game birds. Here one should know whether the bird is young or old, and take care in cooking so that the breast does not get powdery dry, which pheasant has a tendency to do.

I am a great admirer of a book (published in England) that was written by Julia Drysdale, a woman who has spent the greater part of her life on a big game farm in Scotland. Her year begins with grouse on the twelfth of August and goes through until February, so she always has freezers full of game. Mrs. Drysdale is not only an extraordinarily good cook but also the only person I have ever come across who tells you how to test the age of a game bird, notably a pheasant. All young game birds have a small blind-ended passage called the bursa on the upper side of the vent that supposedly plays a part in disease control. When the bird reaches maturity, this vent becomes very much reduced or completely closed. When the bursa is open, you may be sure you have a young bird. To test, insert a burnt wooden match or toothpick into the bursa to see if it is open or closed. If the bird is old, certainly don't attempt to roast or sauté it. Braise it instead.

Young pheasant may be sautéed just like chicken, by browning it on each side in bacon fat or butter, then covering it and letting it cook gently until tender. Or you can flavor it with chopped herbs, or make a sauce for it from the pan juices and heavy cream. Just follow any of your favorite recipes for sautéed chicken.

Mrs. Drysdale has flattered me by using three of my recipes in her book (with credit, naturally), one of them being a sautéed pheasant with cabbage that I started doing years ago. About this recipe she says, "I have used this recipe of James Beard's so often that I have forgotten that it isn't really mine," and then she adds a little wrinkle of her own: "If you would rather skin the pheasant, I think it is better to wrap the pieces in streaky bacon, secured with a toothpick, before you sauté them."

For sautéing, the pheasant should be cut in convenient serving pieces, like chicken. Brown the pieces on both sides in 4 tablespoons butter or bacon fat, then reduce the heat, cover, and simmer for about 20 minutes. Meanwhile, shred a medium-size cabbage and parboil it in salted water for 10 minutes. Drain it very well. Add to the pheasant and cook, covered, for 10 minutes. Season with salt and pepper to taste, add 1 cup heavy cream, and simmer 5 minutes more. Then sprinkle with ½ teaspoon good Hungarian paprika and serve with boiled potatoes. I prefer boiled new potatoes and, failing those, good, waxy older potatoes. I have made this dish many times, and it is equally good with chicken.

Roasting a pheasant is very much the same as roasting a chicken, as far as I am concerned. Usually I don't stuff a pheasant, but I often put an onion or a clove of garlic, a little thyme, and sometimes 2 or 3 slices of lemon, all well smeared with softened butter, inside the bird. I truss the bird very carefully, rub it well with butter, and then put strips of streaky bacon or pork fatback on the breast and tie them securely, to preserve the tenderness and juiciness. I roast a pheasant at 375° to 400°F, the way I would a chicken, placing it on one side on a rack in a shallow roasting pan. I roast it for 15 minutes, then turn it on the other side, baste the bird with melted butter and perhaps some white wine, roast it another 15 minutes, then turn it on its back, baste it well with the pan juices and additional butter, and let it roast for a final 15 minutes. Ten minutes before the end of the roasting time I remove the larding pork or bacon so that the breast will brown nicely. Carve a pheasant with poultry shears, as you would a chicken, cutting it in half or in quarters. The breast is by far the best part of the pheasant, but there are those who like the legs and thighs. To satisfy everyone, either give them half a pheasant or a quarter, according to their wishes. Or, if you prefer, cut off the legs and thighs and carve the breast downward in pleasantly thin slices. You can usually count on a whole pheasant serving two, though a young one may only serve one.

With the older, less tender pheasants, my favorite way of cooking them is to braise them with sauerkraut. I rub the pheasants well with butter and brown them in a combination of oil and butter on all sides until they are nicely colored. For 2 pheasants, wash 3 pounds of sauerkraut well under cold, running water, in a colander, then put in a pot with a few juniper berries, cover with chicken broth, and let simmer for 1 hour. Then push the sauerkraut to the sides of the pot, place the pheasants in the center, and put the sauerkraut around and on top of them. Cover the pan and simmer for 1 to 1½ hours, until the birds are tender, adding more chicken broth to the pot if needed. Serve the pheasant and sauerkraut on a platter garnished with slices of Italian or French garlic sausage that have been poached separately in water, and have a dish of boiled potatoes as accompaniment.

To some people, the most important of all game is venison. This again is a gamble. You may get meat from a very young deer that is extraordinarily tender, or you may get the meat of a more mature animal that has to be marinated or hung for a while before it is really good eating. If you are not a good judge, consult your butcher, who will probably have cut up the animal. For roasting, the saddle is by far the best and tenderest cut, and usually the part of the deer with the best flavor. It may be marinated or not, but like most other pieces of venison, it should be larded with little strips of larding pork that you may soak in Cognac first if you like. Use a large grooved larding needle to run the strips through the flesh, from one end to the other. This takes the place of the marbling fat that one finds in beef or lamb and tenderizes the meat. Roast the saddle on a rack in a roasting pan in a very hot oven (400° to 425°F), allowing about 12 to 15 minutes per pound and basting frequently with melted butter mixed with either red wine or port wine (or, if you have marinated the meat, use some of the reduced marinade for basting). The meat should be very pink, not overcooked. Serve it with squares of fried grits or cornmeal mush or a casserole of barley cooked in chicken broth with mushrooms. If you are going to drink a good red wine with the venison, don't ruin the wine by serving red currant jelly, a custom I deplore.

If you'd like to marinate your venison, combine in a large non-metallic bowl enough red wine to cover the meat, ½ cup good olive oil, 1 onion, thinly sliced, 1 or 2 carrots, scraped and cut in strips, 2 or 3 garlic cloves, 2 teaspoons freshly ground black pepper, 1 bay leaf, and 2 teaspoons of either rosemary or thyme. Marinate the venison for 1, 2, or 3 days before roasting. Use the strained marinade as the basting fluid and, if you wish, reduce it and use it for a sauce.

Braising is a good way to treat other cuts, such as a haunch or shoulder of marinated venison. Remove the meat from the marinade and dry it well. Brown ½ pound diced salt pork in butter in a large skillet. When it is crispy, remove it, add more butter to the pan, and brown the venison thoroughly on all sides. Then place the browned meat in a braising pan with an onion stuck with 2 cloves, the vegetables from the marinade, the salt pork, and the marinade. Cover the pan and cook in a 350°F oven until tender, about 1½ to 2 hours. Remove the meat, strain the pan juices, and thicken them with balls of butter and flour, kneaded together, dropping them into the boiling liquid and stirring until the sauce thickens. Season with salt and pepper to taste, then add ¾ cup port wine. Serve the braised venison with a purée of chestnuts or chickpeas, mixed with cream and butter and seasoned to taste, and braised onions or glazed turnips.

The less good, tougher cuts of venison make perfectly delicious hamburger. I always add a small amount of beef suet when I make venison hamburgers to compensate for the lack of fat. Cook them like ground beef hamburgers. I like to roll them in coarsely ground or cracked pepper before cooking, and flambé them with a little Cognac when they are done. This makes good and interesting eating. If you have children who don't like the taste of roast or braised game, try them on a venison burger and they will probably love it. This way you can break them in to being real game eaters.

I firmly believe that everyone should learn to appreciate that underdone game is one thing and well-done game is another. So experiment. The whole field of game cookery is one of experimentation, imagination, and surprises that makes game eating one of the major adventures of the palate.

HAPPY
HAMMING

Every summer during my youth in Oregon, our family went off to the beach for a holiday. In addition to all the trunks, suitcases, and bundles that were dispatched to the train, a great picnic hamper was packed at the last minute by my mother to keep us going until our new pattern of living was established. In that hamper there was sure to be a delicious cooked ham, simply glazed with mustard, crumbs, and a bit of brown sugar. We would have two good meals from it, and then it would become snack food. It was the type of heavily smoked, heavily cured ham that has come to be known as "country ham."

In America, we have a great tradition of country hams. One of the most famous is Smithfield, which is unique in the world and which closely resembles some Chinese hams. In fact, many Chinese restaurants of top quality use Smithfield ham in their cooking. Smithfields are made from razorback hogs and are cured and smoked in a distinctive way. No ham can be called a Smithfield unless it comes from a designated region in Virginia and is treated to the prescribed processing. It is ham with character and is at its best when well aged. Many people do not like its intense flavor if they have become accustomed to the delicate, rather flabby slices of pink ham that one finds in the average supermarket or delicatessen.

The same can be said for Kentucky hams, similar to Smithfields, which are dry-cured, slowly smoked with green hickory, and aged for months and sometimes for years, a method that goes back in history well over two centuries. I remember some rather extraordinary Kentucky hams in the past that were said to be the result of natural enzymes in the meat and the weather conditions of a certain section of the state. We used to buy them from J. W. Cowherd, an odd name for a man who dealt in pigs. These hams disappeared from the market for a period of years, but recently I was overjoyed to learn they are again available, though not quite the well-aged ham we used to have.

Many other country hams were on the market in the days before World War II, but they are becoming increasingly scarce. Those from Maryland, which are all but extinct, shared the glory of Virginia and Kentucky hams. There were superb hams from Georgia. One company in that state advertised its product as "peach fed." There were also good hams from Missouri, where one discriminating lady sold only "left hams" because she felt the meat was better than that in the right ham; she guaranteed that her pigs were fed on Jerusalem artichokes. Quite a few good hams could be found in New York State and New England, too, but these were standard cured hams, lacking the distinction of the great hams of the South. Another source of varied country hams was Pennsylvania. Some of the most delicious I have ever eaten were produced by Clarence Herr, who worked in a smokehouse in Lancaster that had been in the family for three generations. He does only a small business nowadays and does not

ship any hams, but they can be sampled at his daughter's unique eating establishment in an eighteenth-century farmhouse in Mount Joy, near Lancaster. The restaurant is called Groff's Farm, and it serves magnificent home-cooked Pennsylvania Dutch meals.

Despite the decline of the country ham, we are lucky to still have Smithfields and Kentuckys with us, to carry on one of our most notable culinary traditions. These hams are sold cooked and uncooked. I use a good many during the year and buy both kinds in equal quantity. The uncooked variety, which usually comes from Kentucky, I prefer to age a little longer in the basement before preparing it. To store a Kentucky or Smithfield before cooking, hang it in an airtight container, like a plastic bag, so it is protected from insects or from excessive moisture. It needn't be refrigerated.

If you buy a ham that is properly aged, you will find some mold on the surface when you unwrap it. This mold does no harm whatsoever. It can be easily removed by washing with plain water and a brush—no soap, mind you—or by rubbing with a cloth dampened with vinegar. I must warn you that Kentucky hams, because of their curing and aging methods, are salty. They often appear streaked when you slice them, due to nothing more than a concentration of salt, which helps to preserve and flavor the meat. I happen to like the overtone of salt, although many people don't. But stick with it and you'll become an addict.

The preparation of aged hams used to be quite a ritual. Standard equipment for kitchens was a boiler designed especially to hold a whole ham, though most people simply used a huge copper wash boiler or a cauldron. First, the ham was soaked in cold water overnight, or longer if it was very well aged. Then, it was cleaned with warm water, brushed briskly, placed in the boiler, and completely covered with water. Sometimes a healthy slug of cider vinegar with some brown sugar was added to the pot. It was brought to a boil, reduced to a simmer, and cooked about 20 minutes per pound. As soon as the bones in the hock end pulled loose easily, the ham was done. Finally, it was allowed to cool in the broth.

We no longer have huge ham boilers in our kitchens, so this is the most practical way to manage one: Place the ham in a deep pan, fat side down, add 2 or 3 inches of water to the pan—I often add some white wine or cider—and cover tightly with foil. Cook at 300°F, allowing 20 to 25 minutes per pound, or until the meat reaches an internal temperature of 170°F when tested with a meat thermometer. When done, remove the ham from the liquid and allow it to cool.

Remove the skin, using a boning knife and your fingers, to expose the fat. The ham is now ready for scoring and final glazing in the oven. I avoid the strong flavor of cloves and recommend rubbing the fat with mustard and crumbs.

Many wonderful recipes have been created around our native hams, but probably none is more famous than fried country ham with red-eye gravy.

FRIED HAM WITH RED-EYE GRAVY

Use slices of good country ham ¼ to ½ inch thick. Remove the dark outer edge but leave the fat. (It adds flavor and contributes to the gravy.) Heat a big iron skillet or other heavy pan. Add the ham slices, and cook very slowly, turning them often and keeping the fatty parts toward the center of the pan so they will render faster. When the fat is transparent and beginning to brown, transfer the ham to a platter. Put the drippings into a small bowl.

Add 1 to 1½ cups of water or coffee to the hot skillet, and bring to a simmer. Stir with a spatula or spoon to loosen the flavorful residue adhering to the pan. After it has simmered for 3 or 4 minutes and reduced slightly, add the drippings, and stir until it reaches the boiling point.

This is red-eye gravy. Some people add brown sugar to it, but I prefer it in its natural state. I like to have it with hot biscuits or poured over grits, which lets you savor every delicious, smoky particle.

If you've never ventured into country hams, let me advise you to start at once.

CHAPTER 22

ICE CREAM: THE GREAT AMERICAN EXPERIENCE

What could be more American than ice cream—except, perhaps, the hot dog? Ice cream may be American by adoption, but we have done more to glorify and perfect it, and we've certainly come up with more weird and wonderful flavors and names for it, like Rocky Road, Impeach Mint, and Here Come Da Fudge, than any country in the world. Ice cream is not so much a food as a habit, and the number of gallons consumed each year—786,000,000—boggles the mind.

Ices or iced desserts are very ancient indeed—it seems that where there was snow, there was also the ice. Legend has it that the Chinese were the first to make water ices by mixing snow with the juice of lemons, oranges, and pomegranates, and that from thence their concoction traveled to Persia, where it got its Arabic name, *sharbah*, which later became *sorbet* in French, sherbet in English. Montezuma liked his chocolate iced, with snow brought by relays of runners from the mountains; and the Emperor Nero refreshed himself with honey and fruit juices chilled with snow brought by slaves from the Apennines. It was the Italians who really made a big thing of ices. They discovered that by chilling the liquid in a bowl of snow combined with saltpeter, they got a faster result, and it was they who brought the civilized custom of the *sorbet* to the rest of Europe. When Catherine de Médicis married Henry II of France in 1533, her Florentine cooks lightened the lengthy and stupefying court menus by a judicious injection of refreshing *sorbet*.

Italians also get the credit for inventing that pleasure palace of the masses, the ice-cream parlor. A score of Italians opened cafes selling sherbets and iced creams, as they were then called, in eighteenth-century Paris. One was Signor Tortoni, of biscuit tortoni fame.

There's a certain amount of disagreement about who was responsible for starting America on its long-lived ice-cream binge. While Thomas Jefferson is known to have served it on his return from France in 1789, records show that the French envoy had launched it some seven years earlier at a fete in Philadelphia, and "iced cream" was regularly featured at George Washington's Thursday dinners, for which his accounts mention the purchase of "a cream Machine for Ice." In those days, of course, ice cream was not the firm and compact mixture it is today.

Philadelphians were ice-cream addicts from the start, and Philadelphia confectioners have long been known for the quality and excellence of their product, so much so, in fact, that the word *Philadelphia* before ice cream came to mean the best. I can remember the elegant ice creams, rich in butterfat, made by Sauter's, now, alas, departed. Fortunately, there is still the family firm of Bassett, who have been in business since 1861, to carry on the glorious tradition. At their little stand in the Reading Terminal they sell some of the most luscious ice cream I have ever tasted. Friends of mine rave about their Irish coffee ice cream, made with Irish whiskey—no substitutes for Mr. Bassett.

I've been an ice-cream fancier all my life. One of the high spots of life in my hometown of Portland used to be the Saturday night trip to Baskin-Robbins, where you got to sample before buying. Nowadays, I'm sorry to say, most ice cream is no longer what it used to be. Of the millions of gallons of commercial ice cream sold in this country, far too much is a sorry mixture of dried or condensed milk combined with chemical emulsifiers and stabilizers, artificial flavorings and colorings, whipped and pumped full of air to give it that deceptive overrun—overrun is the volume of ice cream over and above the volume of the mixture, and legally 50 percent of the volume can be air. If you want really good ice cream these days, something that is honest and delicious, made with only the purest ingredients, you should invest in an ice-cream freezer and concoct it yourself. There's nothing to equal the fun and the flow of satisfaction you get from making your own ice cream. I can remember summer Sunday afternoons of my childhood when I sat on the back porch turning the crank of the freezer for dear life, until I thought my arm would drop off, anticipating that blissful moment when it would be frozen and, as a reward, I would get to lick the dasher. You don't even have to put any effort into it, for now we have electric ice-cream freezers, magical robots that do all the work. If you love ice cream, it's well worth buying one. You can, of course, make ice cream in refrigerator ice trays, but it won't have the perfect, smooth creaminess of one churned in an ice-cream freezer. In case you want to try it, here's a recipe for a pretty good refrigerator-tray chocolate ice cream.

Beat the yolks of 4 eggs well and put them in a heavily enameled saucepan. Gradually beat in ¾ cup white corn syrup and 3 ounces (3 squares) melted unsweetened chocolate (melt the chocolate in the top of a double boiler, over hot water). Cook the mixture over medium heat, stirring constantly, until smooth and thick. Remove from the heat and let it cool thoroughly, then flavor with ½ teaspoon ground cinnamon and 1 teaspoon vanilla extract. Whip 1 cup heavy cream until fairly stiff and fold it into the chocolate mixture. Pour the mixture into refrigerator ice trays and freeze in the refrigerator freezing compartment or in the freezer, which will take about 2½ to 3 hours, depending on the temperature.

There are two main types of ice cream, the plain ice cream, made with cream, sugar, and flavoring, and the custard ice cream, often called French ice cream, made with eggs, milk, and flavoring, in addition to the cream, which has quite a different taste and texture. The first recipe I'm going to give you is for a basic vanilla ice cream, just about the simplest of all.

Stir 4 cups light or heavy cream (heavy cream gives a richer result) and ¾ cup granulated sugar together for 5 or 6 minutes, until the sugar is dissolved. Add 1½ tablespoons pure vanilla extract (not the artificial vanillin-flavored kind) or, if you have vanilla beans, slit a 2-inch piece of vanilla bean lengthwise with a sharp paring knife and scrape the tiny black seeds into the ice cream.

Pour the mixture into the can of an electric or hand-operated ice-cream freezer, filling the can only ¾ full to allow for expansion, put in the dasher, and cover the can tightly with the lid. Lower it into the freezer and pack the freezer with alternate layers of cracked ice and rock salt in the proportions of about 1 cup of salt to 6 cups ice (if you can't get rock salt, which is in short supply in some places, coarse kosher salt, sold packaged in supermarkets, works equally well) or use whatever proportions are recommended by the manufacturer of the freezer. Connect the dasher to the crank or shaft mechanism, following the manufacturer's directions, and turn the mixture, by hand or electrically, again following directions, until the ice cream is frozen. Start slowly at first, then increase speed as the mixture starts to freeze and becomes harder to turn. With a hand-operated machine, the ice cream is frozen when the crank can barely be moved. With an electric freezer, the motor will slow down or stop. When turning by hand, do not stop until the ice cream is frozen, or it may be lumpy.

When frozen, disconnect the mechanism, remove the can, and wipe it carefully to remove any salt. Remove the lid of the can and take out the dasher. Press the ice cream down firmly with a spoon, filling the hole where the dasher was, and cover the can again, plugging the hole in the top where the dasher was with a small cork or piece of aluminum foil to prevent any salt liquid seeping through. Drain the saltwater from the freezer, replace the can, and repack with more ice and salt until ready to serve. It can stand for 2 to 3 hours. Of course, if you are going to serve the ice cream right away, there is no need to repack the can in the freezer. This recipe makes about 1½ quarts ice cream.

There are all kinds of ways to vary this basic ice cream, using different fruits and flavorings.

For fruit ice cream, combine 2 cups crushed fruit, such as strawberries, raspberries, apricots, or peaches, with 1½ cups sugar, a pinch of salt, and let it stand for 20 minutes. Stir in 8 cups heavy cream and freeze as for basic vanilla ice cream. If you wish, add 3 to 4 tablespoons lemon juice to the fruit.

For French vanilla ice cream, first you make a custard. This gives you an ice cream of a different color, like pale yellow jonquils. Combine 6 egg yolks, 1 cup sugar, ⅛ teaspoon salt, and 2 cups milk in the top of a double boiler. Cook the mixture carefully over hot, but not boiling, water, stirring it with a wooden spoon, until the custard thickens sufficiently to lightly coat the spoon. Remove the top of the double boiler from the heat and let the custard cool. When cool, stir in 4 cups heavy cream and 1½ tablespoons vanilla extract, or the seeds scraped from a 2-inch piece of vanilla bean. Pour the mixture into the freezer can and freeze as for basic vanilla ice cream.

Should you like chocolate sauce on your vanilla ice cream, here is a very easy one that is absolutely luscious.

Melt 12 ounces semisweet chocolate and 2 ounces unsweetened chocolate in the upper part of a double boiler over hot water. When it is melted, stir in 1 cup heavy cream and 4 tablespoons Cognac until smooth.

Nowadays, when so many people are dieting but hanker for a taste of something sweet, I often serve a sherbet, or *sorbet*, for dessert. While less rich than ice cream, it satisfies that craving and is extremely refreshing. These ices are basically mixtures of fruit juice, coffee, champagne, or puréed fruit and either a simple sugar-and-water syrup or sugar. Sometimes egg white is added to give a fluffier texture. Ice-tray freezing works well for sherbets, but you must take them from the freezer and beat them until smooth two or three times during the process, or they will be grainy. Sherbets can also be turned in an ice-cream freezer until they are just softly frozen—not frozen hard like ice cream. Before serving a sherbet, remove it from the freezing compartment to the refrigerator to soften it up a bit. For lime or lemon sherbet, make a syrup with 3 cups water and 1½ cups sugar, boiling it for about 5 minutes until the sugar has dissolved. Remove from the heat and cool. When it is completely cool, add ½ cup lime or lemon juice.

You can freeze this in a machine or in ice trays. If you freeze it in a machine, freeze it until it becomes mushy, then remove the lid of the can and add the white of 1 egg, beaten until it stands in soft peaks, as for a soufflé. Continue to freeze until softly frozen. If you are freezing the sherbet in ice trays, let the mixture freeze until it is firm around the edges but still mushy in the center, remove it from the trays to a bowl, beat it up well with a fork, a whisk, or a rotary beater, then beat in the beaten egg white and return to the freezer. Freeze a second time until mushy, and again remove to a bowl and beat until smooth. Return to the trays and freeze until firm. This makes six to eight servings.

One of my all-time favorites is a delicious strawberry *sorbet*, which can be made with either fresh or frozen berries.

Wash and hull 3 pints fresh strawberries or slightly thaw 3 packages frozen strawberries. Combine the fresh strawberries with 2 cups sugar (if using frozen, cut the sugar down to 1 cup), 1½ cups orange juice, and ¾ cup lemon juice. Let stand 2 or 3 hours for the strawberries to absorb the flavors. Purée the mixture either by putting it through a food mill, rubbing it through a strainer with a wooden spoon, or whirling it in a blender or food processor. Stir ⅓ cup Grand Marnier into the purée and pour it into refrigerator ice trays. Freeze until about 1 inch of the mixture is firm around the edges and the center mushy, then remove, turn into a bowl, and beat until smooth, as for the lime sherbet. Return to the trays, refreeze, beat up once more, and then return to the freezer to freeze until firm. This makes about eight servings.

So there you have it—the ice-cream experience. As Stendhal remarked, on first tasting ice cream, "What a pity this isn't a sin!"

CHAPTER 23

THE JOYS
OF JAMS,
JELLIES, AND
PRESERVES

While in the southwestern part of France recently, I had occasion to go to the doctor—the family doctor of friends I was visiting. He practices and lives in a lovely, lovely old house that harks back to the sixteenth century, in a tiny village with a gem of a marketplace. After a test, which required my going without breakfast, the charming doctor invited me to share the morning meal with the family in the big kitchen behind his office. Here was a spacious room with a fireplace that must have been all of ten feet to twelve feet in width and an advantageous depth, with *crémaillère*, cranes, and a gigantic spit that could be regulated by counterweights or probably had originally been regulated by dogs. Albeit, the family has now added a modern stove for summer, but in other than hot weather the fireplace is still used to do most of the cooking.

We sat down to a large round table for breakfast and drank from the big bowls that one finds so often in French homes for café au lait or tea and ate toasted country bread and croissants and the most extravagantly rich, lovely prune jam that had been long cooked over gentle fire. I couldn't stop! I wanted to eat and eat it! I had to guard my gluttonous desires and be polite.

Marmalades, preserves, jams, and jellies are prepared in a huge copper preserving pot over low fire and cooked slowly for hours to enrich and reduce the jam. Afterward it was shined and kept clean and used only for preserving. I am afraid such luxury is not possible for most of us these days who have to live in small kitchens and who cannot store tremendous pots to be used in as limited a fashion as that. However, it smacks of wondrous preserves in my childhood, and gave me a great feeling of how little most people care about such delicious additives to our daily diet, and are content to buy preserves and jams that are prepared with corn syrup, pectin, and citric acid. It used to be, and not too many years ago, one could buy very good preserves that were pure sugar and pure fruit. But I am afraid that those days have flown for all of us.

Make your own preserves at home, not necessarily in huge quantities the way they used to be made, but a few of many different fruits. All sorts of jams, marmalades, and brandied fruits are within your grasp to enjoy yourself, others to give away as gifts. As a quaint old Victorian woman once said years ago as she came down the stairs with several jars of preserves, after I had spent a weekend in her guest house, "I want you to taste a little of my sass." Well, sass was an old New England word for preserves—and good that sass was!

If you are a preserver, you will want to follow the span of things in season. Start in the spring with rhubarb, and go on to strawberries, raspberries, currants, gooseberries, apricots, cherries, peaches, plums, prunes, and figs. The scope is tremendous, and the results can be rather awe-inspiring and mouth wateringly good. There are combinations such as the delights of apricots and pineapple. This I find to be one of the most exciting flavor combinations, and one that is satisfying and delicious.

For that delectable delight, you should wash 6 pounds ripe apricots very well. Halve them and remove the pits, reserving some. Cover the halved apricots with 6 pounds sugar, and let them stand for 2 to 3 hours. Crack the reserved pits and remove the kernels to make 1 cup. Drain 2 large cans sliced pineapple, cut the slices in small sections, and add 2 cups of the juice to the sugar and apricots. Bring the apricots to a boil very slowly, stirring with a wooden spatula so they will not burn. Skim off any scum that rises to the top and discard it. Add the pineapple and kernels and cook the mixture down slowly, watching it constantly until the fruit is translucent and the syrup is quite thick. Stir it very often; do not let it burn on the bottom. Test the syrup from time to time on a cold saucer to see if it has set. When it is set, fill sterilized jars with screw tops and seal them firmly. This preserve has a lovely, enchanting flavor, and holds its color and texture. Also, this may be put in small pots to be used for gifts.

Another very similar jam is made with peaches. For this you will need ripe, meaty peaches that have good flavor and sweetness. Cook about 20 unpeeled peaches in boiling water for about 10 minutes. Pour off the water, cool the peaches, and peel them. Put the fruit through a food mill and add an equal quantity—cup for cup—sugar, and ½ cup bourbon, and just a tiny drop of vanilla. Then, in a heavy kettle, bring the mixture to a boil and cook it until it is thick (use the same test of dropping a bit on a cold saucer to see if it jells before taking it off the heat). Be sure to skim off the scum. The preserve may be poured into sterilized jars and sealed with screw tops. For a nice variation, crack some of the pits and add ½ cup of the kernels to it. They are quite bitter, but they give a nice variation to peach preserve. Or, if you don't do that, you may add ½ cup blanched almonds and an equal quantity of seedless raisins to it to produce a different color and quality. They are extraordinarily good to serve with hot croissants or a good hot buttered toast, and even better to spoon over ice cream. The result will be something startlingly good. This also applies to the apricot preserve and most any other.

My father, who was from a pioneer family, grew up with an appetite for rich wonderous delights that were indulgences of the pioneers. He was from a Huguenot family, and his roots went back to Kentucky and the Carolinas. One of his favorite preserves was

pear, and he could sit and eat it with either a main course or as a dessert. I often watched him eat one of his favorite meals, fried chicken, and he would eat the pear preserve on hot biscuits all through that, and then have hot biscuits and pear preserve for dessert. He didn't like my mother's pear preserve very well, so one of his sisters often made a tremendously sweet batch that suited him just fine. They used winter Nelis pears or other hard winter pears so they wouldn't become soft and mushy—as pears are wont to do sometimes when they are cooked.

The recipe was based on a good rich syrup that took 4 cups water and 4 pounds sugar. While cooking the syrup you must wipe the sides of the pan with a brush or cloth so that it doesn't granulate on the sides and thus ruin the texture. After the syrup has boiled for about 10 to 12 minutes, add 4 pounds peeled, sliced firm pears. Cook them until they are more or less translucent and the syrup has cooked down noticeably. You may try the jelling process as described above. However, this will never be a firm jelled preserve. Be sure you don't try to get them to be a solid mass. The pears should hold their form, and the liquid should just turn sort of a pinkish color and be noticeably thick. If you wish, when you take them up and fill sterilized jars, you can add 1 to 2 cloves, a little piece of cinnamon bark, or a small piece of fresh ginger to each jar for a variation of taste. The jars should be sealed at once with screw tops. I will say they are a rich delight and may be used on hot biscuits, toasted English muffins, or would dress ice cream extraordinarily well—especially with a little whipped cream added to the dish and a dusting of ginger. Rich as hell, but good!

Because we lived in Oregon where there was such a wealth of apples, apple jelly was always a standard in our family. Its lovely color provided a beautiful addition to the jellies. There was a time when people unmolded their best jellies and placed them on dinner tables in cut glass or silver dishes, and apple jelly would shimmer in quite a dramatic fashion. Alas, the days of serving jelly and hot breads seem to have passed, and we seldom see that type of service.

To make jelly, you must have a jelly bag. The best ones are made with a thin flannel. Others are lined with a soft flannel, and some are heavy muslin. You can make them yourself, or if you find such convenient shops as Williams-Sonoma, which have a complete line of articles for the kitchen, you will no doubt find jelly bags.

The basics for making various jellies are almost exactly the same, and it is easy and possible to combine two fruits—usually with apple being one of the fruits, because it is high in pectin and complements most other fruits. A blackberry jelly with apple added is very good indeed, as are raspberry and strawberry. It will behoove you to play around with apple jelly and its possible variations.

Apples vary a great deal in their tartness. In these days when apples have been standardized to a very few brands, one must search around a bit for a good tart apple. In the East we have Greenings, Granny Smiths, and, in some places, Gravensteins—which are absolutely perfect for jelly making. And we have Transparents and other varieties that are tart.

For apple jelly use 5 pounds tart apples, quartered and cored (do not peel them), and cook them with enough water to just barely cover them, until soft and almost to the mushy stage. Pour this into a jelly bag and hang it over a large pot or bowl overnight. Or, if you don't have a jelly bag, you can line a large China cap sieve or colander with a clean damp cloth and let it drain through that. If you do use a jelly bag, don't squeeze it if you want a beautiful translucent jelly. When it is drained, add 1 cup granulated sugar to each cup of juice. Put it on to boil until it tests for jelly in a cold saucer (drip a few drops of it in a saucer and let it cool). Another way to test it is to dip a wooden spoon into your jelly. Remove it and you will find at first that it drips off in two streams. But when the two run together and make one stream your jelly stage has been reached. When you have reached the jelly stage, be very careful not to overcook it or you will have a gooey jelly instead of the delicate one that you are looking for. Pour your jelly into sterilized hot jars or glasses. If you wish to unmold it, you will have to have a wide-mouth glass with no ridges that will keep the jelly from sliding out.

If your jelly doesn't seem to be quite as firm as you like it, leave it for a day or two in a cool place and it will concentrate. For a nice variation you may add a leaf of rose geranium, a small piece of cinnamon bark, or a tiny slice of ginger to each glass as you pour the hot jelly in. This will not only give a nice design to the finished jelly, but it will give it a heavenly flavor. Other fruit jellies may be prepared in very much the same way, using the principle of "cup for cup" to make a firm finish for the jellies. Best are quince, plum, and huckleberry. Apple jelly is amusing to serve with roast pork, roasted chicken, or duck, adding a fruity flavor to the meat. It is also mighty good on crisp toast and hot bread and can be melted down and brushed over fruits in a fruit tart.

I have always hated grape jelly. I don't like Concord grapes to eat, and I don't like them in jelly and I don't like them in wine. There is something sort of brutal in the taste of a Concord grape, and I consider the jelly-and-peanut-butter combination the lowest ebb to which eating can fall. Now I like peanut butter, but I think that those two together are just ghastly! However, there is one place that I like Concord grapes, and completely without reason. They are excellent made into a grape conserve. Concord grapes have quite dark, heavy skins that slide off very easily, leaving the pulp and seeds.

So for the conserve, wash about 8 pounds Concord grapes, squeeze out the pulp and seeds into a saucepan or preserving pan, and reserve the skins in a bowl. Measure your grape pulp and skins separately and take note of the overall volume. Cook the pulp and seeds very gently over low heat for about 30 to 45 minutes. Pour the mixture through a sieve, food mill, or colander without overly large holes, to extract the seeds. Then combine with the skins. Add to this an equal quantity of sugar and bring to a boil (watching very carefully) for about 1 hour. Add to this, again, an equal quantity of sugar and cook for about 30 to 40 minutes. Add 2 cups sultana raisins (either the white or dark), 2 cups coarsely chopped black-walnut meats. (Walnuts give quality without equal. If you can't get black nuts, use English.) Add the grated rind of 2 oranges and the rind of 1 lemon. Let these boil together for 15 to 25 minutes or until it tests for jelly and seems thick. Pour into sterilized jars and seal with screw tops. This, I think, is a rich, wondrous conserve that can be used in many, many ways, despite the fact that it is made with Concord grapes. It is delicious.

I happen to be a prune nut. I keep prunes preserved in various and sundry flavor—sometimes bourbon, sherry, Madeira, or Grand Marnier—in my kitchen all the time. Apricots, pears, or peaches may also be used in much the same way as prunes. They come forth as a quick dessert, and I use them in breads, cakes, sauces, meats, and poultry. They are wonderful to keep on hand at all times, and there are always possibilities if you have them on hand.

Recently, I stopped in Auch, in the southwestern part of France, at the great Hôtel de France where the brilliant chef Daguin experiments with local delicacies. He, too, seems to be a prune lover, because there they were in various flavors. The one that intrigued me most had freshly ground black pepper added to the syrup after the prunes had cooked, which gave them an extraordinary zest, decidedly good and different. Simply take 1 to 2 pounds dried prunes (I like to use the pitted ones because they are easier to eat) and just barely cover them with water. Let them come to a boil, and boil for about 5 to 6 minutes. Then add sugar to taste. (I find that for 2 pounds prunes I will add I cup sugar.) Let this simmer for about 5 minutes. Put about 1½ teaspoons to 1 tablespoon freshly ground black pepper into a jar or crock and pour the hot prunes over it. Then I add about ½ cup sherry or Madeira or ⅓ cup Cognac—whatever suits your fancy. Cover the fruit and allow it to mature for a few days. It is good to eat right out of the jar, or to serve with whipped cream as a really splendid dessert. It is also delicious for stuffing a pork roast or to add to pork tenderloins as a contrasting flavor. If you are going to use it for a gift, I suggest very strongly that you find the large pitted prunes, which are pretty expensive these days, but the results are highly rewarding because of the enormous size and appearance. A slice or two of orange and lemon added when the prunes are cooked makes an enormous difference.

CHAPTER 24

CONSIDER
THE OYSTER

Few among those who go to restaurants realize that the man who first opened an oyster must have been a man of genius and a profound observer," remarked that great French gastronome Brillat-Savarin. King James went even further, saying, "He was a very valiant man who first ventured on eating oysters."

How true. It must have taken a great deal of thought and inventiveness to figure out how to open that tight, forbidding shell and then what to do with the strange creature lurking inside. We'll never know if that pioneer approached the oyster the correct way, or if he struggled until he cracked and destroyed the shell before he found that the morsel it contained was one of the supreme delights nature has bestowed on man. I'm glad someone was brave enough, however, because as far as I'm concerned he was responsible for centuries of gustatory enjoyment. There are few things as enticing, as exciting, as varied, and as delicious as the oyster, a mollusk that is found almost everywhere in the world. I've eaten oysters in the Orient, in South America, in France, England, Ireland, and on our Gulf, Pacific, and Atlantic coasts. Practically everywhere I have been, there have been oysters of one type or another.

How intriguing and romantic it is to read tales of people sitting in restaurants in Paris and having tray after tray of oysters opened for them. One gastronomic writer tells us that the average consumption of oysters among the bon vivants of the nineteenth century was somewhere between six and eight dozen a sitting, for some as much as twelve dozen, and this, mind you, was merely a first course.

I can think of no better way to start a meal in good company than with a dozen glorious oysters, well-buttered, paper-thin brown bread, some lemon, and perhaps a sauce mignonette made from crushed pepper, shallots, and vinegar, with a bottle of a flinty white wine such as Chablis or a glass of good ale or stout. Oysters lead to discussion, to contemplation, and to sensual delight. There is nothing quite like them.

In this country, oysters have been part of our lives for generations, flourishing in the waters of New England, Long Island, the southern states, the Gulf, and the Pacific Northwest. Before we had the extensive oyster farms of today, where the spats, or embryonic oysters, are carefully raised in huge beds, these precious mollusks were out of the running for about four months of the year, during the summer breeding season, for it is a rise in the temperature of the water that makes an oyster spawn. Now, with modern methods, they can be served throughout the year in most parts of the country.

My first memories of oysters go back to my childhood. The father of one of my close friends was the man responsible for transplanting the Eastern oyster to the northern Pacific waters. The spats were nurtured in the bays and inlets of southwestern Washington, in Shoalwater Bay, very close to our summer colony on the northwestern corner of Oregon, and during the summer we ate oysters to our heart's delight. Every Friday a great sack of them would arrive, to be shared with various and sundry friends. We ate them raw in great quantities, but sometimes my mother and my friend's father, both of whom were good cooks, would open, crumb, and fry some in lots of sweet butter and we'd have them hot, crispy, and delicious for breakfast after we'd been swimming, crabbing, or clamming. That youthful experience married my taste buds to the oyster forever.

Our own native oysters came from slightly north of the bays, in a corner of Puget Sound. These were the Olympias, the pygmies of the oyster family, each one about the size of your thumbnail, with a flavor like no other oyster in the world. I have tasted many oysters, and, to me, the flavor of the Olympia is one of the finest, if not the finest of all. Olympias are so tiny that they are usually shucked, packed in half-pint and pint bottles, hundreds to a bottle, and distributed that way. There are still a few places where you can have Olympias opened for you. If you want a great breakfast treat the next time you are in San Francisco, wander over to Swann's Oyster Depot on Polk Street, near California, where you can sit at the counter and feast on Olympia oysters with a squeeze of lemon juice. Or, if you are not brave enough to face a raw oyster first thing in the morning, have oyster stew.

After indoctrinating my taste buds with the Olympia and Shoalwater Bay oysters, I was avid for more. As I traveled, I learned to love the English and Irish oysters before I encountered those of our East Coast. In Ireland I had oysters from the cold, cold waters of Galway Bay, which have a very interesting flavor, and in England there were the famous Whitstables and Colchesters. While we are on the subject of Colchesters, here's an anecdote I think might amuse you. Several years ago, while on a magazine assignment in England, I decided I would like to see the Whitstables or Colchesters being harvested. Well, we set out from Colchester on an oyster boat on the coldest day I've ever known in England—and that was pretty cold! I was sure I had dressed warmly enough, but I was not prepared for the chilling winds and bitter cold as we chugged out through the bay into the oyster beds, where we dredged for hours without finding a single oyster. Finally, one of the oystermen noticed my frightful frigidity and brought me a cup of tea. It came in the oldest, most cracked cup I have ever seen, but it was strong and scalding, and it thawed out my frozen body and made up for some of the disappointment of not eating oysters fresh from the water.

The French take their oysters very seriously, picking their favorites as you would pick your favorite painter. There are people who will eat only Belons number 0, 00, or 000, graded according to size in the French manner, with the smallest usually considered the choicest, or who insist on another variety, the Portugaise. They are as finicky about their oysters as they are about picking cheese when the great cheese board comes around. Certain cafes have great baskets of oysters on the sidewalk with a man who opens them to order for you and brings them inside. In Paris, I learned to eat two or three dozen at a time, relishing them hugely. A different kind of oyster one sometimes finds in the south of France is the deep-sea oyster—dredged from the depths of the water—which has yet another flavor that I find most agreeable.

Back in our own country, I finally made the acquaintance of the oysters that have flourished for so long along the Atlantic shores, such as the oysters of Cape Cod, and the Blue Points and Lynnhavens from the waters around Long Island. Before World War II, and before pollution, there were at least eight or ten different varieties of oyster taken from the waters of Long Island Sound and the Long Island bays. I can remember great oyster tastings where one compared and judged the different Long Island oysters, comparing them for salinity and tenderness, but now it has boiled down to just your basic Long Island oyster. Farther south, in Chesapeake Bay, one finds the extraordinarily good Chincoteagues, now, alas, in limited production because of pollution. These have a different shape and a rather different savor from the more northerly oysters. Chincoteagues are great favorites of mine, and I still favor them if I am lucky enough to find some. It is often easier to get the Malpeques from Canada, extraordinarily good, and occasionally available in New York restaurants, although they, too, are in limited supply.

It is sad to think that only about eighty years ago, in pre-pollution days, this country had a wealth of oysters. In the 1890s, it was quite the thing for well-heeled citizens who had settled in the Middle West to contract for a barrel of oysters to be shipped from the East each week. The Burlington, the New York Central, and the Pennsylvania railroads carried oysters in their baggage cars. As far west as Colorado, it was a social event to be invited to an oyster feast at certain homes with a regular supply of oysters. I imagine it must have been about this time that there first appeared on the table that red menace known as cocktail sauce, a dreadful invention loaded with tomato and garlic and onion that, to my mind, is the worst thing that ever happened

to the oyster, or any other form of seafood. Probably, as oysters became fashionable, there were those who just could not face eating them unless they were masked by this rather revolting mixture. Well, it might have made them more palatable to some people, but it ruined them for others. Why anyone would want to drown a delicious, succulent oyster in this red menace is beyond me, but they do. As I said before, oysters are best with lemon juice or a little mignonette sauce, although I will admit of a few additives that do not spoil the glory of the oyster, such as freshly shredded horseradish, freshly ground pepper, or a tiny drop of Tabasco.

While oysters per se are perfection when freshly opened and eaten raw, many different ways to cook them have been developed, some very acceptable. The crisp, crumbled fried oysters I remember from my childhood, if properly prepared and not overcooked, are a delight. Then there is oyster stew in its many versions, some made with milk, some with cream, some with half milk and half cream, plus various and sundry seasonings. Probably the most classic stew is made with milk and cream, and served in heated bowls in which a little pat of butter has been melted. For this, you heat the milk and cream and oyster liquor, add salt, pepper, and a dash of cayenne, pop in the oysters, and let them cook just until the edges curl, then ladle them into the hot bowls and put a dash of paprika on top. Oyster crackers, buttered toast, or French bread, very hot and crisp, are the traditional things to serve with oyster stew.

In the South, around New Orleans, where the Gulf oysters are so good, you'll find an old traditional dish that is an original in American gastronomy. It's known as *la médiatrice*, or the peacemaker, and it was supposedly created when the paterfamilias lingered too long drinking in the bar and needed a peace offering to take home to his waiting wife. The peacemaker was a loaf of New Orleans French bread split, toasted, heavily buttered, and then filled with a generous helping of crisp fried oysters. This clever ploy eventually made its way to the West Coast, changing in the process from a loaf of French bread to a loaf of bread baked in a pan, scooped out, toasted and buttered, and filled with fried oysters. In another variation, the loaf was filled with creamy oysters, but I can assure you this was in no way as good. There is something about the combination of fried oysters and toasted bread, crunchily munched together, that is overpoweringly appealing. I can remember eating oyster loaves when I was quite young at, among other places, one of our best Portland restaurants, which was called the Oyster Loaf and specialized in seafood and oysters. They also did a fabulous oyster omelet, a mass of tiny Olympia oysters crumbed and cooked very quickly in butter, pancake style, then covered with beaten eggs and left to set. It was really more like an oyster frittata than an omelet, and with some freshly ground pepper, maybe a dash of Worcestershire sauce or a squeeze of lemon juice, it made a pretty exciting meal. We very often ordered one for supper after the theater—for in those days restaurants were open after the theater, and supper was a real occasion.

We Americans have gone in for much more elaborate dishes of oysters baked on the half shell. One is another specialty of New Orleans, oysters Rockefeller, originated at Antoine's, in which the oysters are covered with a heavy sauce or paste of chopped spinach and shallots and put under the broiler or in a hot oven for a few minutes. This is a dish I have never been able to take to, for it really overpowers the oyster.

If you like your oysters raw, you owe it to yourself to master the trick of opening them yourself, for oysters freshly opened are preferable to those opened at the fish store and then brought home. You can keep oysters in the shell for a number of days in the refrigerator, provided they are packed in seaweed or covered with something damp. To open them, you need a good oyster knife with a heavy blade and a very heavy point. Look at your oyster and you will see that it is almost triangular in shape, with a point at the end where the hinge holds the shells together. Protect the hand holding the oyster with a folded dish towel or a thick pot holder in case the knife should slip, then push the point of the knife into the hinge of the oyster. Sometimes this takes a good deal of pressure, but after the knife has penetrated, the shells will usually pop apart. If this doesn't work, insert the knife on the curved side of the shell and twist it to raise the shell. The next step, once you have your oyster couched on the half shell, is to slide the knife under the oyster to loosen the muscle, making it easy to remove and eat. Serve your oysters on oyster plates or on a bed of chopped ice, the choice is up to you. Oysters may be somewhat of a luxury these days, but they are one of the most flavorful and exciting natural foods we have and should be enjoyed to the hilt, whenever and wherever you find them.

CHAPTER 25

PERFECT
PASTA

If I could afford the calories, I'm sure I could eat pasta three times a day. It is to me one of the shorter routes to heaven. I have always favored the lovely strings of linguine, spaghetti, vermicelli, and fettuccine and all those other luscious forms of alimentary paste that we combine with sauces and flavorings to make one of the most soul-satisfying of all foods. A plate of good pasta with butter and grated Parmesan cheese, or a little oil and garlic, is a culinary delight that can carry you off to the higher planes of gastronomy. Small wonder that in Italy pasta is a way of life rather than a sometime thing, to be eaten daily—or twice daily. Pasta is so tempting to the nose and the eye and so exciting to the palate and stomach that it makes one wonder why we even bother to eat other things. I'm not referring, naturally, to those poisonous plates of overcooked spaghetti with horrible, artificial-tasting tomato sauce and meatballs so hard they could be bounced off the roof of a building, nor to the so-called pasta that comes gloppily out of a can, with a sauce that tastes as if it had merely looked through a car window at a tomato. I'm talking about perfect pasta, freshly made, properly cooked, spiced with the gutsiness of garlic, and, if you wish, tomato and other seasonings.

I happen not to be a great lover of baked pasta dishes, although I have on occasion eaten macaroni and cheese done in the American way with a rich cream sauce and lots of cheddar cheese, baked to a crusty brown on top but not overcooked within, that has been a true delight. Still, as far as I'm concerned, I'll leave lasagna to others. To me it is an overcooked and messy dish. Give me a plate of fettuccine with nothing more than sweet butter and a grind of fresh black pepper. That's a joy and a delight.

Recently, after years of making my own pasta by arduous hand rolling or with a hand-operated pasta machine, my life has been revolutionized by an electric pasta machine—a most glorious boon to anyone who loves pasta as I do. Who would ever have dreamed of an electric pasta machine? The Italians, of course. They have come up with a machine with plastic rollers for kneading and cutting that is really fun to operate, for it makes the whole process a breeze. I first of all make the dough in my food processor and then roll and cut it with the electric machine, and I can have fresh pasta from processor to table in a miraculous 30 to 35 minutes. It's so easy it's dangerous to start unless you have a lot of willpower, because you'll get so hooked you're liable to make pasta every night.

Here's how you go about it, simplicity itself. To make enough pasta to serve two people pleasantly, put in the beaker of the processor ¾ cup all-purpose flour, 1 large egg, and ½ teaspoon salt. Process for about 30 seconds, until you have a smooth ball of dough. Take it out, give it a little knead by hand, and then start feeding it through the rollers, to knead it electrically, starting at gauge number 6. If you wish to double the recipe to serve four, use 1½ cups of flour, 2 eggs, and 1 teaspoon of salt. However, I have found that it takes more than double the time to make a larger batch of dough in the processor than it does for a small recipe. It is easier and faster to make two small batches, one after the other.

Run the dough through the rollers at number 6 gauge half a dozen times, each time folding over the strip that emerges before feeding it through again. Folding over the dough ensures that it gets a thorough kneading. As the strip gets longer and thinner, fold it over two or three times and keep on putting it back through until it looks and feels silky and has the quality hand-rolled pasta only achieves after many rollings and turnings.

At this point you start to lower the gauge for each rolling, from 6 to 4 to 3 and finally to 2, until you achieve the thinness you like— either the usual thinness of fettuccine or a paper-thin version that is almost translucent (which is what you will get with the number 2 gauge). The thinner the pasta, the tenderer it will be.

It's now time to change over from the kneading to the cutting rollers. There are two, of different thicknesses. One cuts the pasta into strips ¼ inch wide, the other into strips about ⅛ inch. Use the one you prefer. While you change rollers, keep your long strip of pasta moist and supple on a damp towel. If it is very long, as it probably will be, it's a good idea to cut it in half crosswise, otherwise you'll have endless strings of pasta coming out the other end. As you feed the pasta into the cutting rollers, have your hand ready on the other side to catch the long strings as they come out. Carefully arrange them on a dampish towel and sprinkle them lightly with flour so they don't stick together. The next step is the cooking. If you are smart, you will have put a large pot of salted water to boil while you cut the pasta. There should be plenty of water so that the pasta can move around. When the water comes to a rapid, rolling boil, drop the pasta strings into the water, let it come back to a boil, and slowly count to ten—with freshly made pasta, that is all the time it takes to cook. Never, never overcook pasta; it should always be *al dente*, firm to the bite. Drain the pasta well, add the sauce, toss, and eat.

You may use any of your favorite pasta sauces, or you can simply toss the pasta with butter and grated Parmesan cheese, or with garlic (or garlic and anchovies), finely chopped and warmed through in olive oil, which takes no time at all. After draining the pasta, put it back in the cooking pot, add the melted butter and cheese, or the heated olive oil and garlic, and toss well. By tossing the pasta and sauce in the pan, rather than merely putting the butter and cheese or oil and garlic on top, you get everything thoroughly mixed, and the pasta will absorb the flavors faster and better.

Recently, being on a salt-free diet and therefore always experimenting with ways to make more palatable dishes, I made a diet version of pesto that, while not the normal mixture of basil, parsley, pine nuts, garlic, salt, and olive oil, was most satisfying to the palate. I had a good deal of fresh basil in my garden, so I took about 2 cups of the leaves and placed them in the beaker of the processor with 4 large garlic cloves, coarsely chopped, a few drops of lemon juice, and ½ teaspoon freshly ground black pepper. I processed this until the leaves were quite finely chopped, then I added 3 tablespoons of unsalted margarine and let that blend with the rest of the ingredients until it was a beautifully smooth paste. I tossed the pasta with this, served grated Parmesan cheese to those of my guests who, unlike me, were allowed to have it, and it was absolutely delicious, proving to me once more that if the seasonings are right, you don't miss the salt.

The most famous sauce for pasta is something that is very often referred to in cookbooks or restaurant terminology as a *ragù*. This is the classic Bolognese sauce, supposed to be the be-all and end-all of pasta sauces. It is easy to make, has great quality, and once you have learned how to make it, you can play around and make your own variations on the theme. For sauce for six servings of pasta, cut ¼ pound of bacon into small pieces and sauté in a large skillet until it has thrown off most of the fat and is on the way to being cooked, but not crisp. Add 1 tablespoon butter to the bacon and fat, and when melted and bubbling, add ½ pound of very lean hamburger or chopped beef and break it up thoroughly with a fork or wooden spatula. Toss the meat in the fat and stir it so that it browns but doesn't stick together in lumps. Then take ¼ pound of chicken livers, remove the little membrane joining the two halves and any discolored or greenish bits, chop them very finely, and add to the pan. Sauté for 3 or 4 minutes, and then add 1 good-sized onion, very finely chopped, 1 finely cut or shredded carrot, and a small amount of finely chopped celery. Sauté for 3 or 4 minutes, then add ¼ cup concentrated tomato paste, ½ cup white wine, and, if you have it, a little stock—otherwise water. Mix all this very well, then simmer the sauce very gently, covered, for 35 to 40 minutes. Then add a good ½ cup heavy cream, stir it in, and let it simmer 5 or 10 minutes longer. Taste for seasoning and add what is needed. This is good with any pasta, either the fresh pasta made in the electric machine or a good brand of commercial spaghetti, spaghettini, or macaroni. Cook the pasta until it is *al dente*, just bitey, then drain well, return the pasta to the cooking pot, pour over it half the sauce, and toss well. Serve with the rest of the sauce and great quantities of freshly grated Parmesan cheese or Romano cheese. Some people like to add a good pat of unsalted butter to the pasta before putting on the final sauce, and you can, if you wish, add a sprinkling of chopped parsley to each plate as you serve it, which looks very attractive and tastes very good. This is a marvelous blend of flavors, and one of the really great pasta sauces. Sometimes people sauté additional chicken livers and put them on the pasta before pouring over the final sauce; that makes it another type of dish and a very good one, too. If you want a really saucy sauce, a ragù Bolognese is as fine as any can be.

Lastly, here is a pasta dish that represents one of the very best ways to use up the meat from a Thanksgiving turkey. In some versions the pasta is baked, but I think that overcooks it, so I prefer to *gratiné* it under the broiler to get the top browned and bubbly.

For Turkey Tetrazzini, you will first need to make a good rich béchamel sauce. Melt ½ cup (1 stick) butter in a saucepan, and when it is bubbling, stir in ½ cup all-purpose flour. Stir this roux over medium-low heat until it is golden and frothing, then slowly mix in 1 cup hot milk and 1 cup hot chicken broth. Cook, stirring, until thickened, then blend in 1 teaspoon salt, ½ teaspoon freshly ground black pepper, and about ⅛ teaspoon grated nutmeg. Mix in ¼ cup Madeira and ¾ cup heavy cream. Heat through and remove from the heat. Slice ½ pound mushroom caps and sauté in 2 tablespoons butter until just cooked through. Cook 1 pound spaghettini until *al dente* (do not overcook) and drain well. Combine the cooked pasta and the mushrooms with half the béchamel sauce and put in a buttered shallow baking dish. Make a well in the center. Mix 2 to 3 cups diced cooked turkey with the remaining sauce and put it in the well. Sprinkle the top with about ½ cup grated Parmesan cheese and put under a preheated broiler until the top is gratinéed (browned and bubbly). Serve at once. Serves six to eight. With a green salad, some crusty French bread, and a chilled white wine this makes a very pleasant luncheon dish.

CHAPTER 26

PICNICKING
CAN BE A
GOURMET'S
DELIGHT

I'm a picnic lover from way back. Among my greatest joys as a child were family trips from Portland, Oregon, to the beach. At 9 A.M. we would take the train and ride along the Columbia River shore, arriving at the beach about 1 P.M. A picnic lunch would have been packed to eat en route.

I'd get to the station well ahead of train time and make a beeline for my favorite seat on the train's observation-car platform, which was exposed to the air, a view of the river, and, in those days, quite a lot of cinders from the coal-burning locomotive.

I adored that trip, and I knew every inch of the landscape, the river, and the towns and landmarks. Sometimes, if friends were on the train, my meditations were interrupted by conversation. But I most enjoyed sitting by myself, just savoring the fun of the trip—and my solitary picnic. Even if my mother was along, she knew that I liked to have my own little lunch.

I'd eagerly open my package and find sandwiches, separately wrapped in waxed paper. Maybe there would be thinly sliced chicken or home-cured ham on homemade bread spread with plenty of sweet butter, with a touch of hot English mustard on the ham. Or there might be my favorite onion sandwiches, with a little bit of mayonnaise. There was always something crunchy—a crisp dill pickle, celery, or a few radishes pulled from the garden. Dessert was fruit and perhaps a thin, delicious cookie. Even though we were rolling along the track, it was eating in the open and had all the excitement of a picnic for me.

After arrival, there were beach parties to look forward to. My mother loved picnics as much as I did, and she'd had a rack made that was big enough to hold a skillet or two, or a griddle and a coffeepot. The rack would be jammed into the sand over a fire, and we'd grill hamburgers or frankfurters, although more often than not my mother would cook more interesting things.

No matter how many men were in the group, mother was always master of the grill. After we'd gone clamming or crabbing, maybe for a dip in the ocean, we'd come back to wondrous breakfasts of bacon or ham, eggs, and pancakes. Never have sourdough pancakes or sour-milk pancakes tasted as good as they did hot from the griddle with plenty of butter, maple syrup, and good bacon or ham.

Later, when I was living in England, I was invited to some splendid, formal picnics given by well-to-do friends. These were usually picnic lunches before some race meet or horse show. We'd drive to the chosen spot where the domestic staff would have set up in advance a table and chairs, serving tables, and sometimes a portable phonograph or radio for background music. The big hampers were opened and we'd sit down to feast alfresco. There would be cold roast pheasant, grouse, or quail, sometimes hot soup from insulated containers, smoked salmon from Scotland, quail or plover eggs, salads, a plentiful array of pastries and puddings, and excellent wines. While that kind of picnic was grand rather than intimate, it was just as much fun in many ways.

I've had picnics on the road while traveling from New York to the eastern shore of Maryland. Friends and I toted along freshly roasted chicken, which cooled on the way to the picnic spot to perfect eating temperature. Or it might have been a fillet of beef that had been marinated in soy, oil, wine, ginger, and grated orange rind, then roasted quickly over charcoal before being put in the picnic basket. By the time we were ready to eat it, the meat was just tepid and juicy and rare, with a crusty outside that had kept all the exciting flavors of the marinade. We liked to be elegant on these picnics, so we would take along our best crystal wineglasses and huge damask napkins, which were much in vogue in my parents' day.

Another splendid picnic I remember with amusement and pleasure was in France with my friends Henry and Bettina McNulty and the late Alice B. Toklas. Henry brought two magnums of champagne, carefully swaddled in ice. Alice had roasted a chicken in her own particular fashion. Bettina had made a salad and that familiar picnic standby, stuffed eggs. I had wandered through a market near my hotel and picked up a fine duckling *pâté en croute*, bread, and a *jambonneau*. The last was one of the delicious little ends of the ham that the French cook and cover in crumbs, and which are very flavorful and an ideal size for a picnic.

We found a good spot near trees in a lovely grassy meadow and spread a huge tarpaulin and arranged our offerings on it. I don't think that I've ever had a chicken that tasted as marvelous as Alice's— crispy brown, not overcooked, still slightly warm, and deliciously juicy. Alice, who spurned her own chicken, declared that the duck *pâté en croute* was one of the best she had ever eaten. We were all happy with our communal feast. However, while we were in the middle of eating, clouds gathered and a torrential rain started to fall. We moved, food and all, under the tarpaulin, peeked out as we munched and laughed at the weather. We must have been a strange-looking group under there, I in a suit and sweater, Henry in a sports coat, Bettina in a rather fetching sports outfit, and dear Alice wearing a black hat with feathers and a Pierre Balmain coat!

I've done a great deal of cooking on picnics myself, and I've evolved a certain style that I feel easy and comfortable with. I usually take along a couple of hibachis for grilling meats—perhaps hamburgers or good chops or chicken, sometimes marinated, sometimes not. With the meat I usually have fresh vegetables, salads, sandwiches, cheese, and fruit. It's so simple these days to have a cookout picnic. All you need is one of the many types of grills or a hibachi or a folding grill or, in picnic grounds with electric outlets, an elaborate grill with an electric rotisserie. The infinite variety of insulated containers, ice chests, and portable refrigerators that plug into auto cigarette-lighter sockets enable you to use even the most perishable foods. You can dine in the wilds with almost as much menu variety as if you were in a restaurant. You can have hot or cold soups, hot vegetables, hot meats. I've even taken along big containers of chili or Irish stew or a Latin American *cocido*, all good hearty provender for the outdoors.

Then there have been the fishing expeditions, with expert anglers who soon produced big catches for our meals. I can remember the delight of eating blue trout, which had been rushed from the stream, quickly gutted, and plunged into a big pot of boiling acidulated water where they simmered just long enough to cook through, about four or five minutes. The procedure gives the fish the extraordinary blue color for which the dish is named. While this is a rare picnic treat, it is just as easy to prepare as the usual pan-fried trout.

I have two favorite picnics, which I repeat over and over with variations, and which you might like to add to your own repertoire:

For the first one, take along a big insulated jug of cold soup, such as iced gazpacho or cold avocado soup with yogurt, and a portable grill. Rub chicken halves well with oil, garlic, and soy sauce, and wrap them in foil and put in an ice chest. Also include whole ripe tomatoes, scalded so they will peel easily, and sweet onions—such as Walla-Wallas on the West Coast, Mauis, or red Italians—peeled and wrapped in waxed paper. Pop in a dozen hard-boiled eggs and some chilled white wine. Take along a freezer of freshly churned ice cream, repacked with salt and ice so it will stay firm. Include a basket of dishes, flatware, and glasses. Don't forget to take good crusty bread, butter, oil, vinegar, salt, and pepper for the salad, and maybe a little rosemary to sprinkle on the chicken as it broils. And while the chicken broils, make a vinaigrette sauce. Peel and slice the tomatoes, slice the onions, and arrange on a platter and pour the vinaigrette over them. Sip the cold soup first. Munch on the eggs while the chicken is cooking. Then sit back and enjoy the main course.

The second picnic starts with a selection of smoked fish (salmon, sturgeon, and whitefish) and paper-thin slices of buttered dark bread, cut into finger sandwiches to eat with the fish. Lemon, too, of course, and capers, if you wish. For the main course, take along the makings of a hearty beef salad. You'll need a good-sized piece of cold boiled brisket; 6 to 8 new potatoes, boiled in their jackets; 2 Italian red or

sweet white onions; a dozen hard-boiled eggs; some crisp celery; French cornichons (the tiny sour pickled gherkins); 18 cherry tomatoes (or 3 ripe tomatoes, scalded); and good greens. For the dressing, take Dijon mustard, olive oil and wine vinegar, salt and pepper, and a fresh herb, such as basil or rosemary. Mix your dressing at the site, using ¾ cup oil to ¼ cup vinegar, with salt, pepper, a good dollop of Dijon mustard, and the chopped fresh herb. Taste, and adjust to your liking.

For the salad, you can use either a large platter or a bowl. Start by peeling and slicing the potatoes. Slice the onions paper-thin and cut the celery into thinnish strips. Arrange these around the edge of the platter, more or less separately. Intersperse cherry tomatoes or wedges of peeled tomato. Cut the beef into bite-size cubes or strips, and place them in the center along with the eggs, cut in quarters. Surround with a row of greens, or serve the greens separately in a bowl. Garnish with the cornichons and let guests help themselves to the components of the salad and add dressing to their taste. Or, if you are making the salad in a bowl (which is not as attractive to the eye), put in the potatoes, onions, celery, beef, cherry tomatoes, and greens, dress with the vinaigrette, and toss well. Serve with a garnish of egg wedges and cornichons. Serve this palate-pleasing, hunger-satisfying salad with homemade bread, or French or Italian bread, and sweet butter. You can, if you wish, substitute chunks of cold turkey, cold chicken, or cold roast pork for the beef, although to me, the boiled-beef version is the most flavorful. All you need after this is cheese and fruit or, if you prefer, a sorbet or ice cream with some crisp cookies. It's a great dish for a picnic and really very easy; all you have to do at the site is chop, slice, and arrange. Check beforehand to make sure you have all the ingredients. Pack in your ice chest some bottles of lightly chilled Beaujolais, the best wine for this particular salad as it is light on the palate, festive, and fruity.

One of the easiest of all picnics, and one that can be great fun if you like impromptu meals, is what I call a delicatessen picnic. You take along part of the meal and pick up the rest en route. You might start with a cold ham, chicken, turkey, or roast beef, two or three breads (don't forget the bread knife), sweet butter, a selection of mustards, and mayonnaise. Then stop along the road at a likely looking delicatessen or grocery that carries specialties such as good salami or Polish sausage, a selection of cheeses, olives, and pickles, and maybe coleslaw or potato or cucumber salad. Pick up cherry tomatoes and green onions at a vegetable market and cakes and cookies at a good bakeshop. Lay out the makings of your impromptu picnic on a cloth, and let people make up their own combinations. Sometimes the choices can be pretty weird, but that's the fun of it.

If you are picnicking near the sea, or any place where there are good seafood markets, arm yourself with homemade mayonnaise, bread and butter, and maybe tomatoes for a salad, and then splurge on the local specialty—be it freshly boiled lobster, shrimp, or fresh crabmeat. Ask the market to pack it in ice (and to crack the lobsters if you don't have the necessary tools).

These are the kinds of eating adventures that make picnics such a glorious change from the usual routine of outdoor dining. I, for one, still get the same thrill from them that I did when I was a child in Oregon.

CHAPTER 27

THE PLEASURES

OF PIE

Our forefathers, especially those who settled in the north-eastern section of the country and later trekked across the continent to Oregon, California, and Colorado, often ate pie for breakfast. Why not? They liked to finish a meal with something sweet, and after having perhaps porridge, cured meat such as bacon, ham, or sausage, maybe eggs and hot cakes, they would finish off with a nice big wedge of pie.

That sweet tooth made Americans the world's champion pie eaters, although I think that title must have been lost in the last ten to fifteen years. I notice that nowadays in restaurants and diners the number of people who order a piece of pie for dessert, plain, à la mode, or with cheese, seems to have dwindled. I think there's a very good reason for it. Most restaurant pies resemble what the British once called "fruit between two sheets." Pastry has hit an all-time low, heaven knows why. It no longer has the flavor and delicacy of the pie crusts of thirty or forty years ago, either the short crust that literally crumbled at your touch or the flaky crust that melted in your mouth. Now most pastry resembles inferior Leatherette.

Maybe we would be better off if we went back to the traditional pie of our English cousins, the deep-dish kind with only a top crust. The fruit was packed into the dish along with the sugar and flavorings and over it was fitted a crust of puff paste, rough-puff paste, or a rich pastry. Very often this pie was served rather differently. The top crust was carefully removed, cut into even wedges and stuck into the fruit so it looked like the little jagged edges of a crown. Sometimes, especially with apple pies, the minute the pie was taken from the oven the crust would be lifted and a thin mixture of cream and eggs poured into the pie, to cook by the heat of the fruit. Or butter might be placed on top of the fruit, to melt and add flavor to the filling. Practically every pie-baking trick we know of was practiced in those days.

The French are not basically pie eaters, but they do have their own versions—fruit tarts and the classic *tarte Tatin*, one of the most glorious of all apple desserts. First, sugar is caramelized in a very heavy pan (an iron skillet is perfect for caramelizing, deep enough for the fruit, ideal for baking, and generally much more desirable than an ordinary pie pan), then the sliced apples are piled up in layers in the pan, butter and sugar added, a rich crust placed on top and tucked down around the inner edges of the pan, and the whole thing baked in the oven. Almost immediately it is finished, the pan is inverted on a plate so that the crust is on the bottom and the glistening caramelized fruit on the top. Some cooks glaze the top with additional caramel or apricot purée made by heating pure apricot preserves and rubbing them through a strainer, but it isn't really necessary. *Tarte Tatin* may not qualify as everybody's dream of apple pie, but it is an exquisitely delicious version.

I would say that the following is the American dream of an apple pie. Line a pie pan with a good short crust, load it with sliced apples, sprinkle with sugar, dot with butter, cover with a top crust, fluting the edges and cutting a slash in the top for the steam to escape, and bake until the crust is golden brown and the fruit lusciously juicy. Eat hot, tepid, or cold.

It used to be that there was always a hunk of store cheese, or what we now call Cheddar, to accompany a wedge of pie. Then about 1910 or 1911 came the vogue for putting a scoop of vanilla ice cream on the pie and calling it pie à la mode. This became the favored dessert of millions of people, and very good it was.

One of the great controversies about apple pie is to spice or not to spice. I am definitely on the no-spice side. I like sugar and butter, with maybe a few drops of lemon juice squeezed over the apples, that's all. Others think differently. There is the cinnamon contingent (who are so apt to overdo the cinnamon), the nutmeg contingent, and the clove continent. I think all of these spices ruin the flavor completely and add nothing. I've even known people who get carried away and put in three or four different spices, which to my mind is an abomination. Nothing can be better than the pure and simple taste of butter, sugar, and apples—provided they are good apples.

I can think of at least twelve or fifteen versions of apple pie (possibly there are more), from the simple two-crust pie to the pie with the crisscross lattice crust to the apple pie into which a custard mixture is poured during the baking. There's a rather more elegant type of pie in which the apples are first cooked, more or less to a purée, then poured into the tart shell, topped with thinly sliced raw apples, baked, and brushed with apricot glaze before serving. Then, I suppose, you might consider baked apple dumplings—pastry-wrapped apples baked in a rich syrup—to be a kind of apple pie. There are seemingly endless variations on the apple pie theme, including dried-apple pie, which is not too popular with most people, and a famous mock apple pie that must have originated through necessity and has been a part of our pie tradition for almost a hundred years. Mock apple pie, in which broken-up soda crackers took the place of apples, had a great vogue at one time. I did a story about this particular pie a number of years ago and received a most amusing letter from a woman who had been snowbound. Her family was pretty bored with what she had been able to produce in the way of desserts, so she remembered this recipe and reconstructed it, putting the crackers in the pie crust with sugar and seasonings and a touch of water. The family loved it, and said it was as good as the real thing—and with some of the mediocre apples we get today I'm sure you could hardly tell the difference between soda crackers and fruit.

As fruits other than apples were discovered and cultivated in New England and the South, different pies appeared, all of which have become part of our heritage. There was a wealth of wild blueberries and raspberries, certainly strawberries, cranberries, peaches, and eventually pears. All these fruits were made into pies, sometimes in combination. There were blackberry and apple pies and sometimes blueberry and apple pies. The French Canadians developed a tall, rich, wonderful blueberry pie with three crusts, top, bottom, and in the middle. Various parts of the country had their own special pies, like the pecan pie of the South and the shoofly pie of the Pennsylvania Dutch that has a rich, sticky molasses filling and a crumb topping. I remember hearing my father talk about the pies they ate crossing the plains, when he was a child. One was vinegar pie, which had the refreshing tartness we enjoy in lemon pie. There was sweet potato pie and pumpkin pie that I believe was originally cooked in a pumpkin before graduating to a crust, and, of course, in Virginia, Maryland, and New England, with their English traditions, mince pies were the great treats at Christmastime. Then, as we progressed (I suppose you might call it that, although I don't consider it much of a culinary progress), we developed cream pies. These were probably an outgrowth of custard pies, which can be excellent desserts if well made, but the cream pie was more a sort of flavored pudding filling smothered with either meringue or whipped cream and served in large, gooey portions. Presumably, cream pies delighted the palates of those who felt anything creamy and sweet to be perfection, but I have never been able to tolerate them. At one time, you couldn't get away from cream pies. There were plain vanilla cream pies, peach cream pies, coconut cream pies, banana cream pies, black-bottom pies with layers of chocolate- and rum-flavored cream, a veritable avalanche of cream pies.

Today, it seems the only way to get a good pie is to make it yourself. First, you must make a good pastry. There are a dozen different ways of doing this. I am going to give you a basic hand method and a food processor method.

For a two-crust pie (hand method), sift 2 cups all-purpose flour and 1 teaspoon salt into a large bowl or directly onto a pastry board. Make a well in the center of the sifted flour and put in the well ½ cup vegetable shortening and ⅓ cup butter. Cut the shortening and butter into the flour with a heavy fork, a pastry blender, or two knives, or rub it in between your fingers until it forms pieces about the size of a pea. Add ice water, a few drops at a time, and toss the mixture with a heavy fork or your fingers to combine the water evenly with the flour mixture. The dough should be just moistened enough to hold together in a ball, but not wet. The flour and the temperature of the mixture will make a great difference in the amount of water you need, so have ready about ¼ cup water and add it little by little, until the dough holds together. Chill the ball of dough in the refrigerator, wrapped in waxed paper or foil, for 15 to 30 minutes before rolling it out.

Have ready an 8- or 9-inch pie tin. When you are ready to roll, cut off slightly more than half the dough for the bottom crust. Roll it out on a floured board, or between two sheets of waxed paper, to a circle about ⅛ to ¼ inch thick and large enough to fit easily into the tin. Gauge by holding the pie tin over the pastry. If you are rolling between waxed paper, turn pastry and paper over frequently and loosen the paper on the upper side each time you turn it. When your circle is large enough, roll it over the rolling pin (or, if you used the waxed paper, peel off one sheet and holding the other side on the flat of your hand, gently allow the pastry to drop into the pie tin, then peel off the paper on the top) and unroll over the pie tin so that it fits snugly with a little overhang. Don't punch or press it down or the pastry will shrink during baking; just drape it gracefully over the bottom and sides of the tin. Roll out the smaller piece of dough to a circle that will fit over the bottom crust. Now it is time to fill your pie.

For an apple pie, peel, core, and slice 6 to 8 good-sized apples. Arrange them in the pastry shell, dotting them with butter and sprinkling them with sugar. You will need about ½ cup sugar and 4 to 6 tablespoons butter. The butter gives the pie great flavor. Build the apples up to the center in a kind of pyramid, higher in the center than at the sides. Dot the top slices with butter. Moisten the edge of the bottom crust with cold water and put the second circle of pastry over it. Cut off excess pastry around the edges of the tin with a sharp paring knife and then, with thumb and forefinger, crimp the edges of the crust together. Cut a vent in the top crust for the steam to escape. If you want a brilliantly shining crust on your pie, brush the crust with 1 egg yolk mixed with 1 tablespoon cream before putting the pie in the oven. This gives a lovely golden finish and makes it look very professional.

Preheat the oven to 450°F. Bake the pie for 12 or 13 minutes, then reduce the heat to 350°F and continue baking until the crust is nicely browned and the apples have softened. This depends on the type of apples you are using. The pie will take from 25 to 40 minutes to bake, so test after 25 minutes by inserting a small skewer in the vent to check the softness of the apples.

You can serve your apple pie hot, tepid, or cold, with aged Cheddar cheese or ice cream or good, rich heavy cream. If you like cinnamon in apple pie, sprinkle the apples with ½ to 1 teaspoon cinnamon before putting on the top crust. To my mind, the pie will be much better without it.

Now here's the method for making a rich pastry in the food processor. Put in the beaker of the processor 2 cups all-purpose flour, ½ cup (4 ounces or 1 stick) *frozen* butter, cut in pieces of 1 tablespoon size, and ¼ teaspoon salt. Process the mixture for about 10 seconds. Then add 2 whole eggs and 1 tablespoon lemon juice and continue processing until a ball of dough forms on the blades. If the dough seems too soft, sprinkle with 1 to 2 tablespoons flour and process until combined, about 6 seconds. Refrigerate for ½ hour before rolling out as before. This makes enough for a two-crust pie or for two 8- or 9-inch pastry shells.

Totally different from the familiar apple pie is the famous Pennsylvania Dutch shoofly pie, one of our most traditional pies. This is a pie that I really love to eat now and then, when I'm in that part of Pennsylvania. Although it has had many bad imitations, it can be a delight when perfectly made. The recipe I'm going to give you is from *Betty Groff's Pennsylvania Dutch Cookbook* (Macmillan), and you can be sure that it is completely authentic and really good because Betty Groff, a great friend of mine, is a Mennonite who lives in Lancaster County, Pennsylvania, and runs a restaurant there in her farmhouse home. She's a terrific cook, and I know you're going to like her shoofly pie.

First, make the crumb topping. Combine in a bowl 1 cup unsifted all-purpose flour, ½ cup light brown sugar, and ¼ cup vegetable shortening, and cut with a pastry blender or rub with your fingers until it forms fine crumbs.

Dissolve 1 teaspoon baking soda in 1 cup boiling water in a second bowl. Add 1 cup golden table molasses and ¼ teaspoon salt and stir to blend well. Pour the liquid mixture into an unbaked 9-inch pie shell (using the pastry recipe I gave you) and sprinkle the crumb topping evenly over it. Bake in a 375°F oven for 10 minutes, then reduce the temperature to 350°F and bake for a further 30 minutes or until set. When the pie is given a gentle shake, the top should remain firm. Serve warm with whipped cream or ice cream.

Pie is the foundation of our national dessert menu, an American fixture. At its best, pie can be blissfully good and deliciously flavorful, one of the most soul-satisfying of all our eating experiences.

CHAPTER 28

COMPOSED

SALADS

There are two types of salad, of which the most familiar is the tossed salad, the kind that is vigorously tossed and turned until all the different ingredients are blended together with the dressing, and the greens are what the French call *fatigue*. It is then allowed to rest a minute or two in the bowl before being heaped onto salad plates. A tossed salad is probably the favorite of all salads in America, and though often it is made well, much more often it is made badly. All too frequently one finds that any old oil and vinegar have gone into the dressing and the salad has been gussied up with herbs and spices and seasoned salts to a point where you can hardly recognize anything.

Our subject is the *salade composée* or composed salad, quite the opposite of the strenuously tossed *fatigue* salad. The salad is composed in two senses of the word: composed of a variety of ingredients, and allowed to compose, or rest itself, rather than being agitated like a tossed salad.

Both tossed and composed salads are appealing to the eye, but the composed salad can be almost a work of art if you go about it in the right way and have a feeling for arrangement. Arrangement is one of the secrets of a perfect composed salad. It must have a blend of colors. It should have attractively cut ingredients. It demands to be put on a beautiful platter or in a bowl so that it becomes almost the centerpiece for the table or buffet. A composed salad on a huge platter can be a breathtaking sight, which makes it ideal for large parties.

Almost anything goes into a composed salad—any vegetable, any green, and any combination thereof. The vegetables can be raw, blanched, cooked, and cooled; they may even be canned. The greens can be the whole swing of the lettuce family, from leaf lettuce to red lettuce, to oakleaf lettuce to romaine, to iceberg to other greens like chicory, Belgian endive, watercress, spinach, and arugula. Any of these lovely greens, in juxtaposition, so that they contrast one another, will be part of your composed salad.

Among the vegetables that you can use are tomatoes, cucumbers, green beans (blanched or cooked to a crisp tenderness), tiny raw green peas, raw broad beans (if they are young and tender), raw zucchini, or blanched or cooked zucchini. Grated carrots are a colorful fillip to a composed salad. Then there are turnips or jicama—that crispy, tender root from Mexico with a succulent flavor and delicious taste— both, of course, finely cut. Artichoke hearts and bottoms are good in a composed salad, and so are tiny cymling squash. In fact, practically any vegetable you see in the market will find its rightful place. I can visualize a perfectly beautiful composed salad of red bell peppers, broiled until the skin blackens and shrivels, then peeled, sliced into thin strips, and arranged on a bed of greens with, let us say, crisply cooked green beans, previously marinated in oil and vinegar, then perhaps slices of avocado and a garnish of chopped parsley, tarragon, and basil. It's a challenge to work out your own effective combinations of color, taste, and texture for a salad of this kind.

Or, a fruit plate might be your salad—but not with a sweet dressing. I pray you. Use a vinaigrette or cottage cheese or sour cream dressing, unless it is for a luncheon and that's the one dish you're having. Then you might have a sweet dressing, perhaps a poppy seed dressing made with lemon juice, honey, poppy seeds, and spices. Your fruits can be fresh and raw, poached, or canned. Poached or fresh peaches are good. If fresh, they should be marinated with a touch of lemon juice so they don't discolor too much before they are served. Cherries, pears, pears with cheese—all these can take their place in composed salads.

Peel, cut, and arrange the fruit with care, considering the placement of colors and shapes against one another, so the platter is appealing to the eye. Exercise your flair for composition. For instance, if you have crescents of melon (a fruit equally at home with vegetables, by the way), play them off against the shapely rounds of halved peaches, ovals of halved and cored pears, thin slices of apple (marinated in lemon juice so they don't turn color), and perhaps sliced or halved bananas and pineapple in long fingers or the traditional slice with a hole in the center. Strawberries, raspberries, blueberries, and cherries (whole, naturally) can be sprinkled here and there over your completed salad. Put the dressing in the center of the platter in a halved melon or a pretty bowl. Or, if you are using cottage cheese, a big mound in the center with a little garniture of small berries or mint leaves would make a nice appearance.

Oranges and grapefruit lend themselves to composed salads of all kinds. One of the best is a delicious combination of orange sections, shrimp, and red onion rings, tossed with or arranged on greens and served with a sharp vinaigrette. The orange gives the shrimp a piquant acidity and the blend of flavors is fascinating. Grapefruit, with or without avocado, also teams well with seafood.

Seafood is a natural for the composed salad. Try crabmeat with artichoke hearts or bottoms, and with zucchini and cucumbers, and lobster with very finely cut celery. Salmon and cucumbers might have been made for each other. They're an unrivaled marriage. Cold salmon with mayonnaise and a cucumber salad, or perhaps with a cucumber and sour cream salad, or shreds of cucumber in yogurt, make a lovely summer meal. Nothing is more beautiful than a platter of cold poached salmon with a cucumber salad, lemon slices, and a garnish of hard-boiled eggs and black olives. The pale pink of the salmon and the pale green of the lettuce and cucumbers against the bright yellow egg yolks and the shiny black slivers, arranged with an artist's eye and touch, are ravishing.

Meats can be the basis for a hearty composed salad. Pork, veal, and beef are all good candidates. Leeks, which few people associate with salads, are excellent in combination with cold boiled or roast beef. Ham enters into an astounding number of salads. Baked or boiled ham, cut into long julienne strips, diced or cubed—it makes no great difference how meats are cut provided the pieces are uniform—is one of the most versatile of meats. Poultry, too, whether chicken, turkey, or duck, is perfect salad material. You might compose a salad of diced cold duck, orange sections, celery root cut in fine julienne, and thin rings of Italian red onion on a bed of romaine, with mayonnaise. Another delectable combination is diced cooked potatoes, anchovy fillets, capers, and chopped basil, arranged on lettuce leaves with vinaigrette sauce and scarlet tomato quarters.

Eggs are invaluable as a garnish, but they can also be the basis for a salad, in combination with other things. One way is to toss chopped eggs, shredded beets, and chopped onion with a pungent mayonnaise and arrange on greens with a garnish of hard-boiled eggs, olives, onion slices, and perhaps strips of herring.

Certain cheeses lend themselves to composed salads. I've mentioned the role of cottage cheese in a fruit salad. Cream cheese, to my mind, is not very attractive, but Gruyère cheese, grated or shredded, is a welcome addition. One of my favorite salads is made with chopped green onions, shredded Gruyère cheese, and sliced stuffed olives on a bed of greens with vinaigrette sauce. Then there is the famous Swiss salad of diced cheese mixed with a little finely cut celery and a very zippy mustard mayonnaise served on greens, which makes a surprisingly satisfying meal.

Nuts add their own special little note to a composed salad, as a decorative touch and a special texture. Part of the joy of eating a composed salad it that you have not only contrasts of color, but various and sundry textures to pleasure the bite. A salad with the yielding softness of poached salmon, the crispness of lettuce, the butteriness of avocado, and the crunchiness of roasted nuts is an excitement to the eye, the tongue, and the palate. This is the true purpose of a good *salade composée*.

At a Los Angeles restaurant called L'Ermitage, I had one of the most delicious salads I've ever eaten. The manner of presentation was for one person, but it can easily be adapted for a group by changing the style slightly. The basic ingredients are julienne slivers of cold baked or boiled ham and cold white meat of chicken, a tiny bit of celery, a hint of onion, and almonds. The salad was served in a medium-size avocado halved crosswise, not lengthwise as they usually are, so it formed two standing cups. In these were piled mounds of the salad which had been mixed with a sour cream mayonnaise dressing flavored with finely chopped parsley and tarragon. I thought what a lovely variation one could make by heaping the salad on a platter lined with greens and arranging around it a ring of avocado slices, dipped in vinaigrette sauce, and marinated raw mushroom caps. For the mushrooms, use ½ cup oil, 2 tablespoons wine vinegar, a teaspoon or more of salt, ½ teaspoon of freshly ground black pepper, and 2 tablespoons of Dijon mustard, mixed well together. Put the raw mushrooms in a bowl, pour the vinaigrette over them, cover the bowl tightly with plastic wrap, and shake thoroughly so the dressing mixes into the mushrooms. Leave them to marinate for 2 to 3 hours, shaking the bowl every now and then. Arrange the mushroom caps around the salad, with the avocado, and add a garnish of chopped parsley, cherry tomatoes, and additional avocado slices. You could serve this for a buffet, as a first course at lunchtime, with hot, crisp French bread or rolls, butter, and a glass of white wine, perhaps one of the delightfully clean, fresh, fruity whites that are now coming our way from Monterey in California. Finish off this delectable luncheon with strawberries marinated in orange juice and a little port wine, then covered at the last moment with whipped cream. If you prefer something simpler, just have melon with a squeeze of lime, or, if it's the season when cantaloupes are particularly good, cantaloupe with port wine in it, which gives the melon a quite outstanding quality.

For an all-vegetable composed salad, you might use the idea I gave you earlier of arranging toasted red pepper on your bed of greens and then adding mushrooms, avocado slices, and crisply cooked young green beans, all laved in vinaigrette. Flavor the vinaigrette for the mushrooms with mustard, that for the avocado with garlic, and that for the beans with finely chopped onion, and give the pepper nothing but a little oil and vinegar so their own distinctive flavor is not masked. Can't you just see that beautiful platter, with the contrast of red against green and the pale yellowy-green avocado, pearly mushrooms, and glistening green beans? Add a garnish of thinly sliced, peeled ripe tomatoes and chopped fresh basil, and there you have yet another magnificent composed salad.

There are dozens and dozens of ways to work with vegetables, fruits, meats, seafood—foods that are in themselves beautiful, flavorful, and colorful. All it takes is an eye, a palate, and a little imagination to become an artist at the *salade composée*.

CHAPTER 29

ALL HAIL THE SANDWICH

Although we think of the sandwich as an American institution, mainly because it has become one of the more widespread, popular, and glorified items of food in these United States, it had its beginnings in England. It was the inspired invention of the man from whom it took its name, the Earl of Sandwich. Loath to leave his card game for the dining table, his gambling lordship ordered the club steward to bring him meat between slices of buttered bread—and so, fortuitously, was born one of the world's favorite foods.

The English, great sandwich eaters, are perhaps most famous for the paper-thin, dainty sandwiches served at the tea hour, a gastronomic event in the Victorian and Edwardian eras that still continues, though in a shrunken version of its former glory. These tea sandwiches were made with delicious breads spread with sweet butter and such delicacies as thinly sliced cucumber or tomato, watercress, mustard and cress, pâté de foie gras, potted salmon, chicken, or ham. There was always a copious quantity of these delicate sandwiches on the tea tray, in addition to the various and sundry other tidbits. I can well remember when one would go to various hotels in London because they were said to have the finest cucumber sandwiches or watercress sandwiches. It was quite the vogue to discover a new contender.

Years later, when I was in the hors d'oeuvre business in New York,

I tried to introduce these delicate, elegant little sandwiches (which are excellent cocktail party food), but while we had a few customers who ordered them regularly, they went begging, because, for the most part, people preferred the more elaborate and gooey hors d'oeuvre with cocktails, rather than a good, tailored sandwich.

While the sandwich has entered into the cuisine of many countries, it reached its zenith in this melting pot of ours, where it came, conquered, and flourished. Our Italian-American groceries and Jewish delicatessens have taken the simple sandwich and expanded and elaborated on it until it is now legend. We have had, of course, since the turn of the century, two very popular hot sandwichs—the hamburger and the frankfurter. The frankfurter, rejoicing in such names as the dog, the wiener, and the red hot, has never ceased to be immensely popular since it first appeared at the St. Louis Fair. At the beach or in the bleachers, wherever people gather in large groups for any length of time, the hot dog takes its bow, graced by mustard of varying degrees of hotness, tastiness, and excellence. Sometimes the humble dog is good, sometimes so-so, sometimes absolutely inedible.

The hamburger, which probably started in Hamburg, Germany, as a plain ground-beef patty, has had a meteoric career and is now big business. There are two or three American fast-food chains that turn out billions—or at least millions—of hamburgers a year. Some are standardized so that you may buy a hamburger anywhere in the United States, or in Canada, and find practically the same flavor and the same bun. Commercial hamburgers vary from thin, greasy patties that are tragic travesties of the real thing to well-plumped, meaty, hearty hamburgers that are just delicious. My favorite hamburger is the bacon-cheeseburger served at the New York restaurant Maxwell's Plum, a large cheeseburger topped with crisp bacon and served on a toasted bun—just gloriously good.

The epic of the sandwich world is undoubtedly the Italian-American hero, otherwise known as the submarine, the grinder, the torpedo, the poor boy, and the hoagie. It is said that these gargantuan sandwiches got their name from someone who looked at one and said, "You've got to be a hero to eat it." Well, you almost do. A famous food store in New York called Manganaro's will prepare for you truly heroic hero sandwiches, three feet, six feet, or up to nine feet in length, all in one loaf. Who eats a nine-foot sandwich? Not one person, certainly. They are cut up to serve a whole party. There are infinite variations on the filling for the hero sandwich—bologna, salami, provolone, prosciutto, mortadella, green peppers, lettuce, slices of tomato and onion, pickled hot peppers, crushed olives, pickled vegetables, and other kindred things are tucked into split and buttered loaves of Italian bread—a stuffed bread in every sense of the word. I've had them with chicken and turkey, sometimes with a sort of coleslaw. Here are three particularly good fillings:

- Spread the split loaf with a layer of mustard-seasoned butter. Add a layer of thinly sliced skinned mortadella, a layer of thinly sliced onion, a layer of prosciutto, a layer of thinly sliced provolone cheese and a few hot peppers, put the two halves together, and press.
- Split and butter the split loaf. First place a layer of thinly sliced salami, then a layer of sliced tomatoes, then sliced mortadella, then hot peppers, then sliced pepperoni, and lastly a sprinkling of Italian parsley, then press the halves together.
- Split a long loaf of Italian bread, rub each half with garlic and brush with olive oil. Add a layer of Italian tuna (packed in olive oil), a layer of sliced onions, a layer of Italian anchovies, a layer of hot peppers, a sprinkling of Italian parsley, a layer of sliced tomatoes, a sprinkling of chopped fresh basil, and a little lemon juice. Dot with pitted olives and press the halves together.

Then there's the hot hero, which is usually made with thin slices of veal, sautéed green peppers and onions, sometimes with fish, green peppers, and onions.

If you travel across from Italy into the south of France, you'll find a very similar sandwich called *pan bagna*, which means bathed bread. If properly made, this is a splendid feast. Sometimes it is made with a round loaf, sometimes a long one, lavishly brushed with good fruity olive oil, then filled with onion, strips of green pepper, tomatoes, sometimes tuna and always anchovies, and pitted black olives. Then the loaf is crushed down so that it is firm to the bite, with the rich fruity flavor of the olive oil spreading through. Even during the war, when the average bread tasted like sawdust, you could buy a *pan bagna* and the interior garnishings were so delectable that they took the curse away from the bread.

Then there are the delicatessen sandwiches, some of which almost resemble the hero, and might, in fact, be called Jewish heroes.

One distinctive and unequaled product of the Jewish delicatessen is the bagel, the round, fresh, doughnut-shaped roll perfect for sandwiches and exquisite toasted. The Jewish gift to the sandwich world, one of the choicest of all traditional sandwiches, all the more so because it is a truly local invention, is bagels and lox, a split bagel, spread with cream cheese, with paper-thin slices of onion and almost transparent slices of lox or smoked salmon. Sometimes it is belly-lox, rich and oily, sometimes the more delicate, not too heavily smoked Nova Scotia or Scotch salmon. Any way you like it, it's a great invention.

Aside from the bagels, the delicatessen offers the most beautiful dark pumpernickel and Russian rye breads, which have become standard in the sandwich picture. With thinly sliced corned beef, or tongue, or spicy pastrami, they make superb sandwiches. One famous New York delicatessen used to have pastrami on one half and chopped chicken liver on the other, and put them together to make an extraordinary taste experience. Then there are the wonderful pickles (or cured pickles, as we know them) and coleslaw that add so much to the basic sandwich.

Coleslaw, not sauerkraut, went into the original Reuben sandwich. I well remember the first Reuben sandwiches I had, and I rather wish I couldn't remember that far back because most Reuben sandwiches today aren't a patch on them. They were made on pumpernickel bread with corned beef, sliced turkey, coleslaw, Swiss cheese, and Russian dressing—truly skyscraper sandwiches—and the blending of flavors and the overall oozing of the Russian dressing made pretty exciting eating. Nowadays you get a standardized, uninspired sandwich of dried-up corned beef, sauerkraut, and cheese of varying degrees of excellence on rye bread, toasted until all you can taste is warmed-over sauerkraut. It's too bad, because corned beef can have such a special, distinctive flavor.

Somewhere between the delicate English tea sandwich and the monumental hero come the open-face sandwiches of Denmark and Germany, which are not only delicacies for the palate but often works of art, arranged with great taste and imagination for the appreciation of both the eye and the taste buds. One sandwich may be just rows of pink baby shrimp, grouped in a geometric design on a slice of bread and garnished with a feathery bouquet of dill, or little curls of smoked salmon or ham. A platter of these open-face sandwiches is like a garden of food, although I have found to my sorrow a number of times that they can be more beautiful to look at than to eat.

There are so many things that can go to make up a sandwich, ranging from the peanut butter and jelly beloved of children (and, by the way, if you like peanut butter sandwiches, try peanut butter and onion, or peanut butter, onion, and crisp bacon) to lovely smoked whitefish or sturgeon on dark bread, or, if you are really in the money, crisp toast with butter, caviar, and lemon juice—expensive but a revelation.

Among the memorable sandwiches I have eaten in my life are the small sandwiches of cooked scampi with mayonnaise served at Harry's Bar in Venice, so delicious that one wanted to eat them forever. In fact, just about the only sandwich I have no stomach for is what my family would have called a "stepmother sandwich," the kind I used to see in lunch boxes when I went to school—gross, unpleasant hunks of meat and cheese on slabs of bread, put together without any thought for aesthetic value or the effect it would have as it passed through the mouth and hit the taste buds. It's depressing to think that children are brought up on such awful sandwiches.

The toasted sandwich, sometimes open, sometimes closed, has become a great feature in the United States. How familiar is that ringing call at the lunch counter, "BLT down—hold the mayo," which means a bacon, lettuce, and tomato sandwich, toasted, without mayonnaise. Or, "Tuna fish down"—a toasted tuna fish sandwich. The French have probably the most elegant of all toasted sandwiches—the *Croque Monsieur*, made with thin slices of ham and Emmenthaler or Gruyère cheese enclosed in bread and sautéed in butter until crisp, brown, and buttery on the outside, and the *Croque Madame*, exactly the same except that thin slices of chicken breast replace the ham.

We also have what used to be called "broiled sandwiches," such as a cheese sandwich or a cheese-and-bacon sandwich, run under the broiler to melt the cheese and crisp the bacon. Earlier in the century, one of the most popular sandwiches was the cheese dream, a slice of tomato on bread, covered with American cheese which was melted under the broiler and then graced with crisp bacon.

Sandwiches are meals. Sandwiches are snacks. Sandwiches can be savory or sweet. They are one of our major glories—and also sometimes one of our major disgraces. So to end this dissertation, here are two great and classic American sandwiches, as they should be made.

The clubhouse sandwich, usually abbreviated to club sandwich, is one of the oldest composed sandwiches in the American repertoire. At its best, it can be perfection.

Contrary to what most people think, this should be a two-decker, not a three-decker, sandwich. That was the original version. The perfect clubhouse sandwich consists of 2 slices of crisp, hot, buttered toast between which you put a crisp lettuce leaf, if you want it (some like it, some hate it), 2 or 3 slices of cold breast of chicken or turkey (chicken is traditional, but either is usable), 2 or 3 slices, depending on size, of ripe, peeled tomato, and 2 or 3 slices of crisp bacon—and I do mean crisp. Mayonnaise should be served on the side, so that you can slather it on to your heart's content or omit it, as you will. Some are purists and will take only butter on their sandwich, while others insist on the lubrication of mayonnaise. The sandwich should be cut in half and served with a sweet pickle and an olive. For this sandwich, it is mandatory that the filling is cold, the toast should be piping hot. Some people have been known to serve the innards, or filling ingredients, on a platter and make the toast to order, letting people sandwich their own, which I think is a very good idea.

A true chicken sandwich is a joy. It's a great classic and one that is seldom presented well made or well flavored. It should be made with good homemade bread or top-quality baker's bread—fresh, well grained, and not sweet—from which the crust is removed after the sandwich is made. On the bread (spread with unsalted butter) go slices of chicken breast, lightly salted and peppered, and mayonnaise should again be served on the side so that you may add it if you wish. After the crust is removed, the sandwich should be cut into fingers and served, to be traditional, with olives and pickles.

CHAPTER 30

MAKING YOUR
OWN SAUSAGE

To us it's sausage, to the French *charcuterie*, to the Germans *wurst*, and to the Italians *salsicce*, but whatever it's called, this is one of our great international foods. I have often said that I'd be perfectly happy eating nothing but sausages. I have never taken the time to try it, and I'm not sure whether I still feel that way, but there is nothing that tempts me more than the sight of a rosy-pink, juicy knockwurst steaming on a plate with a bit of warm potato salad, pungent with vinegar and oil, and sprinkled with parsley. Or I might find myself hankering for a big fat Polish kielbasa poached in Beaujolais with chopped shallots and served forth with sauerkraut or red cabbage, or paper-thin slices of mortadella wrapped around bread sticks and eaten with a glass of wine. These things start my gastric juices rolling and my taste buds quivering.

Making sausage is almost as much fun as eating it. You learn about the different grinds of meat and the different subtle spicings, and whether or not the sausage you are making should be partially cooked or smoked. There are many, many kinds of sausage that can be made at home, and if you really get interested, it's well worth getting a book on this engrossing subject. Some sausages you can make are the Italian *coteghino*, earthily seasoned with salt, pepper, and garlic, and the Italian sweet or hot small link sausages. These are simple to make and season to your own particular taste. There's no set formula for seasoning, because, as you know, these sausages vary from one butcher to another, and you might just hit on some subtle change that will make the sausage your own creation. Mostly these sausages are redolent with basil and anise and hot pepper, in the case of the hot type, or perhaps coriander for the sweet, and they are delicious served with sautéed or roasted peppers, or with eggs, or with a rich tomato sauce containing roasted peppers and the Italian cornmeal dish called polenta. Little link sausages are very easy to cook. Prick the skins well with a fork. Put them in a skillet with water to cover, bring them to a boil, and let them cook for 1 minute, then drain and continue to cook over medium-low heat on top of the stove or in a 350°F oven until brown. Or prick the skins well again and brown them under the broiler. The initial blanching in water draws out the excess fat and heats the sausages through so they cook in much less time. To my mind, they also have a better flavor when precooked this way.

Another of my favorite forms of pork sausage is the type the English call a "banger," as in that popular dish "bangers and mash." This is a sausage about 1½ to 2 inches long, made with good fresh pork and a rather delicate seasoning. After being poached, "bangers" are finished off in the oven or in a skillet on top of the stove, and then served on a bed of rich, luscious, buttery mashed potatoes with some hot mustard on the side. When well made, these are as delicious a sausage as you are likely to find anywhere, but, unfortunately, some English butchers add meal to them, which is cheating in the worst way because it gives another consistency entirely and a rather dreary blandness. The butchers in the great food halls of Harrods, London's famous department store, make authentic bangers, using the original, unblemished recipe given to them by my friend and fellow cookbook author, Elizabeth David.

There are many other delicious sausages that you can either buy or make at home. The kielbasa, so dear to the Poles and the Russians, is a sausage made from a mixture of meats, with little chunks of fat in it, and it can be found fresh, to be cooked, or dried and slightly smoked, in which case it can be heated through or eaten as it is. Then there are the German frankfurters, knockwurst and bratwurst, which can be poached or broiled. Nothing makes a more delicous meal than broiled bratwurst with crisply sautéed onions. Yet

another type is the Swedish potato sausage, traditional at Christmastime. These are quite different in flavor and texture, and very easy
to make yourself.

All sausages, of course, start with a mixture of ground meat, the
sausage meat that in its simplest and most everyday form we eat
for breakfast, cooking little patties in their own fat until they are
deliciously brown and crisp on the outside, and eating them with
scrambled or fried eggs, waffles, or hot cakes. Homemade sausage
meat is a much more delectable thing than the kind you buy packaged
in a store, and the recipes I'm going to give you can be formed into
patties and cooked, as well as being stuffed into casings for link
sausage.

Among the basic equipment you need for making your own sausages, the first essential is a good meat grinder or a food processor
and a sausage stuffer. There are also electric meat grinders that have
sausage-stuffing attachments. Or, for stuffing by hand, you can buy
a huge sausage stuffer about 2½ feet long that resembles a giant
hypodermic needle. The sausage casings fit on one end, and at the
other there's a pusher for forcing the meat into them. This sausage
stuffer is sold by various kitchen shops around the country.

Casings, either the natural ones made from animal intestines or
the edible-plastic type, are sold by the yard. The best way to get them
is either to talk to your local butcher and ask him where he buys his
casings and if he would order some for you, or to look in the yellow
pages under "sausage casings." You should wash the casings well,
especially the animal ones, before you fill them. Just slip one end over
the faucet and let the cold water run through them, giving them a
thorough bath.

You can make your own sausages the length you want and then
twist the casing well between each one to separate the sausages, or
you can make each sausage and tie it off firmly at either end with a
double knot, then cut the string. This is a little more trouble, but it
is wiser if you are making large sausages. Before cooking the sausages,
prick the casings lightly with a fork so that they don't burst and
spread the filling all over the place.

If this is your first venture into sausage making, I suggest you
begin with the two simple recipes for sausage meat given below. After
you have tried them once or twice, begin thinking of various ways
you might like to vary the seasonings and then experiment with
different combinations of herbs and spices. In the summer, you may

want to use fresh garden herbs, such as basil, sage, thyme, or parsley, all of which give the sausage another quality. However, if you use fresh rather than dried herbs, the sausage should be cooked and eaten quickly, unless you smoke, cure, or freeze it. Homemade sausage can be kept for three months in the freezer. Make it into sausages or form into patties first.

PORK SAUSAGE MEAT

Combine in a bowl 2 pounds coarsely ground pork with 30 percent fat, 4 very finely chopped garlic cloves, 1 tablespoon salt, 2 teaspoons dried basil, 1½ teaspoons anise seed, and 1 teaspoon freshly ground black pepper. Mix everything well together with your hands. Then test for seasoning. Make a small patty of 1 tablespoon of the mixture, sauté it in 1 tablespoon butter until completely cooked through, and then taste it for seasoning. *Never, on any account, taste raw pork.* Adjust the seasoning to taste, adding whatever you feel the mixture lacks. This is a rather spicy Italian type of sausage.

PORK AND VEAL SAUSAGE MEAT

Combine in a bowl 2 pounds coarsely ground pork with 30 percent fat, 1 pound ground veal (from the leg or shoulder), 6 finely chopped shallots, 1½ teaspoons fennel seeds, 1 teaspoon crumbled dried sage, 1 teaspoon thyme, 1 tablespoon salt, and 2 teaspoons freshly ground pepper. Mix thoroughly with the hands and test for seasoning as in the previous recipe.

TO MAKE LINK SAUSAGES

Wash the casings well. Dry them and cut into 4-foot or 5-foot lengths. Slip one end of the casing over the tube of the sausage stuffer and tie the other open end tightly with string. If you are using an electric meat grinder and sausage-stuffer attachment, you can grind the meat and seasonings together, forcing the mixture into the casings at the same time. Should you wish to do this, grind a little bit of the meat and seasonings first and test it, as above, to make sure your seasoning is right. Or grind the meat and seasonings together once, test, then put through the grinder a second time.

Whether you are stuffing by machine or by hand, you must gauge the amount of stuffing you force into the casing for each sausage so as to get an even shape and size. For your first attempt with the plunger type of stuffer, work slowly until you have it perfected. When one sausage is completed, twist the casing twice or tie it with string. Turn off the machine at this point. When all the casing is filled, remove the casing from the stuffing tube and tie this end.

There are times when you want a sausage without a casing. For instance, if you are using the sausage meat as a stuffing for cannelloni, you merely form the meat into little sausage-shaped fingers.

CANNELLONI WITH HOMEMADE SAUSAGE

Make 12 to 16 crêpes, according to the recipe given in "Economical, Versatile Crêpes" (see page 103), or your favorite crêpe recipe. Form the pork sausage meat mixture into sausage-shaped fingers about 3 inches long and ¾ to 1 inch wide. Heat 2 tablespoons butter and 2 tablespoons oil in a skillet and sauté the little sausages until lightly browned on all sides and cooked through, shaking the pan so they roll over but don't flatten out. Test by making a tiny cut in one sausage to see if the meat is completely cooked.

Spread one side of each crêpe with soft ricotta cheese, sprinkle with Parmesan cheese, and add a grind or two of pepper. Put a sausage on top and roll up the crêpe. Place them side by side in a baking dish, seam side down, packing them close together so they don't unroll. Pour tomato sauce over them, sprinkle with grated Parmesan cheese, and bake in a 375°F oven for about 15 minutes, or until the cheese is melted and the sauce bubbly. Serve two to three crêpes a person.

TOMATO SAUCE

Heat 2 tablespoons olive oil in a saucepan, add 2 finely chopped garlic cloves and 2 small onions, finely chopped, and sauté for 3 minutes, until soft but not brown. Add 20 ounces canned solid-pack Italian plum tomatoes [about 1½ 14-ounce cans], 2 teaspoons dried basil, salt, and freshly ground black pepper to taste. Bring to a boil, reduce the heat, and simmer for 30 minutes. Add a small [6-ounce] can of tomato paste, correct the seasoning, and cook for 15 minutes, then increase the heat and let the sauce cook down until it is reduced and rather thick. Stir frequently to prevent the sauce from scorching.

I hope I have intrigued you with the possibilities of sausage making. As you become more practiced, you can increase your scope, making and seasoning your own meat mixtures. You'll find that sausage making is not only fun, but a real gastronomic achievement that your friends will be delighted to share. Surprise them with a gift of your own homemade charcuterie.

CHAPTER 31

THERE'S
NOTHING LIKE
A GOOD STEW

A stew is a ragout is a braised dish, and in one of the definitions given in the dictionary, it is also a "hot bath." This very aptly describes a great many of the watery stews dished up in some restaurants and homes that, sadly enough, have made stew something to shun for the most part, unless you make it yourself and can ensure a dish that is rich, savory, and agreeable to the palate.

Stews figured a great deal on the menus of our ancestors. Homesteaders and pioneers traveling by wagon train would trap animals and birds, and stew them, giving them a long, slow simmering that made the meat tender, rather than resistant to the tooth. While we no longer have to worry about that, there is still nothing quite as satisfying and cockle-warming as a good stew. One of the most popular of all lunchtime menu items throughout this country is Irish stew, with beef stew a close second. A navarin of lamb or a beef *à la bourguignonne* will attract another group, but they still qualify as stews. A good stew is a great leveler. I find that one of the most perfect dishes for a New Year's celebration at home is an oxtail ragout. This rich, hearty stew pleases the palate and satisfies and soothes a stomach wearied by the taxing round of holiday drinking.

As far as I am concerned, one of the most important factors in making a good stew is to start with good broth. Making a broth is no horrible problem. If you are going to be home for a day of catching up on household chores, you can put a broth on to simmer and forget it for four or five hours, at the end of which time you'll have a flavorful stock with no trouble at all. For that matter, you can start it in the evening when you are preparing dinner, and leave it overnight on the slowest possible heat. Turn it off early in the morning and then go through the niceties of straining it and removing the fat from the top. If you go about this intelligently, you can have enough stock not just for one stew, but for several, and the excess can be frozen for future use.

To make a good stock, buy about 5 pounds of bones, including in this about 3 pounds of shank or shin of beef so you have meat on some of the bones, 2 marrow bones, and for a richer texture, a veal knuckle. Put these in a big roasting pan and either put them under the broiler or in a 450°F oven and brown them, turning them from time to time with tongs so they get a nice color on all sides. You'll get quite an appetite from the lovely odor they give off during the browning. Transfer the browned bones to a 12-quart (or larger) stock-pot or soup kettle and add 5 quarts of water, 1 large onion stuck with 2 cloves, 1 well-washed and trimmed leek, several scraped carrots, a sprig of parsley, 1 teaspoon of dried thyme, and a bay leaf. Bring all this to a rolling boil and let it boil for about 10 minutes. Notice that when it begins to boil the liquid will throw a scum that settles on top. Take a skimmer of some kind and carefully remove and discard the scum. Then reduce the heat, cover the pot, and let the broth simmer at the lowest possible temperature that will produce a tiny bubble in the liquid (the French call this a feeble ebullition) for 4 to 5 hours—or overnight—disregarding it completely as long as it retains that faint bubbling. When the broth is finished, taste it for seasoning as you have not yet added any salt or pepper. Add salt to your taste, let it cook for a few minutes, then retaste and see if it has the proper amount of salt or needs more. You can now add pepper, or you can save that for later, when you make the stew. Strain the broth and discard the bones. If the meat on the shank bone is still flavorful, remove it and use for a beef salad or for hash. Allow your broth to cool in the coldest spot you can find, or in the refrigerator, until the fat forms on top. When it is cold and set, remove the fat. You will now have a rich, clear, fat-free broth.

Now let's say we are going to make a beef stew, as fine a dish as one can find, provided it is properly cooked. For eight people (or for six with leftovers), you will need 4 pounds of beef, cut into 1½-inch cubes and trimmed of all fat. This could be an inexpensive cut like bottom round, chuck, or brisket. Dredge the cubes lightly with flour and brown in hot fat in a large skillet over fairly high heat, a few at a time, shaking the pan and tossing the cubes around so that they get deliciously browned on all sides. Or if you want to eliminate the calories in the fat, you can brown the meat under the broiler. In this case, don't dredge the cubes with flour, but arrange them on the broiling pan and place the pan about 4 inches from the heat. Turn the cubes several times until they are well colored on all sides.

When the meat cubes are brown, transfer them to an 8-quart pot. Add 2 bay leaves, 1 teaspoon thyme, 6 crushed garlic cloves, and about 3 quarts of your prepared broth, enough to just cover the meat. Bring to a boil, let boil a minute or two, as you did with the stock, removing any scum that forms on the surface, then reduce the heat to a simmer, cover the pan, and simmer 1 hour. Then add to the pot 16 to 18 small, peeled, white onions (if you cover the onions with boiling water and let them stand for 5 minutes, they will peel much more easily, and do not cut off the root end, just a tiny bit, because this prevents the onion from falling apart), 1 cup diced celery, 4 potatoes, peeled and sliced paper-thin, and 6 carrots, scraped and cut into long thin strips or sliced into rounds. You may also add 1 or 2 turnips, peeled and quartered, if you wish. Let the meat and vegetables

simmer for 1 more hour, then test the meat for tenderness with a fork or the point of a knife and the broth for flavor. Add salt and freshly ground black pepper to taste and, if the meat seems fairly tender, 3 or 4 more potatoes of medium size, diced or cubed. Cover the pan again and cook until the potatoes and all the vegetables are done and the meat tender. Meanwhile, heat 2 or 3 packages of green peas in a minimum of water until just heated through. Transfer the cooked stew to a large serving bowl or tureen and serve it in deep soup bowls, giving each serving 1 or 2 spoonfuls of the green peas and a little chopped parsley.

Have plenty of crisp French or Italian bread, which you have rubbed with garlic and heated through in the oven, and a hearty salad. This is a beautiful dish, gutsy, varied in flavor, and thoroughly delicious, and you'll find many people asking for seconds.

If you would like to be really old-fashioned, just about 15 minutes before you serve the stew, make a batch of dumplings. Sift 2 cups flour with 3 teaspoons baking powder and ½ teaspoon salt, and add enough whole milk to make a soft dough. Drop this dough by spoonfuls into the simmering stew, cover the pan tightly, and cook for 13 to 15 minutes without removing the cover. These light dumplings are marvelous for absorbing the juices. When you serve the stew, add a dumpling to each bowl.

Another tremendously popular dish that can, by a stretch of the imagination, be called a stew is braised short ribs of beef. Good short ribs, available in most butcher shops, have the blade bone in them and are pretty streaked with fat and lean. Because of the fat and bone, allow 1 pound per person. Heat 4 tablespoons butter and 3 tablespoons oil in a big skillet, flour the short ribs well, and brown in the hot fat on all sides. Or you can do this in the broiler, as you did for the beef cubes. Transfer the browned short ribs to a braising pan or kettle. Brown 6 medium onions, cut in thickish slices, in hot fat until they have taken on a rich brown color. Turn them well and be careful not to let them burn; you just want them to develop a beautiful color. If you sprinkle the onions with 2 teaspoons sugar, they will brown and glaze more quickly. When they are colored, transfer them to the pan with the short ribs, add 4 or 5 peeled and crushed garlic cloves, 2 or 3 bay leaves, 1 teaspoon rosemary, crushed to a powder in the palm of your hand or with a small mortar and pestle, 1 or 2 thinly sliced carrots, and 1 thinly sliced turnip. Add just enough of the prepared broth to barely cover the short ribs, bring to a boil, reduce the heat to a simmer, cover, and cook gently over low heat, or in a

325°F oven, covered, until tender, that will take from 1¼ to 1¾ hours. Taste, add salt and freshly ground black pepper, and, if you wish, 3 or 4 tablespoons of canned Italian tomato paste, stirring it in well. If the short ribs are tender, remove them to a hot platter and spoon the sauce over them. If you want to thicken the sauce, knead butter and flour together, using equal quantities, about 2 tablespoons of each, form into small balls, drop them into the hot sauce, and stir until the sauce boils and thickens to the point you like. Serve these savory short ribs with plain boiled potatoes, or with lightly buttered homemade noodles, to absorb the lovely juices.

Earlier on, I mentioned Irish stew, a delectable and simple dish that originated in Ireland, was adopted by the French, and, while it hardly comes under the heading of French cooking, can be found in the books of such famous chefs as Escoffier, Montagne, and Raymond Oliver. A good Irish stew is both delicate and satisfying and as honest in flavor as any dish could be.

Once more, broth is an important part of the dish, so buy some lamb bones and 1 pound neck of lamb to make a stock. Put the lamb and bones, 1 onion stuck with 2 cloves, 1 scraped carrot, 1 peeled turnip, 1½ teaspoons thyme, 1 sprig parsley, and 2 quarts water in a pot. Cook for 2 hours, strain the stock, remove the bones and vegetables, cool or chill the broth until the fat rises to the surface, then remove all the fat.

For a rather elegant Irish stew to serve six, have a shoulder of lamb boned, and cut away most of the fat. You should have about 3 to 3½ pounds of meat. Cut this into 1 × 2-inch strips. For an Irish stew, the lamb is not browned, as this is, so to speak, a "white" stew. Thinly slice 3 to 4 peeled onions of medium size and 4 peeled medium potatoes.

Put a layer of sliced onions in a heavy pot, then a layer of lamb, sprinkle with 1 teaspoon thyme, add another layer of onions, a layer of potatoes, a layer of lamb, a layer of onions, a layer of potatoes, continuing until you have used up all the meat and vegetables. Barely cover the topmost layer with your lamb stock, add 1 bay leaf, 1 tablespoon salt, and 1 teaspoon freshly ground black pepper. Bring to a boil and boil for several minutes while you remove the scum from the surface. Reduce the heat, cover the pot, and simmer for 1 to 1½ hours, At the end of 1 hour, test the meat with a knife or a fork and taste the broth for seasoning to see if you need additional salt and pepper. When the meat is tender, but not mushy, the stew is cooked. Irish stew needs no thickening, because the potatoes will thicken it just enough. There are some people who like to shred a little carrot into Irish stew for color, but I think it is much better without. This is not a glamorously flavored dish, but one with the good, honest, pure quality of the lamb, onion, and potato. Serve it in bowls or soup plates with a healthy sprinkling of chopped parsley and eat with a spoon and fork. A good Irish stew is something you can be proud to serve for a Sunday brunch or a late supper after the theater, or for most any kind of informal gathering. Here again, you could add dumplings if you wish, following the directions given for beef stew. Many people feel dumplings are a necessity for any kind of stew that has a lot of juice.

Stews don't end with meat and poultry. Fish stews are immensely popular all over the world. One that I am particularly fond of is made with frozen rock lobster tails, either clams or mussels, whichever can be found in the market, and shrimp. It's quick, easy, and an all-time winner that everyone adores. You can serve it as a first course or a main course. For a first course, serve it in soup plates with crisp French bread to mop up the glorious juices. If you serve it as a main course, you could have rice with it, or freshly made noodles tossed with olive oil and grated Parmesan.

For this seafood stew, thaw and shell 6 lobster tails. Cut each one in half the long way. Chop 6 garlic cloves rather coarsely. Heat ½ cup olive oil in a good-sized sauté pan or braising pan, add the garlic and lobster tails, and toss them around well in the oil. You do not want to brown them, just sear the outside. Then add to the pan 2 cups canned Italian plum tomatoes, 1 cup dry white wine, 2 table-spoons chopped fresh basil or 1 teaspoon dried basil, 1 teaspoon freshly ground black pepper, and 1 or 2 strips of lemon rind. Let this come to a boil, reduce the heat, and simmer, uncovered, for 4 to 5 minutes. Taste and see if it needs salt. If so, add 1 to 2 teaspoons salt. Then arrange in the pan 24 to 30 well-scrubbed littleneck or cherrystone clams (or the same number of well-scrubbed mussels), hinged side down. Cover the pan and let them cook in the sauce until the shells open. Any clams that do not open after, let us say, 5 or 6 minutes probably are not going to, so don't serve them. Now add to the pan 2 pounds (about 18) raw shrimp that have been shelled but the tails left on. Cover the pan again and let the shrimp just cook through, no more than 3 to 5 minutes. Be very careful not to overcook the shrimp, or they will be tough and tasteless. Remove the cover, stir ¾ cup chopped parsley into the stew, and either transfer to a tureen for serving or serve it directly from the pan into soup plates, to be eaten with French bread, heated until crisp. This will serve six to eight as a first course, four as a main course. To serve more people as a main course, just add more of each seafood and have it with rice or noodles. This is an interesting change from the usual bouillabaisse or *cioppino*, and you can even make it at the table in an electric skillet if you like.

Now you can make a vegetable stew, first taking those that need the longest cooking time, tossing them in olive oil or butter with herbs and seasonings, covering them, and cooking them a little, then adding other vegetables that need a shorter cooking time. Again, the vegetables should not be overcooked, but still a little bit crunchy to the bite. It's great fun to dream up your own combinations.

You can also make a type of stew with dried fruits, spiking it well with sherry or Cognac. First make a simple syrup with 2 cups sugar and 1 cup water, letting it cook a little (those are the proportions, which you can double if you have a lot of fruit to cook), then add your dried fruit—prunes, apricots, peaches, pears, nectarines—cook them at a simmer until almost soft. Then add a good slug of some liquor—Cognac or port or sherry or any other flavoring you like— and let the fruits cook a bit longer after it is added. You should let your conscience be your guide as to the amount of spirit you use. You want a rich liquor flavor but the fruits should be stewed, not drunken, and not smothered by liquor. Chill the stewed fruit and serve with heavy cream, sour cream, yogurt, *crème fraîche*, whatever you feel like.

Stewing is an essential part of our cooking, and a good stew, to my mind, is about as attractive a dish as you can offer.

YOGURT
CULTURE IN
THE KITCHEN

I first became aware of yogurt quite early in my life, although then we didn't call it yogurt. There was a widespread susceptiblity to new foods and sometimes to what were called "fad foods" in Portland, Oregon, where I grew up. I must have been about ten when talk began about something that sounded mysterious and intriguing to me: Bulgarian milk. Apparently, people were making Bulgarian milk from a culture and eating it with what we then called health food. This was the time when bran muffins were in their first peak of popularity, and there was much discussion of roughage.

I finally had my first taste of Bulgarian milk and adored it. The cool, rather silky texture and sharp overtones of flavor captivated my young palate. Oddly enough, I loathed milk and refused to drink it after I was three, but I liked the soothing texture and interesting taste of Bulgarian milk. Although I didn't have it very often, when I did it was a treat. I would eat it with fresh, crisp radishes, green onions, and other such garden ingredients, and with good homemade bread and butter. I never lost this youthful fascination with Bulgarian milk. Many years later when I was living in London and Paris and discovered that yogurt and my old friend Bulgarian milk were one and the same, I had a second fling with it, which has lasted ever since. In those days no meal in Europe was complete without a cheese tray, and I noticed in France that containers of yogurt would come on the cheese platter, for some people ate yogurt rather than cheese. When I bought yogurt, I preferred to have it for breakfast or lunch and still do.

It's a funny thing about yogurt in this country. Although its popularity seems to be growing by leaps and bounds, it is mostly eaten as is, or in frozen form, and seldom used in cooking. There are also a great many Americans who don't seem to take to it at all, perhaps because the name seems as foreign to them as Bulgarian milk did to me. I'm amazed that yogurt doesn't have greater acceptance in the kitchen. We have been such faithful users of sour cream and cottage cheese for so many years that it strikes me as odd that what is probably the pleasantest of all the cultured milk products is not as popular as it deserves to be.

There is, of course, a great vogue for eating flavored yogurts. Some of the berry types, strawberry and raspberry, are okay if made with good-quality yogurt. But when you get into the artificially flavored yogurts, I cannot understand how some people find them pleasing to the palate.

Of course, that's not to say that you can't flavor your own yogurt with pure ingredients of your choice. Fruits and yogurt are very complementary, and you can breakfast or lunch extremely well on a banana or strawberries or blueberries with yogurt. If you're not worried about sugar and calories, fold a good orange marmalade or strawberry or raspberry jam into yogurt, and eat it with a piece of toast or bread and butter. Raspberries and peaches shine when combined with plain yogurt—and perhaps a little sugar, if you feel it is necessary—as a delicious summer dessert. As I learned in my Bulgarian-milk days, eating yogurt with crispy vegetables is a delight. You can make a little salad by mixing crisp radishes, bits of green onion, shredded carrots, and a little watercress into yogurt for a light and refreshing lunch. Cool cucumbers and yogurt, too, are natural partners; you'll find them used together for soups, salads, and as an accompaniment to curry in the Middle East and India. I remember dining in Teheran where the great specialty was an Iranian kebab of lamb, seasoned and marinated in yogurt before being broiled, with the yogurt still clinging to the meat. This was served with crisp vegetables and herbs. Once I had the dish with a platter of all the different kinds of available fresh herbs in little bouquets, with additional yogurt on the side. How good that tasted!

It is very easy, you know, to make yogurt. If you have a yogurt maker, all you do is add the culture or some commercial yogurt to milk that has been brought to a boil and then cooled to lukewarm. Pour it into the jars and keep it at a controlled temperature until it ferments and thickens. You don't even have to own a yogurt maker. For a low-calorie yogurt just reconstitute skim or nonfat dry-milk solids, put in a pan, and heat to a temperature of 180°F. Remove from the heat and cool until the liquid is about 112° to 113°F. Remove the skin from the top of the milk and mix a little of the warm milk with 2 or 3 tablespoons commercial yogurt (for a quart of milk). Stir this into the rest of the milk, mix well, and pour into a clean, warm, widemouthed, vacuum-insulated container. Cover and leave undisturbed for about 5 hours. It is very important not to touch the container during that period lest the mixture separate. The yogurt should then be refrigerated for several hours to thicken further. Making your own yogurt is really a very simple process and certainly much less expensive than buying it.

You can turn your yogurt into a delicious yogurt cheese to use in lieu of cream cheese or cottage cheese. Turn a quart or a pint of yogurt into a cheesecloth-lined sieve set over a bowl. Let it stand for about 30 minutes, by which time most of the excess liquid will have drained away. Then form the cheesecloth into a bag by bringing the ends together and tying them tightly. Now hang the bag from the faucet over a sink and let it drain for 8 to 12 hours, by which time you will have a nice firm cheese. Some people add salt, but I find the flavor delicious and tart and hardly in need of any seasoning. Remove the cheese to a bowl and use it as you would cream cheese, cottage cheese, or ricotta. It's good as a filling for lasagna and in other recipes that call for ricotta. Yogurt cheese will keep well in the refrigerator [stored in an air-tight container] for at least two weeks. You can serve it plain, or add finely chopped herbs such as chives, parsley, and thyme, or a mixture of the three. This pleasant and unusual cheese is only about 300 calories a cup, and, of course, it has no additives or preservatives.

Lately I have been using yogurt a good deal in bread making, substituting it for water, milk, or buttermilk. For a loaf of white bread I substitute a cup of yogurt for a cup of water or milk. If the dough is too stiff, just dilute it slightly with a little water. This makes a loaf with the wondrous tang of a good, tart sourdough, and you don't have all the bother of making a sourdough starter. It also makes the most flavorful toast I've had in a long time. I use yogurt intsead of milk in corn bread, instead of buttermilk in Irish soda bread, and in place of heavy cream for baking-powder biscuits.

X   To make yogurt baking-powder biscuits, sift into a bowl 2 cups flour, 4 teaspoons baking powder, and 1 teaspoon salt. Blend with 4 tablespoons vegetable oil, and then add enough yogurt to make a rather soft dough. I like to pat or roll this into a square and cut square biscuits. Put them on a buttered baking sheet and bake in a preheated 450°F oven for about 10 to 12 minutes. These biscuits have a sharp quality and a most exciting texture; they are as delicious as ones made with heavy cream, but without the calorie count.

Yogurt added to cooked sauces in place of sour cream yields a velvety texture and a light, refreshing, and not-at-all rich quality. If your sauce is spiked with a sharp, hot flavor such as cayenne, Tabasco, or curry powder, the yogurt smooths out and mellows the flavors in an almost magical way; the sauce will be much more subtle than if you had used cream or sour cream. However, yogurt will curdle if it reaches the boiling point or if the heat is too high. It is best to stir the yogurt into the sauce over gentle heat for the last minutes of cooking, just enough to blend and heat through.

I also find that yogurt is admirably suited to cold summer soups, adding a richness and silken smoothness, which belies its low calorie count. Try folding yogurt into soups made with cucumber, avocado, or fresh peas cooked in chicken broth, puréed and chilled, and you'll find they take on a new and very pleasant quality. A last-minute sprinkling of finely chopped mint also does wondrously good things to yogurt soups, for the flavors are decidedly complementary. Vichyssoise, made in the classic way with leeks and potatoes cooked in chicken broth, puréed, and chilled until very cold, is sensational if you pop a dollop of cold yogurt in at the last minute, with a sprinkling of chopped chives. Another variation I like is to add some watercress when cooking the vegetables.

Never underestimate the importance of yogurt in salad dressings. Blended with a highly herbed vinaigrette, it makes an exciting dressing for certain salads, almost like adding cheese to the dressing, but with an entirely different flavor.

For a salad for four, mix together 2 rounded teaspoons Dijon mustard, ½ teaspoon freshly ground black pepper, salt to taste (you can omit this if you are avoiding salt), ½ cup olive oil or vegetable oil, and 1 to 2 tablespoons wine vinegar (some people do like more vinegar). Blend well, add ½ cup plain yogurt, and beat well for about 2 minutes, until thoroughly combined.

You may pour this dressing over a green salad, a sliced tomato and onion salad, or any cold vegetable salad. Add appropriate chopped fresh herbs, then toss the salad and serve. For a salad of tomato and onion, fresh basil is, of course, the answer. For a good green salad, I like an ample amount of coarsely chopped fresh tarragon and a touch of chopped shallot or garlic. For a beet and onion salad with greens, I would add finely chopped hard-boiled egg to the yogurt before mixing it into the vinaigrette and then a goodly amount of chopped parsley—preferably the flat-leafed Italian type, but failing that, curly parsley—and perhaps a few chopped chives. This provides an exciting finish to the otherwise dull routine of salad making. I sometimes feel that the eternal green salad with vinaigrette sauce has become a cliché and a bore. I like to vary my salads and my dressings because I find the variety is more palate pleasing.

Chicken and various meat salads dressed with mayonnaise are much more intriguing if you use half mayonnaise and half yogurt. Indeed, my favorite poultry salad is made with comfortable chunks of good chicken (or turkey) mixed with finely cut macadamia nuts and served with a mixture of mayonnaise and yogurt. For a garnish I use quartered hard-boiled eggs and more macadamia nuts, and I arrange the salad on greens such as watercress or romaine. This makes an exceedingly pleasant departure from the usual chicken salad over-loaded with finely chopped celery, which is often an excuse for using more celery than chicken. If you're going to have a chicken salad, make it a bountiful one; don't economize on the chicken. Cut it in good bite-size chunks; don't chop it. Nothing looks messier and more anonymous than a finely textured chicken salad; you want to see what you are eating. If you like, you can spike your mayonnaise-yogurt dressing with chopped tarragon, a great partner for chicken, or with fresh basil, in which case I would skip the egg and garnish the salad with sliced ripe tomatoes or little cherry tomatoes.

Seafood salads, too, benefit from the mayonnaise-yogurt combi-nation. Flavor the dressing with finely chopped garlic and onion, chopped hard-boiled egg, a little chopped pickle, chopped parsley, and any other herb you wish, such as basil, tarragon, or chives. Blend well and let stand in the refrigerator for several hours before tossing the seafood with the dressing. Shrimp, crabmeat, and lobster are all delicious with this dressing. This flavorful dressing is great with cold salmon or cold striped bass, either as a salad or with the whole fish, served on a platter and accompanied with a good potato salad, coleslaw, or Russian salad. This last is made with tiny cubes of cooked carrot and potato, finely diced cooked green beans, and little green peas, bound with a pungent mayonnaise. Stuff tomatoes with Russian salad to serve with cold meats, fish, and poultry.

Next time you make coleslaw, dress it with the mayonnaise-yogurt mixture, which is just superb with cabbage. Blend the two well, mix with the shredded cabbage, and let it wilt in the dressing for several hours before serving. As a flavor variation, mix chopped parsley, chives, or thinly sliced green onion into the dressing. For a spicier coleslaw add a good amount of Dijon mustard. If you like a sweet-and-sour taste to your coleslaw, you can add a touch of sugar, or mix finely chopped orange or pineapple into the yogurt before blending it with the mayonnaise for a more complex sweet flavor.

Yogurt has so many good qualities. It is versatile, refreshing, and stimulating to the palate, low-calorie, and healthful, and a most exciting addition to just about everything you cook: soups, sauces, salads, marinated poultry and meat kebabs, dressings, and desserts. Once you start using yogurt in the kitchen, you'll find it a great blessing and you'll wonder how you ever got along without it.

CHAPTER 33

SUMMER
VEGETABLES:
ASPARAGUS TO
ZUCCHINI

One of the most glorious of all the sights of summer is the parade of fresh young vegetables in the markets and the garden. Every month brings something new—crisp, juicy snow peas; succulent fresh green peas; tender zucchini and summer squash; purple eggplant; fat ears of corn and ripe tomatoes bursting with juice. When I go to the markets, either here or in Europe, I find it hard to resist buying a little of everything I see, taking it home and making myself a platter of *crudités* or vegetables *à la Grecque*. There are so many vegetables to try, each with its own distinctive flavor and texture, that I often think I could spend weeks feasting on nothing else.

During the times I have lived in Provence, some of my happiest hours have been spent wandering around the great outdoor markets of Nice and Cannes where local produce mingles with the best from all over France. The stalls, piled with perfect, dewy-fresh vegetables and fruits, are a most ravishing symphony of color. Bouquets of rosy radishes nestle next to *haricots verts*, the baby green beans so beloved by the French, exquisite bunches of miniature carrots with their feathery tops, baby eggplant and zucchini and immature violet artichokes, so tiny and tender they can be eaten raw. In the market at Grasse, I came across a great idea I wish our markets would copy. The ingredients for a ratatouille, the incomparable Provençal vegetable stew, were sold ready-packaged with the onions, eggplant, zuc-chini, peppers, tomatoes, and garlic in a plastic bag. For *salade Niçoise* you could buy a package of the greens and vegetables, to which you would only need to add the tuna, hard-boiled eggs, olives, and anchovies.

While American markets seldom have vegetables as young and tender as those you find in France, if you grow your own, as so many people are doing in these inflationary times, you can know the rewards of picking green beans and zucchini while they are still tiny, dollar-size pattypan squash, green peas at their point of perfection, and your own vine-ripened tomatoes, or plucking radishes, little carrots, and scallions from the earth, washing them off, and eating them while their flavor is fresh, pure, and unsullied by time. All the laborious hours of digging, planting, weeding, and watering are more than repaid.

One of the pleasures of eating out in Provence is the "bouquet of *crudités*" that many restaurants present as a first course, a bevy of raw, crisp vegetables beautifully arranged in a basket, to be eaten with salt and pepper, or oil and vinegar, a spicily flavored mayonnaise, or the special local dip called *tapenade*, an earthy mixture of anchovies, black olives, capers, garlic, olive oil, and tuna spiced with mustard and a dash of Cognac. To me, there is no more appropriate, refreshing, and delightful a way to start a summer luncheon. Arrange your selection of raw vegetables with an eye to contrasts of color and shape in a long shallow basket or large pottery bowl, or on a big platter. Some of the likely candidates for *crudités* are raw asparagus tips, minute raw artichokes (often to be found in Italian markets), tiny green beans, whole baby carrots or carrot strips, cauliflowerets, strips of celery and cucumber, fingers of zucchini, endive leaves, green onions, radishes, cherry tomatoes, small, firm white mushroom caps, thin slices or strips of raw white turnip, watercress, and if you can find them, young fava or broad beans, either shelled or left in the pod for guests to shell and dip in coarse salt. If the day is hot and the vegetables likely to wilt, put cracked ice in the bowl or platter to keep them cool and fresh. If you use a basket, be sure to line it with aluminum foil to prevent drips. With the *crudités*, pass a dish of coarse salt, oil, and wine vinegar for those who like to make a little vinaigrette sauce, a pepper mill, and perhaps an anchovy mayonnaise for a dunk. For the anchovy mayonnaise, mix into 2 cups homemade mayonnaise, 12 to 14 finely chopped anchovy fillets, 2 finely chopped garlic cloves, ¼ cup chopped parsley, ¼ cup chopped fresh basil or 1 teaspoon dried basil, 1 tablespoon coarsely chopped capers, and 1 teaspoon Dijon mustard. Taste for seasoning—with the anchovies and capers you probably won't need salt, but you may need a touch of pepper or a dash of Tabasco.

Another favorite summer first course of mine is vegatables *à la Greque*. This style of preparation, which originated in Greece but has now become completely identified with the French cuisine, is one of the easiest and most agreeable ways of cooking seasonal vegetables. They are poached in a highly flavored liquid until tender, but still crisp, and cooled in the liquid, after which they can be served right away or kept refrigerated in containers for a couple of weeks and brought out as and when you need them. Among the summer vegetables that lend themselves to this treatment are tiny whole artichokes or artichoke bottoms with the choke removed, whole green and wax beans, asparagus spears, young carrots, tiny pattypan squash and whole or halved baby zucchini, green onions, cubes or fingers of eggplant, to which you can add celery hearts, firm white mushrooms, and tiny white onions. At other times of the year, you might use whole or halved leeks halved or quartered fennel bulbs, and the buds of cauliflower and broccoli.

For the poaching liquid, combine in a large skillet or shallow pan ½ cup olive or peanut oil, ⅓ cup white wine vinegar, ⅓ cup dry white wine, 1 teaspoon salt, ½ teaspoon freshly ground black pepper, 1 bay leaf, 1 or 2 peeled garlic cloves, a dash of Tabasco, and 1 teaspoon dried thyme, tarragon, oregano, or basil. Place the desired vegetable in the pan, add just enough water to barely cover, bring to a boil very slowly, then reduce the heat and poach until just crisply tender. This makes enough liquid for 1 pound green beans or 1 large cubed eggplant or 8 artichoke bottoms, or an equal amount of other veg-

etables. You can use the same liquid to poach a selection of vegetables, but cook them separately as they all require slightly different poaching times. Let the poached vegetables cool in the liquid, then transfer them to a serving dish and chill lightly in the refrigerator. Serve sprinkled with chopped parsley. For a dinner party, you might cook three or four vegetables, such as green beans, zucchini or eggplant, onions, and mushrooms and serve them either as a first course or in place of a salad or vegetable.

Another good way with vegetables is to serve them as vegetables vinaigrette. They may be either raw or cooked. Asparagus, artichoke bottoms, green or wax beans, baby beets, broccoli, cauliflower, celery hearts, green onions or onion slices, small whole zucchini or sliced zucchini should be cooked first in chicken stock or mushroom broth until tender but crisp, cooled and chilled in their liquid. When you are ready to serve, drain them, transfer to a serving dish, and give them a good bath of vinaigrette sauce made with salt, pepper, and 3 or 4 parts olive oil to 1 part wine vinegar. Sprinkle with chopped herbs and serve the vegetables vinaigrette as a salad, with grilled meats, as a first course, or as part of a cold buffet. If you use green or red peppers, these are better if not cooked but merely divested of their tough skin. Put them under the broiler until the skin chars, then scrape it off, seed the peppers, and cut them in thin strips before covering with the vinaigrette sauce. Raw vegetables, such as fava beans, shredded red or white cabbage, grated carrots, thinly sliced celery, seeded cucumbers (thinly sliced or cut in strips), sliced tomatoes, and sliced mushrooms need only to be dressed with the vinaigrette.

Green beans also make a very pleasant purée. For this, break off the ends of 3 to 4 pounds of young green beans, cut them into ½-inch pieces, and cook in boiling salted water until slightly over-cooked—softer than you would usually make them. Drain well and purée in a food processor or by putting them through a food mill or a fine sieve. Transfer the purée to a heavy pan in which you have melted 6 to 8 tablespoons butter and mix into the butter gently over medium heat. Then stir in 3 to 4 tablespoons heavy cream or yogurt, salt, and freshly ground black pepper to taste. Serve sprinkled with chopped parsley.

Of all summer vegetables, corn is probably the American favorite. Eaten with lavishments of butter, salt, and pepper, it is one of the most satisfying foods we have. When it comes to cooking corn, my preferred method is to put in it a big pot of cold water and bring it to a boil, then serve it without further ado or cooking. In this way you never get that unpleasant "starchy" taste from which so much overcooked corn on the cob suffers. As a variation on this, try cooking the ears in half water and half milk.

Corn is extremely good roasted. You can roast it on the outdoor grill either in or out of the husk. If you husk the corn, brush it well with melted butter or wrap the ears with bacon secured with tooth-picks, and grill over fairly brisk heat, turning several times, until lightly browned here and there. Cooking time varies according to size, but allow 5 to 10 minutes.

For roasting in the husk, choose ears of uniform size. Peel back the husks and carefully remove the silk. Replace husks, tie the ends with twine, and soak in cold water to cover for 30 minutes or more. Remove from the water, arrange on the grill, and roast over rather brisk heat for approximately 15 minutes, turning three times. Serve with plenty of butter, salt, and pepper.

Eggplant, a very prolific summer vegetable, is delicious if baked in its skin on the charcoal grill. Turn it frequently until it is soft and tender, about 35 minutes to an hour, according to size. Remove the charred skin, split the eggplant, and serve with butter or a well-seasoned tomato sauce. If you can find in your market or grow in the garden the small eggplant similar to those of Italy and the south of France, they are ideal for foil cooking. Wash them off well, cut off the top or stem end, and split. Arrange each one on a square of heavy aluminum foil with ¼ teaspoon chopped garlic, a slice of onion, and 3 or 4 cherry tomatoes. Season to taste with salt and pepper, add 1 tablespoon olive oil and ¼ teaspoon thyme or finely chopped fresh mint and perhaps a slice of lemon. Wrap securely, making a neat package, and grill in the foil pouch for 20 to 25 minutes, turning once or twice. Put the little packages in individual baskets and serve one to a guest—the packages can then be opened easily and the vegetables eaten from the foil without any loss of the natural juices that have collected inside.

Many other summer vegetables can be grilled this way in foil and served as an accompaniment to charcoal-broiled meats and poultry. Zucchini is one. Pick the tiniest you can find, about 3 or 4 inches long and ½ inch in diameter. Three of these babies are enough for one serving. Trim the ends, put them on squares of foil, add 1 tablespoon olive oil and 1 finely chopped garlic clove for each package, sprinkle with salt and pepper, wrap, and grill for about 30 minutes. Or, for a foil version of ratatouille, put on large squares of foil 1 small zucchini, a large cube of eggplant, a slice of onion, a strip of green pepper, a chopped garlic clove, and half a small peeled tomato. Season with salt, pepper, and basil, wrap, and grill for 30 to 35 minutes, moving and turning the packages to prevent the vegetables from sticking to the foil and to blend the flavors inside. These are delicious with grilled butterflied leg of lamb or shish kebab.

Baby beets also lend themselves to foil cooking. You don't have to peel them, just scrub them well. If they are really tiny, allow 3 to 4 a person. Put on the foil with a pat of butter, seal, and cook on the grill for 30 to 45 minutes, according to size. Serve with additional melted butter, freshly ground black pepper, and chopped fresh dill or chives. Or serve them with sour cream or yogurt and finely chopped parsley.

The vegetables of summer are one of our greatest seasonal treats. Enjoy them to the hilt while they are young, fresh, and in their prime.

PART III

HOLIDAY SPECIALS

CHAPTER 34

TASTEFUL

HOLIDAY

BUFFETS

As one who goes to, and gives, a goodly number of parties each year, I'm in a position to see how entertaining patterns have changed, and I'm happy to report that it seems the day of the "doot" is done. If you are wondering what I'm talking about, doot is my name for those bits of this and that on tired little rounds of toast, or squiggly mixtures squeezed onto crackers through a pastry bag that become soggy and dreary five minutes after they are put together. Some call them canapés. There was a time when at most cocktail parties it became something of an endurance test to refuse and resist these tiny horrors that were constantly pressed on you.

Not to mention punch bowl after punch bowl of rich, thick, gooey eggnog that you are faced with on holiday-party rounds. And what was served with that sweet eggnog? More sweets—slices of fruitcake, pound cake, or cookies.

During one stage of my early life, my father used to give an enormous Tom & Jerry party every Christmas. That thick batter with a splash of whiskey and a great deal of boiling water is something best forgotten.

Some years of those holiday "treats" left me determined to do—and fare—better. When I was living on my own in a small New York City apartment, I decided to give a big holiday party that would get away from all the traditional stuff, and see what the results might be. I remember sending out a mass of invitations, something like eighty-five, which was pretty daring considering the size of my quarters. I filled my enormous old bathtub with champagne bottles and crushed ice.

Then I set up a very posh electric grill, one that looked rather like a stainless-steel dollhouse. It was a very efficient affair with a spit that would turn a rather heavy weight, such as an eight- to ten-pound turkey. So I set to and grilled turkey after turkey. This, with a couple of baked Kentucky hams and very good bread, was it. I had no Christmas decorations, just masses of long-stemmed American Beauty roses. The party was a huge success, and no one seemed to have the slightest desire to leave. They drank every drop of champagne and ate all the turkey and ham.

Thus began my campaign for bigger and better holiday parties with less gloppy drinks and more good solid food. While I don't begin to take the credit, I do think I started a healthier trend. More and more I find people are doing an intelligent job of entertaining. It may be because they have less help, or because they are smarter about party giving and take a greater interest in the kitchen. Nowadays I go to more good parties that stress wine and intriguing food. While these are still cocktail buffets, or whatever you wish to call them, they give you an opportunity to enjoy the company of other people and celebrate the holiday season with some sanity. When you have substantial food and lighter drinks there is much less chance of falling flat on your face as you leave the party, or waking up the next morning with a wooden head. It's an enlightened and considerate way to entertain—and it is fun.

So when you are planning your holiday parties, take a gastronomic inventory, and decide what you can serve that is substantial, good to eat, a bit different, and not too difficult to prepare. The turkey-and-ham routine was all right in its day, but it is now ancient history. The two were linked for so long that they had to divorce, because anything repeated over and over becomes dull and a bore. It is all right to put out one or the other, a good ham or a good turkey, but one really needs to think of new foods that are pungent and delicious.

For one party, I can remember making a huge platter of stuffed eggs that I replenished twice during the time people came and went. They were hearty and satisfying and stood up well against the drinks, but they took a hell of a long time to prepare. If you don't mind that or have lots of willing little hands in the kitchen, they can make a good beginning.

At that same party, I had an enormous kettle of chili, which I served in small cups on saucers, with spoons. The variety of flavors in a fine, fiery chili does something very exciting to the palate—and don't feel that you are ruining wine by serving it with chili. Wine can be drunk with many pungent dishes, and chili is no exception. A well-chilled light white or light red goes very nicely with it. Or you can serve beer, or perhaps a more alcoholic tequila drink. Chili is always a good companion to holiday entertaining and you don't have to worry about making too much; it tastes even better reheated the next day and the day after that. For one large party I made a five-day chili, adding various and sundry things to the pot every day for five days—diced beef, chopped beef, diced pork, onions, garlic, green chilies, and chili powder among them—and I can honestly say it was one of the most wondrous chilies that ever happened.

Recently I did two enormous parties, one a business party for 300 people that worked extraordinarily well. You could use the same menu for a much smaller affair and cut down on the number of foods. I think you'll find the combination of things particularly interesting. As my local market will cook certain meats to order, I had it prepare corned beef and London broil. Each was served in a different room, and we carved them in thin slices that were cut into small pieces to pick up in the fingers or eat on bread. We had excellent rye and pumpernickel, large loaves that were sliced at the bakery, and French bread that we sliced at the party, but no butter or special condiments, just mustard for the beef. Corned beef, roast beef, and London broil are all excellent party foods, solid enough to fill people up through the drinking stage.

I had also ordered some delicious smoked chickens from a smokehouse in upper New York State, and these were cut into pieces and arranged on platters so people could eat the bony parts with their fingers or the breast pieces on French bread. The moistness and smoky taste of the birds made for irresistible finger food and everyone devoured the chicken without being afraid to pick the bones in public.

Of course, with so many people, we had lots of other food. We made two batches of each of four different pâtés and a big crock of rillettes, a gloriously rich and smooth French country pâté of pork, which is one of the most luscious things I know for Christmas or any cocktail buffet. Then we had two huge salmons that had been cured with salt, sugar, pepper, and dill for that great Scandinavian delicacy *gravad laks*. The deep-pink salmon, thinly sliced on the diagonal and enhanced by bright-green bouquets of fresh dill and parsley at either end of the board, looked too beautiful for words. With it we had bowls of the traditional Scandinavian sweet-and-sour mustard sauce, the perfect complement to the exciting flavor of the salmon, and buttered rye bread.

When the party ended after four hours, there was nothing left but a six-inch piece of *gravad laks*. I don't think I have ever seen people eat so much at a party. All we served with the food was a well-chilled white wine. For this kind of buffet you don't need a fancy wine, just an honest California jug wine that is to your taste. I find that nowadays everyone is perfectly happy if all you serve is wine, although it's sometimes a good idea to keep some hard liquor in reserve.

Another large party, planned for the christening of a very smart new professional kitchen shop, was a buffet that could well be duplicated for the holidays. *Gravad laks* was again on the menu. But because the shop had kitchen facilities in view of the guests, we did some cooking on the spot. We broiled butterflied legs of lamb and roasted 125 fresh quail. The birds were split in half and the wings removed, and then brushed well with a mixture of olive oil and Dijon mustard, wrapped with bacon, put on baking sheets, and given 18 to 20 minutes in a 400°F oven. These, like the smoked chicken, were a huge hit as finger food. The minute they came out of the oven, the guests picked them up, using paper napkins, and ate them—the quail halves were gone in no time, though even if they had stayed around and got cooler, they would still have been as good to eat. The sight of the trays of tempting roast quail and the mouth-watering aroma of the broiling lamb that wafted over the room certainly gave everyone at the party an appetite, and the food disappeared fast.

We also put out bowls of marinated shrimp—large, juicy, and so impregnated with the flavor of the marinade that they needed no dipping sauce—and big pots of chili that people relished enormously. I purposely cut down on the heat of the chili, feeling that a mildly hot chili would be more pleasing to most palates than one that was fiery hot, and the only objection came from a nine-year-old boy who told me I should have made it hotter! When I explained to him that if you were catering to a great many people you don't follow your own tastes but those of the majority, he rather reluctantly admitted I was right. With our menu we offered only red and white wine, and not a soul asked for liquor.

If you are planning a holiday party, my advice is to think in terms of good, hearty, filling foods. You could marinate and cook a large eye-of-the-rib roast or a thick piece of London broil for your buffet, using this teriyaki marinade, which is one of my favorites. Combine 1 cup peanut oil, 1 cup soy or teriyaki sauce, 6 finely chopped garlic cloves, a good-sized piece of fresh ginger root, grated or shredded, and about ⅔ cup of Madeira, sherry, or red wine. Blend well, then add your eye-of-the-rib roast and marinate for 24 hours (more, if you like), turning the meat several times in the marinade. Remove the roast from the marinade, dry it well, arrange on a rack in a roasting pan, and roast at 500°F for about 50 minutes, or until the internal temperature, tested with an accurate meat thermometer, reaches 125°F for rare beef. Now I warn you that roasting at 500°F will play havoc with the inside of your oven, so I trust yours is a self-cleaning model. During roasting you can brush the meat with some of the marinade from time to time, although this is not really necessary, for 24 hours marinating enables it to absorb quite enough flavor.

After you remove the roast from the oven, let it rest for 1 to 2 hours before carving. It will be just about tepid and a pleasant temperature to eat. Serve with sliced French bread and mustard.

For London broil, use the same marinade, but give the meat only about 3 hours marinating time for a thick cut. Broil a thick cut about 5 inches from the broiling unit, giving it 20 minutes a side. Test with your meat thermometer as it should be rare, the same 125°F temperature as the roast. If you like a zesty, spicy flavor, put a lot of freshly ground black pepper on the meat before you broil it. Carve London broil on the diagonal in paper-thin slices and eat on rolls or French bread.

The same teriyaki marinade can be used for a butterflied leg of lamb. When the butcher bones and butterflies the leg, ask him to leave the shank bone in. Marinate the lamb for 4 or 5 hours, turning it in the marinade, then broil about 6 inches from the heat for 30 to 35 minutes, 15 to 18 minutes a side. Turn at least once during the broiling time so the meat is evenly cooked. It will be rare in the thicker parts, better done in the thinner, with a lovely crisp, crunchy outside. Test the internal temperature about 5 minutes before the end of the broiling time by inserting a meat thermometer in the thickest part of the meat—it should register 135°F for rare, 140°F for medium-rare. Serve the lamb medium cool (not as cool as the beef), and carve on the diagonal in slices about ¼ inch thick, to be eaten on French bread or toast. Broiled butterflied leg of lamb is extraordinarily good buffet fare.

You don't need a vast array of dishes for a holiday buffet. Three or four substantial, tasty things will do, perhaps *gravad laks* (if you can get fresh salmon), marinated shrimp or smoked salmon, one broiled or roasted meat or a fine baked country ham, or roast quail or smoked chicken, duck, pheasant, or turkey. You'll find that companies and smokehouses that sell by mail are excellent sources for the kind of foods you need for a holiday buffet, such as smoked poultry, country hams and Smithfield ham, smoked salmon and other smoked fish, fresh crayfish, quail and other game birds, corned beef and prime meats, prosciutto and Westphalian ham, Italian, Polish, and Portuguese sausages, and also for wheels of the best American cheeses, like Maytag Blue, aged Vermont, and New York State Cheddar.

If you love to cook, you'll have a lot of pleasure creating your own buffet food from your own kitchen. If you don't, you can always find someone to prepare it for you, to bake a ham or roast a cut of beef, so all you have to do is tend to the carving. To start you off, here is a recipe for *gravad laks*, which will keep for several days in the refrigerator after curing, and one for a coarse, high-seasoned Provençal *pâté de campagne*.

For *gravad laks*, buy an 8-pound fresh salmon (if the fish is very large, have an 8-pound piece cut from the center). Ask for the skin to be left on and that the salmon be split lengthwise and the backbone and the small bones around it removed so you have two sides of boneless salmon. Place one piece, skin side down, in a dish or casserole large enough for the fish to lie flat.

Combine 1 cup coarse (kosher) salt, ½ cup granulated sugar, 1 ounce saltpeter (sold in drugstores), and 2 to 3 tablespoons coarsely ground black peppercorns. Rub half this mixture well into the flesh of the salmon and top with 1 or 2 large bunches of fresh dill. Rub the second half of the mixture into the flesh of the other piece of salmon, and lay it over the dill, flesh side down, reforming the shape of the fish. Cover the salmon with heavy foil, put a board or a large plate on top, and weigh this down with canned goods. Refrigerate for 36 to 48 hours, turning the salmon over once a day so it cures evenly. When you turn it, baste with the liquid that will have been drawn out by the curing process. Each time, cover and weigh down again. At the end of the curing time, remove the fish from the liquid, scrape away the dill and seasoned mixture, and dry the salmon well on paper towels.

About four hours before you are going to serve the salmon, make the mustard sauce. Put in a bowl 8 tablespoons seasoned German mustard (the kind that is very spicy, but not hot), 2 teaspoons dry mustard, 6 tablespoons sugar, 4 tablespoons wine vinegar, and ⅔ cup vegetable oil. Beat well with a small whisk until it has the consistency of a thin mayonnaise (the mustard will thicken the sauce). Mix in 4 or 5 tablespoons finely chopped fresh dill, and refrigerate for 3 or 4 hours to mellow the flavors.

To serve, arrange the salmon pieces on a carving board, flesh side up, and slice thickly on the diagonal, detaching the flesh from the skin as you do so. Garnish one end of the board with a bouquet of fresh dill, the other end with a bouquet of fresh parsley. Serve with the mustard sauce and buttered rye bread. This will serve up to thirty people.

For the *pâté de campagne*, combine in a bowl 2 pounds very coarsely chopped lean pork, 2 pounds rather finely chopped veal, 1 pound ground pork liver, 1 pound diced fresh pork siding or fat bacon, 6 finely chopped garlic cloves, 3 eggs, a pinch (⅛ teaspoon) each of ground cloves, nutmeg, and cinnamon, 1 tablespoon basil, ⅓ cup Cognac, 1 tablespoon salt, and 1½ teaspoons freshly ground black pepper. Mix thoroughly with your hands. To test for seasoning, make a small patty of 1 tablespoon of the mixture, and sauté it until thoroughly cooked through in 1 tablespoon butter or oil. Taste, then adjust seasoning in the raw mixture, if necessary. Line a 2½-quart straight-sided terrine, soufflé dish, or heavy pottery or ovenproof-glass baking dish with strips of bacon or salt pork. Fill with the meat mixture, and place more bacon or salt pork strips over the top. Cover with foil and set the dish on a baking sheet to catch any drips. Bake in a 325°F oven for 2 to 2½ hours, removing the foil after the first hour. When done, the pâté should come away from the sides of the dish. Remove from the oven and allow to cool for 1½ hours, then cover the top with foil and a board or plate. Put canned goods on the board or plate to weigh it down. Leave for several hours, until firm and set, then refrigerate until ready to serve. Serve from the dish, cutting the pâté in thick slices with a sharp, heavy knife. Serve with French bread or toast.

With your holiday buffet have plenty of red and white wine, and if you can afford it, champagne. Good food and drink are all it takes to make a good party—that's my formula for holiday entertaining.

CHAPTER 35

TURKEY, THE
ALL-AMERICAN
BIRD

It seems that turkey, in one fashion or another, and Thanksgiving as we celebrate it today have always been synonymous. There *are* those who give thanks every year that they don't have to eat turkey. Evidently they grew up on it and were turned off by bad cooking, and by having to eat turkey soup three days later and all the other leftover bits and pieces. That's too bad, for a perfectly cooked turkey is a toothsome thing.

Turkey didn't become the national bird until less than a hundred years ago. Wild turkeys were extraordinarily plentiful in the early days of the colonies, when there were great harvest festivals and festivals of thanksgiving, a perpetuation of the age-old harvest festivals of Europe and other parts of the world, and the bird became a symbol of harvest time. The native American wild turkey is, of course, the ancestor of our present domesticated bird, which is described in extravagant merchandising phrases as full-breasted, prebasted, butterball, and the like. Nowadays you can buy turkeys fresh or frozen, ready-stuffed or unstuffed; you can buy turkey parts and boneless turkey roasts—and all this is an outgrowth of that accommodating bird that roamed and flew the forests many generations ago.

Today we are not talking wild turkey, but domestic turkey—the regular kind with which you are going to celebrate Thanksgiving, which you'll get from your butcher or some favorite source for good turkeys. Personally, I like fresh-killed turkeys better than frozen ones, but that's purely a matter of choice. In various cities throughout the country, New York, San Francisco, and Los Angeles, for example, fresh-killed birds are readily available. They are, to my mind, better flavored, pleasanter to work with, very often fatter, and they make more agreeable eating than the frozen members of the family.

I don't always agree with people who want small birds. Provided the oven is big enough to accommodate it, I like to roast a bird of about sixteen to twenty or even twenty-two pounds, because, I must confess, I like cold turkey, if it is perfectly cooked. With a larger bird, you get much larger thighs and legs and oyster—that wonderful little tidbit that lurks in the backbone and is perhaps the choicest morsel of all.

One of the great faults with most turkey is that it is overcooked. It seems people are afraid the bird is raw if there's the slightest tinge of pink at the joint of the thigh and the leg. That is idiocy, if the flesh is a delicate pink, not blood-red, the dark meat is moist and, we trust, the white meat, too. The deadliest thing that can happen to a turkey after you have spent all that time stuffing it, nursing it, buttering it, and basting it is to bring it forth to the table looking dreamily crisp-skinned, brown, and luscious and then slice into the white meat and find it powdery, dry, and overdone.

If you have never cooked a turkey, be sure first that your *batterie de cuisine* has everything you need. You'd better measure your oven and your pans before you choose your turkey, and buy accordingly. A turkey weighing between sixteen and twenty pounds is a good-

sized bird and you need a good-sized pan to accommodate it. The large broiler pan from some ovens, with a folding rack in it, will take a large turkey, but you'd better make absolutely certain.

Naturally, you are going to stuff your turkey, if it isn't already stuffed, so first decide which of a delicious array of stuffings you are going to have. There are heaps of them. Some are made with bread crumbs, herbs, plenty of butter, onions, and seasonings. Others contain chestnuts, oysters, or sausage meat, or are made with corn bread and with bits of greens, sometimes shredded lettuce or zucchini. I think that perhaps the most interesting of all is a good bread stuffing with variations, and I also adore corn bread stuffing. Go through the repertoire of stuffings and make up your mind ahead of time so that you can shop for everything you need. Then, since this is a holiday and you can't rush out at the last minute and buy something you overlooked, you had better decide on the other parts of your dinner menu and make a list.

Personally, I like a holiday meal that is both simple and elegant. I like my turkey and a good stuffing and gravy, and I like something very simple but very expensive first: caviar, if I can afford it, otherwise delicious smoked salmon or some beautiful oysters, if I can find time to open oysters just before dinner. Or I might settle for a wonderful vegetable mixture of some sort, or a composed salad. With the turkey and stuffing, I have only one vegetable, unless I have to bow to popular taste and give my guests potatoes as well. Left to myself, I'm tempted to have a purée of parsnips, or mashed yellow turnips with lots of butter, swirled with sautéed mushrooms. I'm not a pumpkin or apple pie enthusiast, so for dessert I might have a pumpkin mousse, maybe an apple torte, or again I might choose to have just cheese, fresh fruit, nuts, and port wine.

Let's get back to our turkey. We've chosen our stuffing and the bird is ready for preparation. The first step is to put the gizzard, heart, neck, and wing tips in a pan with salt, an onion stuck with 2 cloves, a sprig or 2 of parsley, maybe a sprig of thyme, and about a quart of water and make the broth. Bring the liquid to a boil, skim off any scum that rises to the surface, reduce the heat, and let the broth simmer for 1 to 1½ hours, to give you a good rich stock for your gravy. You may remove the heart and gizzard and plunge the liver in at the very last for just about 5 or 6 minutes, then chop these very finely to be added to your gravy, or to your stuffing if you like. Now you have the broth made, a very important part of your preparations.

I happen to have a trick that I think works very well for turkey, chicken, and all kinds of birds, including game. I cut a lemon in half and then rub it inside the bird, all over the cavity. This tends to sweeten the interior and to give a little zest and a nice fresh quality when the stuffing goes in. It's a minimum amount of flavor for maximum satisfaction, as far as I'm concerned. To get your bird ready for stuffing and trussing, you will have cut the little wing tips off and cut the neck out, if it was there, and add these to your stock ingredients. If there should be any pinfeathers—rather remarkable these days—pick them out with a pair of tweezers. It used to be that one singed the turkey over a flame and then picked out the pinfeathers because the turkeys were handplucked.

Now, have we chosen and prepared a stuffing? If not, a basic crumb stuffing is hard to beat. Sometimes it is fun to have two stuffings in the bird, one in the neck cavity (in which case the skin around the neck has to be left on) and the other in the large cavity. Or you can have but a single stuffing in both large cavity and neck. Again the skin around the neck should be intact when you buy the bird as it has to be folded under and sewn.

Let's make our crumb stuffing first. For an 18-pound bird, you'll need 15 to 16 cups stuffing if you are using just one. If you are using two stuffings, you'll need 10 cups for the cavity and 5 cups for the neck. I'm very fond of stuffing, so I often make extra and bake what's left in a buttered, covered casserole.

For crumb stuffing for an 18-pound turkey, you'll want about 12 to 13 cups of crumbs, freshly made from good homemade bread or French or Italian bread—you can use part whole wheat and part white if you like. You can make the crumbs in a blender, you can make them with great ease in a food processor, or you can grate them by hand on a heavy grater. Naturally, the process will be greatly speeded up if you use a blender, even more with a food processor. You can use some of the crust, too, for crumbs. It adds flavor and a certain nuttiness. Next you need 2 to 2½ cups of finely chopped shallots, if they're available. Second choice would be green onions or, failing both of these, onions. Next you'll need a good pound of melted butter, because stuffing needs butter.

Then comes the subject of herbs. I have played around with several. Tarragon is extraordinarily good in stuffing. Thyme makes a good stuffing and so does sage, if carefully handled—or you can use half sage and half thyme, for balance. Too much sage is overpowering, just enough is exciting. I think it is best to mix in a small amount of sage, if you use it, and taste the stuffing to be sure you have enough but not too much. I like to add lots of parsley, at least ½ cup of finely chopped parsley. Then salt—the amount will depend on how much salt is in the bread. You should mix first, then taste and decide, but certainly the stuffing will take a tablespoon or more of salt. It's interesting to note that our forefathers used a great deal of nutmeg in cooking, much more than we do. Nutmeg is often thought of as something to be put in desserts, but it isn't limited to that. It is delicious in turkey stuffing and combines well with other flavors, so we'll add to our stuffing seasonings perhaps ¼ teaspoon of nutmeg, plenty of freshly ground black pepper, and then, to give it a little alcoholic treat and a good flavor, ¼ cup of Cognac, bourbon, or Scotch.

First sauté the shallots or onions in 12 tablespoons (1½ sticks) of butter until the butter melts down. Add more melted butter to this, then your seasonings—tarragon, thyme, sage, whatever you are using, including the chopped parsley, salt, pepper, and nutmeg. Mix in your bread crumbs and more melted butter, enough to make a moist but not sticky mixture, then the Cognac, bourbon, or Scotch. Your stuffing is now ready, except perhaps for tasting and readjusting the seasoning, and perhaps adding a little more butter and, if you desire, the chopped giblets from the broth.

If you are making a second stuffing for the neck, you'll need 2 pounds of ground pork, about 60 percent lean to 40 percent fat, 2 finely chopped garlic cloves, 2 teaspoons salt, 1½ teaspoons freshly ground black pepper, ¼ teaspoon nutmeg, 1 teaspoon dried thyme, and, if you like the flavor, ½ to ¾ teaspoon anise seeds (these may be bought anywhere), with about 2 tablespoons of Cognac, bourbon, or Scotch, whichever you are using in the bread stuffing. Mix these very well together and, lastly, mix in ¼ cup of chopped parsley. When everything is well mixed, make 1 or 2 tablespoons of the mixture into a little patty and fry it quickly until cooked through, then taste for seasoning, to see what is needed. Then, and only then, add 1 small head of Boston lettuce, finely shredded, or ½ head of romaine, finely shredded. Mix this well with the pork and seasonings and stuff the neck part of the turkey with it. Mold it in and around and fold the flap of neck skin over so it fits perfectly. Fill the rest of the bird with the bread stuffing. Do not overstuff the bird with the stuffing, as it will expand in cooking.

Now you're ready for the trussing and tying. When the cavity is filled, fold a piece of foil into a square and slip it under the skin of the vent so that it covers the stuffing and holds it in. Then, with a trussing needle and heavy thread or fine twine, sew up the vent tightly. Turn the bird over on its breast and with the needle and heavy thread sew the end of the neck skin over the turkey so that it secures the stuffing. Now take a long piece of string and wrap it around the wing joints of the turkey—not across the breast—and bring the two ends of the string down to the tail part of the bird. Turn the bird on its back, cross the two pieces of string under the tail and bring them up to the legs, wrapping one piece of string around each leg several times at the end of the drumstick, them pull them together and tie firmly. You will now have a compact, trussed, and tied bird with the vent and neck flap securely sewn, the wings tied to the bird, and the legs and tail tied together.

Massage the bird well on all sides with plenty of butter or bacon fat, if you have some on hand. It's very important to rub the fat well into the skin before you roast. I like to roast the turkey on a rack in a shallow pan that will hold enough fat and drippings to baste the bird. I like to place it on one side to begin with, giving the side that is upward a final rub with fat, and I think 350°F is a very good roasting temperature. There is really no hard and fast rule for roasting. Some people say it must have 25 minutes per pound, others say 20 minutes or 18, or recommend roasting to an internal temperature of 185°F. I think the test is in the bird and your fingers have to tell you. Protect them with a cloth or paper towel before testing. The drumstick and breast meat should feel soft when pressed with the fingers and the drumstick and thigh joint should move easily. If you puncture the skin at the joint of the leg and thigh, the juices should run clear.

I usually give an 18- to 20-pound bird 1 hour on one side at 350°F, then very carefully turn it over onto the other side, baste well, and rub with a little more butter or bacon fat, then give it an hour on the second side. I then salt the whole bird, turn it on its back, baste well, and either rub or brush the breast and legs with fat. Give it enough additional roasting time to produce a bird that tests faintly pink at the joint when the skin between leg and thigh is pierced. If you use a meat thermometer, thrust into the fattest part of the thigh so that it does not touch the bone, the temperature should register between 175° and 180°F. Should your bird brown too quickly, slip a piece of brown paper or aluminum foil over it and baste often. People who say turkeys are self-basting are wrong. Only basting will give a turkey that lovely color.

When the bird is cooked, remove it from the oven and let it stand on a platter in a warm place for 15 to 20 minutes before you attempt to carve it. This will give the juices time to settle, and meanwhile you can be making the gravy and finishing off the vegetable dish you have chosen. Then, satisfied that you have done your very best, you can sit down and enjoy the fruits of your labors.

CHAPTER 36

SPIRITED

DRINKS FOR

A FESTIVE

CHRISTMAS

You can't celebrate Christmas without eating and drinking, and this cooking lesson is going to be on Christmas drinks and
the foods that go with them.

Certain drinks associated with Christmas are almost as old as the
festival itself. One is the wassail bowl, which took its name from the
salutation with which one drank to someone's health in medieval
England—"was-hail," meaning, be hale or in good health. In the
sixteenth century, it was the custom to carry a wassail bowl, a hot
spiced ale drink with apples floating in it, all around the town, singing
"Wassail," and offering a libation to everyone, a rather charming
custom.

While I don't see many of us wandering around with a wassail
bowl today, we do have in this country two or three great traditional
drinks. One is the eggnog, much renowned in Virginia and Maryland,
which gradually became the universal Christmas drink. People all
over the United States serve eggnog at holiday time—some make it
well, some make it badly, but most people make the outstanding
mistake of serving sweet things with eggnog, which is sweet, rich,
and luscious enough in itself. They think it is the time to show off
all their Christmas baking, so they give you cookies and fruitcake
and that kind of thing, when they would be far better off serving

little sandwiches of chicken, ham, or turkey, salted nuts, and similar savory nibbles.

However, if you do insist on serving some kind of cake or cookie, there are two good choices I would recommend, neither very sweet. One is Scottish shortbread, which is not difficult to make, and a delicious accompaniment for a holiday punch.

To make a very good shortbread, mix 3 cups of sifted all-purpose flour, ½ cup of sugar, and 1 cup (that's 2 sticks) of soft butter together, either with your hands or in the electric mixer. Add 1 egg yolk and knead it in well.

Divide the mixture into 4 parts and roll each into a square or a circle, about ½ inch thick. Prick with a fork. Cut each circle into 8 triangles or each square into 8 smaller squares, place the pieces on a lightly buttered and floured baking sheet, and bake in a preheated 350°F oven for 15 minutes, then reduce the heat to 300°F and bake for 30 minutes longer, until the shortbread is a delicate light brown. This makes 32 little pieces of shortbread. Or, you may bake the 4 circles, first crimping the edges with your fingers as you would do with pie crust, then cut them into 8 triangles while they are still warm, and return the pieces to the oven until the edges are lightly browned.

Another traditional accompaniment to eggnog that I like very much is seedcake. It is rich, but not too sweet, and it makes better eating than gooey fruitcakes or Christmas cookies.

To make seedcake, cream 1 cup (2 sticks) of butter with 1 cup of sugar until very light and fluffy, using an electric mixer, if you have one. Add 5 eggs, one at a time, beating well after each addition. Sift 2 cups of all-purpose flour with ½ teaspoon of salt and 1 teaspoon baking powder. Add the dry ingredients to the butter-sugar-egg mixture and beat for 2 minutes at low speed in the electric mixer, or by hand with a wooden spoon, giving it about 100 strokes. Add 2 tablespoons of caraway seeds and continue beating for another minute.

Pour the cake batter into a buttered and floured 9-inch tube pan and bake in a preheated 350°F oven for about 45 minutes, or until the cake tests done (when a straw or small wooden skewer inserted into the center comes out clean). This is a nice cake to have in reserve for the holiday season and if you keep it in a tin with a tight lid, it will stay fresh for quite a long time. Serve it thinly sliced with eggnog or other punches, or with tea or coffee.

The first eggnog recipe I'm going to give you is an old Virginia recipe, and it is so thick, rich, and creamy that you can barely take more than one glass.

Separate 12 eggs. Beat the yolks very, very well with an electric beater or by hand until they thicken and turn a light lemon color. Then beat in 2 cups of sugar and continue to beat until the mixture makes a ribbon when you test it with a spoon. Add, very slowly, 1 quart of Cognac and 1 pint of Jamaica rum, beating all the while. Add 3 quarts of heavy cream and fold in 6 of the egg whites, beaten until stiff but not dry and crumbly. Beat the remaining 6 egg whites in a bowl, add 1 cup of superfine sugar to them and then 1 quart of heavy cream. Fold this into the first egg-yolk-and-spirit mixture.

Traditionally, this eggnog was allowed to stand in a very cold room for 6 to 8 hours before serving. One or 2 hours in the refrigerator will suffice, but my advice is to chill the cream, the Cognac, and the rum before you add them; this way you will have a colder drink that will not have to rest so long after it is blended.

Serve this superbly good but indecently rich eggnog in a beautiful crystal bowl, sprinkle it with freshly grated nutmeg, and ladle it into chilled glasses or little punch cups.

If you find this eggnog too creamy for your taste, here is another that is equally good but a shade lighter. You might say it is completely American in that it uses good bourbon whiskey rather than Cognac and Jamaica rum.

Again, you will need a dozen eggs. Separate them, and beat the 12 yolks very well until they are light, lemon-colored, and thick. Add

½ to ¾ cup of sugar and continue beating until good and thick. Then slowly beat in 1 quart of good bourbon and 2 quarts of liquid—either 2 quarts of heavy cream or 1 quart of heavy cream and 1 quart of milk. Add some freshly grated nutmeg and a pinch of mace. Then beat your 12 egg whites until quite stiff and fold into the mixture. Now taste. You may need more sugar or more bourbon, or you might like to add just a dash of Cognac to the eggnog for interest. Here again, let me advise you to have all the liquid ingredients cold, and then chill the eggnog in the refrigerator for an hour or so before you serve it. I prefer this eggnog to the Virginia one and I think you will, too. Remember, you can adjust the sugar content according to your palate. For a pleasant finishing touch, have a nutmeg grater on hand and grate nutmeg freshly over each cup or glass as you serve it from the bowl. That fresh spiciness is a delight to the nose as well as the taste buds.

Another Christmas drink that has been extremely popular for more than a century is the Tom & Jerry, originated by a famous bartender named Jerry Thomas, who must have been an experimenter of the first order, for he created quite a few drinks.

Separate 12 eggs. Beat the yolks very well and then beat into them 1 cup of sugar. Into this, beat about 4 jiggers of Jamaica rum. Beat the egg whites until very stiff, add 3 tablespoons of sugar to them, and beat until you have a meringue. Add a touch of Jamaica rum to this and then fold the meringue into the egg-yolk mixture. This is your batter, the essential in making a Tom & Jerry.

To serve, you need some attractive mugs or heavy cups, spoons, boiling water, fresh nutmeg, and a nutmeg grater. Put in each mug about 2 tablespoons of the batter, then a good jigger of either bourbon, Cognac, or Jamaica rum, fill the mug with boiling water, and stir until blended. Grate nutmeg over the top.

This is an invigorating, heartwarming drink, very cheering on a cold and snowy Christmas Day, after you have done the rounds of relatives and friends.

Another excellent hot drink, neither rich nor heavy, is grog. This was originally enjoyed by sailors in the British navy, but somehow it made its way to France. I well remember on cold mornings in Paris, many years ago, going to one of my favorite bars at about eleven-thirty and having a grog to warm me up. Paris can be very raw in the winter and a grog really hit the spot.

Grog should be made in a heavy glass, such as an old-fashioned glass, and it is advisable to put a spoon in each glass before adding the boiling water, as this tempers the heat of the water and prevents the glass cracking.

For each individual grog, put 1 lump of sugar, a dash of bitters, and a slice of lemon in each glass. Let the sugar melt down or crumble, then add a jigger of Jamaica rum or, if you prefer, whiskey. Then add the boiling water, stir with the spoon, and drink.

A grog party can be a great deal of fun at Christmastime. Grog is different, heart- and body-warming, and an excellent addition to your repertoire of festive drinks. With this, too, it is advisable to eschew all those gooey delicacies that are heavy on sugar and fruits. Instead, have salted nuts and appetizers that are sharp and cheesy, and maybe slices from a flavorful country or Virginia ham, with thin slices of bread.

So, whatever you choose to drink at Christmas, here's wassail to you and have a wonderful holiday.

CHAPTER 37

THE STIRRING CEREMONY OF CHRISTMAS PUDDING

When I was growing up in Oregon, Christmas was always a very festive time at our house, and in the many years since then I have tried to maintain that wonderful feeling, for I love the principle and traditions of Christmas. I get rather tired of the public Christmas of cards and shopping and all the things that, to me, encroach upon the intimacy and personal side of the season and make it a wearisome and commercial travesty. I have no objection to Christmas decorations, and I like the fact that we have holly wreaths and mistletoe boughs and Christmas trees, but I think the celebration of the holiday itself should be very private, a time to gather around you the people you most like and most want to see at this special season.

Most of my childhood memories center around the foods and feasting of Christmas. We had great respect for the past, especially the old English customs and foods. Our fruitcakes, mincemeat, and Christmas puddings were made a year ahead of time and kept moist, fruity, and mellow throughout the following year by repeated dosages of Cognac or bourbon. As you uncovered these puddings and cakes to give them their monthly ablution, your nose was entranced by that spicy, liquory, heady aroma that is associated only with Christmas foods, reviving memories of that happiest of all seasons.

Each year early in November we made great crocks of mincemeat.

Those days were a fascination to me. First there was the cooking of the meat for the mincemeat, which in our home was always beef and beef tongue. These were boiled, the stock was reserved for sauces and soups and stews, and the meat was finely cut or shredded and chopped by hand, then mixed with several kinds of raisins, currants, and candied fruits, and quantities of liquor. We never put apples in the mincemeat until we took it out of the crock to use it, because my mother felt it kept better this way. I remember that we would save bottles of liqueurs that had been sent to us as gifts but were not to our taste for after-dinner drinking, and they greatly enhanced the mincemeat while being themselves overpowered by the other flavors.

We always made both black and white fruitcakes. I preferred the white ones that had more or less of a pound-cake base studded with lovely pale fruits like pineapple, sultana raisins, bits of citron peel, and pecans, although the dark, heavy, black fruitcake could be a delight, too, if properly made. We often added chocolate to ours, which gave them color, mellowness, and depth of flavor. It was very exciting to the palate and the tooth to bite into one of these cakes, dense with good fruit and with that hardly perceptible overtone of chocolate. This dark fruitcake was also kept for a year and given more or less regular anointings of Cognac or rum or bourbon, the spirits best suited to it.

Our Christmas puddings followed a different procedure from those I make today. I have long since changed my method of making them because I no longer have the space to keep puddings and mincemeat and fruitcakes for a year. Now I mix the fruit and crumbs and flour and suet for my Christmas pudding at the beginning of December and then anoint it each day for five or ten days (or longer, if possible) with additional Cognac, which is absorbed by the fruit, giving the finished pudding far greater flavor and richness.

If you are a traditionalist, on the day you make the pudding, you must follow the age-old English custom of stirring the pudding. This is really a household ceremony. Everyone in the house grasps the big wooden spoon in turn and stirs and makes a wish for good luck. So, when you follow the recipe I am going to give you for my Five-Day Plum Pudding, line your family up and get them stirring after you add the eggs.

To make the pudding, chop ½ pound beef suet (beef fat) very fine and sprinkle it with ½ cup flour. Clean ¾ cup seeded raisins, 1 cup sultana raisins, and ½ cup currants and dust them lightly with flour. Make 3 cups fresh bread crumbs. Chop ½ pound mixed peel (orange,

lemon, and citron) very fine and dust with flour. Grate the rinds of
1 orange and 1 lemon, squeeze the juice from each, and combine
rind and juice in a large mixing bowl with the chopped suet, raisins,
currants, bread crumbs, chopped mixed peel, 1 cup flour, 6 to 7 tart
apples that have been peeled, cored, and chopped, ½ cup ground
filberts, 1 cup brown sugar, ½ teaspoon cloves, 2 teaspoons cinnamon,
1 teaspoon ground ginger, 1 teaspoon mace, and 1 teaspoon salt. Mix
well, add ½ cup Cognac or rum, and put the bowl in a cold place or
in the refrigerator. Leave for 5 days, each day adding ¼ cup more
Cognac or rum and stirring the mixture well each time. On that last
day, stir it well again. Beat 6 eggs slightly and stir them thoroughly
into the pudding mixture. At this point, get the family to give it a
good-luck stir.

If the batter seems too thick (it should be well bound together and
thoroughly mixed, but not a tight dough), thin it with a little beer.
Pour the mixture into molds or pudding basins (it will fill a 6-cup
mold and one or more 4-cup molds) or into 1-pound coffee tins,
leaving some room for expansion. Cover with the lids of the molds,
or if there are no lids, cover the molds or pudding basins with cloths
that have been wrung out in hot water and then dusted with flour,
and then cover the cloths tightly with aluminum foil. Or if you use
coffee cans, cover the tops tightly with foil. You don't want the steam
condensing on the tops of the pudding. Stand the molds, basins, or
cans on a rack in a deep saucepan (you may have to use 2 saucepans
and racks) and add boiling water to come halfway up the sides of
the molds, basins, or cans. Cover the pan, bring the water to a boil,
and boil for 6 hours, adding more water if it boils right down. If you
are serving the pudding right away, unmold it onto a heatproof
serving platter, ready for flaming. If you aren't, remove the pans from
the heat and let the puddings cool in the pans. Keep them in a cool
place or the refrigerator until needed. To reheat, put on a rack in a
pan of boiling water, as before, cover, and steam for 2 hours.

To serve, unmold onto a warm, heatproof platter. I like to serve
pudding with a benediction of warm Cognac or rum or bourbon
poured over it and ignited so it flames beautifully, and I usually
sprinkle the pudding with a little sugar first. So heat ⅓ cup of your
chosen spirit (don't let it boil or the alcohol will be dissipated and it
won't flame; just heat through to release the fumes in a small pan),
touch a match to it, and pour it over the sugared pudding. Bring to
the table flaming away. Some people circle the puddings with a wreath
of holly leaves, but I have had too many conflagrations from holly

and burning alcohol to consider doing that anymore. I once placed a great sprig of mistletoe in the center of the pudding before flaming it, and much to my horror the flames consumed the mistletoe and left it in ashes on the pudding. So if you want a sprig of holly or mistletoe on your pudding, add it after the flames have died out.

Christmas pudding is very heavy and should be served in very small portions with either a hard sauce or a custardy Cognac sauce, preferably after a not-too-elaborate and filling dinner. I often wonder how, in the old days, people managed to eat their way through a huge holiday meal that started with oysters or caviar or foie gras, went on to soup and then a turkey or goose with at least three vegetables—potatoes and sometimes sweet potatoes as well, mashed rutabagas or turnips, creamed onions, sometimes corn and a green vegetable—with hot rolls, salad, and possibly cheese. How anyone managed to eat Christmas pudding after that is beyond me. If they did, it was a gastronomic achievement of the first water.

When it comes to Christmas desserts, I have seen some wonderfully weird marriages of flavor. My father always lifted the crust of hot mince pie and put a cube of butter and a piece of Roquefort cheese underneath, which I considered a horrendous mixture. I have seen people take calorie-rich plum pudding and add ice cream and whipped cream to it. This, I think, is gilding the lily—or the pudding. I do want sauce with my pudding, because it sort of lightens the load of the heavy pudding, so to speak, and you don't feel it is just too much eating, but I want either a good Cognac sauce or a good hard sauce, which is perhaps the most delectable addition of all. It has pungency and flavor and it is such fun to watch it melt down on the hot pudding. I make my hard sauce with brown sugar. First I cream ¾ cup of butter extremely well, and then I beat in as much light brown sugar as it will take, about 1½ to 2 cups. The mixture must be very firm. I then stir in Cognac, bourbon, or rum to taste. You can beat in a tiny pinch of cinnamon at the end, if you like, but I prefer it without. Or you can use white sugar instead of brown, although I consider the brown makes a better sauce. After the sauce has reached a light, creamy, fluffy consistency, chill it well. Present it in a bowl with a little candied fruit on top—not maraschino cherries—and pass it with the pudding. Or you could make a Cognac sauce that is very good, too, more like a rich custard. Combine in the upper part of a double boiler 1 cup heavy cream, 3 egg yolks, 2 tablespoons sugar, a pinch of salt, and ⅓ cup Cognac. Stir over hot water until slightly thickened and serve in a bowl.

I usually find that if I don't follow the traditional route and experiment with my holiday menu, I can come up with something that is more fun for me and for my guests. I am apt to go all out and spend money with no thought of tomorrow. One of my favorite extravagances is to have a hearty supply of fresh caviar with lemon and plenty of crisp toast and, for those who really must have them, chopped onion and sour cream. With this I like vodka, chilled in the freezer until icy cold. Then, after everyone has had their fill of caviar, I like to sit down to a sturdy rare roast of beef or a perfectly cooked goose with a chestnut, apple, and prune stuffing, the skin deliciously brown and crisp and the meat tender and juicy. With the beef I would have puréed potatoes, beaten until light and fluffy with plenty of butter and cream, and one other vegetable, perhaps a purée of parsnips (this makes two puréed vegetables, but they are completely different) or braised onions with Madeira, both great favorites of mine. I serve a beautiful red wine with the meat course and with the cheese that follows, and then we all have a pleasant rest and break before the pudding comes flaming into the room and is served forth— at which point I consider one needs French champagne as a *digestif*. End with strong espresso coffee. This is my own idea of a traditional Christmas dinner for today. You might call it "tradition according to Beard," I suppose, but nevertheless that is how I like it. Just one thing more. I think it is rather fun, when the pudding comes in, to

have some crackers on the table. I don't mean soda crackers, but the kind you pull, the little tubes covered with gaily colored crepe paper and designs with snappers at each end that make a sharp pop when you pull them. Inside the cracker there's a paper cap and a favor and sometimes a motto or message like the kind you get in fortune cookies. Christmas crackers are a tradition established in England generations ago that many of us have followed faithfully throughout the years.

When you make your Christmas pudding, make it in quantity and set aside some of the pots or molds to give to friends. It's a perfect gift, one of the things most appreciated. There's something very warm and nice about receiving a pudding from your kitchen, wrought with your hands, perfectly packaged and sent for someone else's Christmas dinner. Or it might be a jar of homemade mincemeat for a pie, or a small fruitcake, or a loaf of homemade bread. These mean so much more than the silly bits of giftery that one finds in the shops, for they restore the personal equation to giving that one misses so much these days. Nothing could be more symbolic of the season and the traditions of Christmas than your own pudding, offered with love. Happy pudding—and don't forget the hard sauce.

CHAPTER 38

MEMORIES OF

CHRISTMASES

PAST

I have quite a necklace of Christmas-dinner memories, strung one by one over the years. Some were fun, some rather grim, and others overwhelmingly memorable. Perhaps the most memorable was the supper for almost 200 merchant marines during World War II, when I was stationed in Panama. We couldn't manage a sit-down dinner, so we had a buffet and an enormous Christmas tree. The tree was maybe the most affecting part of the supper for many men who hadn't seen one for years. We served gallons of really good eggnog and all sorts of Christmas viand—little turnovers with a minced-meat filling, cold birds, and other cold foods. I remember that above all the seamen praised the hot rolls made by my cook, Margaret Tingling. It seemed that the men would never stop eating the delicate, puffy little gems, baked to a turn and waiting a rich dollop of butter. The emotional reaction to these home-cooked delicacies and the traditions of Christmas was deeply moving.

Another of my happy memories is of a Christmas picnic in the South, for which we toted the food and drink about 100 miles to a lovely picnic spot overlooking the ocean. We toasted each other with champagne and ate not turkey but roast squab, one a person. Instead of the traditional mashed potatoes and vegetables, we had an extremely good potato salad and a salad of ripe tomatoes and cucumbers, with homemade bread and sweet-and-sour pickled prunes we'd made in the fall. Our dessert was a luscious white fruitcake laden with pineapple, ginger, white raisins, and almonds, and a brandied chestnut ice cream we had brought along in its freezer. You might say we were being traditional, but in a different, easier way. I almost think I'd rather repeat that picnic every year than sit down to the conventional traditional spread.

Then I remember a Christmas in Provence that should have gone well but was a miserable flop. I'd spent a goodly sum on a magnificent goose, and we started dinner, appropriately, with fresh foie gras. This was to be followed by our goose with a very special stuffing, sautéed apples, and other accompaniments. Alas, one of the members of the household was in a foul mood and another hated Christmas, so our glorious goose was merely a shell for the stuffing. No one could get through it. Two days later, I turned it into a pretty good soup. So much for the Christmas spirit!

Whenever Christmas approaches, past dinners come into your mind, and by now I have found many ways to skirt the possibility of an unhappy Christmas. First of all, I sit down and consider what Christmas dinner should be and what I want it to be. Should it be turkey? Usually I vote that out. I think turkey is for Thanksgiving and maybe for the Fourth of July, but not for Christmas, where you want something special.

Should it be goose? Goose is a festive bird, and if it is a good freshly killed fat one, it will seethe and sputter in a most appetizing way, exuding all the precious fat, which should be drained off and saved for sautéing potatoes, for baking, and for other purposes. But somehow the geese of today, except for an occasional one, seem to lack the wondrously rich flavor always associated with goose. The liver, or foie gras, which usually precedes the goose, invariably outshines it. Goose, it seems to me, is best made into a hash.

Little birds, such as plump quail, sparingly stuffed and quickly roasted so the flesh is still pink and moist, make a wonderful Christmas feast. They should be consumed by family and close friends, with fingers replacing knife and fork, so as to savor all the goodness and get the last scrap of meat from the delicate bones. And there should be plenty of them—two or even three a person. Nowadays, with quail farms abounding, these delicious little birds have become more easily available fresh, so there is no need to use the frozen birds. I once ate quail that had been boned, stuffed, and pulled together at four points so it came to table looking like the little knapsacks you'd carry on a stick if you were wandering through the woods. The bones had been cooked down to a rich broth to make a sauce enriched with heavy cream, the chopped giblets, and a goodly splash of Madeira; the sauce well became the flesh and the stuffing. Served with a purée of chickpeas or a purée of chestnuts, this is a remarkably delicious and quite different way to present quail.

Above all, Christmas must bring back certain memories of the days of childhood, when the family sat down together for Christmas dinner. Being part English and brought up with a great many English traditions, I always associate Christmas with two very special foods, without which Christmas never seems quite the same to me. For the main course I want a noble joint of beef, prime ribs roasted beautifully rare and served forth with a golden, puffy Yorkshire pudding, and roast potatoes browned in the beef fat. With the beef I must have yellow turnips, either cubed and buttered, or mashed and mixed with *duxelles*, that heavenly mass of chopped mushrooms cooked down with a few chopped shallots and lots of butter until they turn deep black, with a fragrance and flavor that is the pure essence of mushroom. Swirled into the yellow turnips, *duxelles* look like dark veins in marble; this is a beautiful thing to behold. Lacking turnips, I'd settle for a purée of parsnips drenched with butter and whipped smooth with a little Madeira, then baked with a few crumbs or chopped nuts on top.

Then, because it is a taste and texture memory without which no Christmas dinner could be considered complete, I'd have a dense, dark Christmas pudding, heavy with fruit and saturated with spirits, ablaze with brandy, and served with either a hard sauce or a foamy brandy sauce. Roast beef and Yorkshire pudding, plum pudding and hard sauce, these are the foods that maintain the tradition of Christmas past and warm the cockles of one's heart on this great day of joyous celebration.

To start with? Well, here I think you can be nontraditional, and I almost always am. If I can afford it, I like to start with fresh foie gras or caviar. This spells celebration to me. With the caviar I want thin toast, lemon, and vodka chilled to the icy point where it almost pierces the palate. If I have foie gras, I either want a very cold, almost frappé bottle of Sauternes, or a favorite fine champagne—and plenty of time to linger over it. If I am at home, I time my roast so that I can enjoy the first course at leisure, with good conversation and the benison of friends to share the celebration.

If these luxuries are beyond your pocketbook, or don't suit your palate, other good first courses would be a homemade pâté, or a rich clear consommé with tiny shreds of noodle, or a double-strength chicken consommé with little cubes of avocado. These are satisfying without being surfeiting, and they introduce the serious eating of the day in a very delicate way. Or you might have fresh crabmeat with a rémoulade sauce or a mustard mayonnaise, served on crisp romaine or Bibb lettuce leaves. With crabmeat, drink a brisk, well-chilled white wine or champagne.

To many people, Christmas is not Christmas without salted nuts (homemade, of course) and maybe olives. I don't feel they are needed at the beginning of a hearty meal, though after dinner a few salted nuts might go along with coffee and brandies. Nor do I think bread has any place at the Christmas table, except for the thin, crisp toast that goes with caviar or foie gras or consommé. Center stage belongs to the main course, a fine roast of beef from the first three or four ribs.

There are many different ways to roast beef. If you have a well-insulated oven, you may roast the beef, as I like to do, at 500°F allowing 5 minutes a rib and 5 minutes for the oven. Then immediately turn the heat off and leave the meat in the oven for 2 to 3 hours without opening the door. At the end of that time it will be deliciously rare and juicy. I don't advise following this method unless your oven is self-cleaning, for it makes a terrible mess.

An alternate way is to roast the beef at 450°F for 35 minutes, then

reduce the temperature to 350°F and continue roasting until the internal temperature registers 120°F when a meat thermometer is plunged into the meatiest part of the roast, not touching the bone. Either of these cooking methods will give you rare, well-flavored beef. If you want to do that unspeakable thing of cooking your beef well done, I can't help you. As far as I'm concerned, if you cook beef to an internal temperature of 150°F, it is ruined.

However, I don't advise going to the expense and trouble of a large roast of beef if your family is small, only two or three people. Instead, splurge on a good thick 2½-inch porterhouse steak. You won't have all the leftovers you get with a roast of beef. But you can still have your Yorkshire pudding, which is merely a popover batter cooked very quickly in a pan of very hot beef drippings until it puffs and turns golden, and all the other things that go with roast beef.

Now to the carving. When you present your fine roast of beef at table on a hot platter, it should not be bone side down, but arranged so the larger end of the beef eye is on the platter and the smaller eye uppermost, facing the carver. No decorations, please. Carving takes room, and save for a few sprigs of watercress tucked on the platter for appearance' sake, there should be nothing the carver has to push out of the way. Experienced carvers will first cut along the ribs to loosen the meat, so that when they slice toward the rib the slices will free themselves and fall onto the platter where they can be lifted with knife and fork to a warm plate. Be sure the slices are thin. Those great slabs of beef called American cut, almost as thick as small steaks, really rob you of the true flavor of good roast beef. They may look impressively chunky and promise a hearty meal, but the flavor of the beef will lack the delicacy you get with a thin slice. Time your Yorkshire pudding so that it rises in the pan to inflated golden glory just as the carver finishes. Then rush it to the table and serve with the beef and the roast potatoes and the turnips with *duxelles* and puréed parsnips. No gravy, please. The beef needs only a little of the pan juices. You won't need salad and you certainly won't want bread.

What a deliciously festive combination. Anglo-Saxon to the hilt. Indulge yourself with a really beautiful wine. A fine Bordeaux of a good vintage, such as a Château Latour or a Château Mouton-Rothschild, is magnificent and carries on the great British tradition of claret with beef. However, should you not want to spend a lot of money, there is absolutely nothing wrong with a fine Cabernet Sauvignon from a top California winery, for each year these wines are increasing in quality and excellence. The choice is yours: French wines breathe tradition; California wines are building their own tradition.

Take your time with the perfect Christmas dinner, and let the flow of wine bring mellowness and reminiscences of other days, other groups, other Christmases. Then, if you and your guests feel like it, bring forth a platter of excellent cheese, and another Bordeaux from your wine cellar. It is all part of the relaxation, good talk, and fun of Christmas dinner.

Then clear the table and bring on the dessert. As I say, there would be no Christmas for me without the sight of that great pudding, with heated brandy poured over it, brought flaming to the table, and served at once with a luscious hard sauce. (Don't forget to start the pudding five days before serving.) To wash down the hot pudding, you could have a fine sweet Sauternes, or a demi-sec champagne, or a good well-chilled California dessert wine, such as a Muscat de Frontignan. After dessert clear the table once more and serve strong, rich coffee and with it the funny little bits and pieces of Christmas—nuts to crack and enjoy with raisins, Christmas cookies, candies, and chocolates. This is the time for them. Let people sit long and relax as they sip a fine brandy or a regal port, while the digestive system does its stuff. It's a special day. Treat it as such.

I wish you a joyous and gastronomically exciting Christmas. Include me among your toasts as you drink your wine. Happy Christmas feasting!

CHAPTER 39

THE THIRTEEN DESSERTS OF CHRISTMAS

Simone Beck Fischbacher is one of France's best-known woman writers on food. In fact, she is on a par with Madame St. Ange and several other greats in French gastronomic history who have written a great deal about food. Simone, better known to her hordes of friends as Simca, lives on an ancient farm in Provence surrounded by age-old olive trees and small vineyards. She grows vegetables and small fruits, and she teaches, lectures, and tours the world regularly.

Simca also has been dwelling at Bramafram, her home seat in Provence, in addition to teaching in Venice, on several Mediterranean islands, in Australia, and in the United States, including Hawaii. I've know Simca for fifteen years or so, both in New York City, where she has taught in my house, and in France, where I've stayed in her house as well as in Julia Child's neighboring house. Both are on the same property in an exquisite little valley between Grasse and Cannes in a village called Plascassier—it is as romantic as it sounds. I have been there at all seasons of the year and have learned the traditions of the seasons. I also have lived in another part of Provence in a section near Avignon and learned another side of Provençal living. In all, there is a rather mystic quality evident in the ancient traditions.

Christmas in Provence calls forth a great many traditions; some seem to be older than time. Some have spread to Simca's region, and others are highly localized. There is everywhere, I might add, a feeling of well-being. Feasting and drinking are a part of the celebration of this joyous and colorful season, which has its deeply religious turn as well. For months or several months before Christmas season you will see little animals and figures displayed in shops. These are hand-made by artisans of the region and are figures for a crèche. They vary from quite tiny, almost infinitesimal ones to fairly good-sized animals and figures. Some are beautifully painted while others display an artistic nonchalance that makes them rather wonderful examples of rustic art.

The food side of Provence at Christmastime is quite different from that of other sections of France and certainly from England or the United States. Because France is basically a Catholic country, the celebration of Christmas Eve is not one of turkey, ham, sausage, and such delectables that turn up in other parts of the European world. It is simple, it is not meat, and it is distinguished and distinctive in its way. Called the *Gros Souper*, or big supper, it is an elaborate evening meal, which includes all kinds of very special Provençal dishes. First there is a huge bowl of *aïoli*, the wonderful garlicky mayonnaise called by some the "butter of Provence." On Christmas Eve it is served with snails, salt codfish either sautéed in olive oil with little onions and garlic and olives or simply boiled and served in one piece, and all kinds of vegetables—artichokes, zucchini, carrots, celery, and potatoes. There might be interesting breads specially baked for such an occasion, not the same breads that would necessarily be found in Germany, Italy, England, or the Scandinavian countries, which are high in spice and filled with fruits and peels, giving them an entirely different and more festive feeling.

One outstanding part of such a meal is unique in the world as far as I know. It is called *Les Treize Desserts*, the thirteen desserts. In a tiny cottage in the mountains these sweet things might be brought forth on a simple board or tray. In a great house they might come forth on silver or copper trays, and the extent and elaborateness with which the thirteen desserts are brought forth is a part of the tradition.

Les Treize Desserts always seem to include a few things that are exactly the same. There are figs, some of which have been partially dried and glazed at home, while others have been bought and are the most beautiful dried and glazed figs one can find. And there are dates in great profusion but very seldom loose. More often they are picked from the trees, four to six on a branch, and then beautifully arranged. Very often there are chocolates, and in the south there are likely to be little boxes of a particular candy know as Calison dates, which come from Aix-en-Provence. These are always packed in little white boxes, which are oval or diamond-shaped. On each box is the name of the town or village from where it came. Having several boxes with the names of different places shows that you took the trouble to travel around collecting things for Christmas. It is a nice feeling.

You may often find on the trays of *Les Treize Desserts* the luscious and beautiful candied fruits that one finds especially around Nice and Cannes, and to a certain extent in Grasse. There is a place in Cannes where they glaze and candy whole melons and pineapples, mandarin oranges, and cherries, which are luscious to look upon and wickedly delicious to sink one's teeth into. It is difficult to find the same combinations of fruit and candies and sweetmeats in any two houses.

Often served as part of *Les Treize Desserts* are crispy, crunchy cakes called *pompe a l'huile*. In many ways they may resemble the Christmas desserts one finds in Italy, Mexico, and certain other countries. If you don't want to collect thirteen desserts, *pompe a l'huile* is one that could be served with dried fruits. Here is the recipe:

Sift together 1 teaspoon salt, 1 teaspoon baking powder, 2 table-spoons sugar, and 4 cups flour. Beat 2 eggs very, very well and beat into them 1 cup milk. Gradually combine the dry and the liquid mixtures and then add ¼ cup melted butter. Turn out onto a floured board and knead for about 5 or 6 minutes, or until the dough is very smooth and elastic.

Divide the dough into 28 or 36 balls and roll them out to 4 to 6 inches in diameter. Have ready a pan of deep fat heated to 370°F. Drop in the circles and let them brown delicately on both sides. Remove carefully and drain on absorbent paper, then sprinkle with powdered sugar. Some people like cinnamon, but I much prefer them simply sprinkled with sugar.

These crispy cakes should be served fresh and almost warm, because they don't keep well. They're short, crunchy, delicious, and I think you'll find your guests will gobble them up.

One year at Simca's there were five of us who had not really planned a great celebration of Christmas Eve because three were going to the theater, one was going to the traditional old Mass celebrated with live animals, and none of us was quite sure what time we would join for our supper and celebration. We didn't even have a tree. I remember that the theatergoers arrived back first. I was next door and returned to find them building a Christmas tree from potted plants that had been sent to the house for Christmas or taken from the garden. It was perhaps as charming a Christmas tree as I shall ever see.

We started with a great rich soup, which had been cooked for a considerable time and then cooled and reheated so that the flavors blended extraordinarily well. It was a treat and a joy as a beginning of *Gros Souper*. By that time it was past midnight and was Christmas, and we followed this luscious soup with homemade foie gras and without stint I might say. I don't know how any of us slept that night with the amount of foie gras that entered our tummies, but it was delicious. With the exquisitely prepared goose liver we had toast and a glorious wine, which we smacked our lips over.

As if that were not enough, we tossed a salad and had some exquisite cheese. Then Simca disappeared and returned with champagne and a luscious tray of *Les Treize Desserts*, not a monumental one, but a tray for four. These were Calison dates in their own little boxes, and there were exquisite candied fruits and chocolates which had been made in the kitchens, and there were tiny cakes made from almond flour, butter, and nuts. The cakes were so thin one could hardly hold them together. There were tiny mandarins, and there were branches of dates, and there were home-cured figs. It was a real feast, and we sat long with champagne and finally with some coffee. I'm afraid we wandered home to our respective houses at a very early hour. In fact, I think some of the more dutiful of the group merely washed their faces, changed their clothes, and went off to early Christmas Mass as a beginning of another day's celebration.

Les Treize Desserts brings something intimate, it brings something friendly, it brings a different keynote for the Christmas season. On another occasion at Simca's house there was a New Year's Eve party for about forty people, and she came forth with several trays heaped with luscious things, which were deep in flavor and highly meaningful in shape and form, and mindful of the lore and traditions of the holiday season. *Les Treize Desserts*, with its many little meanings and tastes and the joys of surprise, has struck me over the years as being one of the choicest ways to add to a Christmas meal. Somehow it means more than a flaming pudding, and it is much lighter for the tummy.

While Simca does not include a Christmas menu in her lovely *New Menus from Simca's Cuisine*, one picks up luscious bits and pieces, which she adores serving and which one might well include with *Les Treize Desserts* at Christmas. I hope everyone will bring out a tray or trays of *Les Treize Desserts* this Christmas with proper things to drink, and will think of this brilliant woman who represents the women of Provence and the women of France as very few do. She is a woman who knows food, who revels in cooking it, who knows wine, and revels in sharing it, and whose outgoing charm has captured people all over the world.

INDEX